ARCHAEOLOGY
IN SOUTH YORKSHIRE
NUMBER 13

A review of archaeology in South Yorkshire 2005/2007

Edited by
Dinah Saich and Louisa Matthews

South Yorkshire Archaeology Service

Published by South Yorkshire Archaeology Service

ISBN: 978-0-9557341-0-6

The South Yorkshire Archaeology Service is maintained by the Metropolitan Borough Councils of Barnsley, Doncaster and Rotherham and the City Council of Sheffield. During the period covered by this report, the Service was administered by Development Services at Sheffield City Council.

Cover illustration features a photograph of samples for archaeomagnetic dating being taken by the Department of Archaeological Sciences, University of Bradford, from the smaller Phase 2 kiln at Rectory House Farm, Laughton-en-le-Morthen, superimposed on a plan of the kiln and drawings of sherds from a commemorative mug found at 17-39 Mowbray Street, Sheffield.

Design and layout by Greg Ward Design & Photography. Tel: 01709 852814

Printed by B&B Press, Aldwarke Road, Parkgate, Rotherham, S62 6DY

Printed on recycled paper and board

CONTENTS

LIST OF ILLUSTRATIONS

COLOUR SECTION

INTRODUCTION

This Annual Review covers two financial years: 2005/6 and 2006/7. The development boom in South Yorkshire was in full swing and the South Yorkshire Archaeology Service was stretched to the limit, keeping up with the volume of development-led investigations generated. The last annual review, which also covered a two year period, reported on 180 cases; this review reports on 230 cases where some level of archaeological input was required as part of the development process. Some of these cases were for large redevelopment proposals that generated a considerable volume of work in themselves.

The quantity and quality of new archaeological information gathered demonstrates how important it is that archaeology is now routinely considered a material part of the planning process. In Jump, Barnsley, the process of assessment, evaluation and then mitigation at Roebuck Hill, in relation to a proposed housing scheme on a greenfield site, produced evidence for multi-period occupation and use of a site where no archaeological evidence had previously been recorded. In Doncaster, the ongoing investigations of two large developments on greenfield sites at West Moor Park, Armthorpe, and at the Catesby Business Park, Balby Carr, provided further detail on the Iron Age and Romano-British period rural settlements identified here. In Rotherham, the evaluation and excavation carried out at Rectory House

Farm, Laughton-en-le-Morthen, in relation to a housing proposal within the core of the historic village, produced confirmation of Laughton's pre-Conquest origins and confirmed its continuing importance post-Conquest. In Sheffield, a variety of brownfield redevelopment sites produced evidence for the cementation process of producing steel and the crucible method of refining that steel (primarily for cutlery and edge tools), allowing us to begin to build up a proper understanding of the development of these important processes and their place in the history of the Sheffield metal trades.

Alongside these development-led projects, the Archaeology Service continued to look for opportunities to widen our knowledge and to find ways to disseminate that knowledge to the wider public. Our work on the English Heritage-funded characterisation project continued (see '*Archaeology in South Yorkshire Number 12*' for an introduction to this project). During the period covered by this report our Characterisation Project Officers completed the mapping of Sheffield, Rotherham and Doncaster and work had commenced on Barnsley. We also worked with consultants *in*Heritage to secure Aggregates Levy Sustainability Funding for an outreach project in Doncaster. This focused on the results of excavation, where Iron Age and Romano-British evidence had been recovered, in advance of mineral extraction. Outputs, including a children's comic 'Look out! The Romans are coming', can be downloaded from the project website:

www.doncaster.gov.uk/romansonthedon

The Archaeology Service acts as a centre of advice and expertise for those carrying out any kind of archaeological research within South Yorkshire and, during this period, many people have made use of the Sites & Monuments Record that we maintain. This holds information on the results of all the development-led fieldwork reported on in the 'general' section of this and previous volumes, as well as on many of the research-led projects reported on in this and previous 'research' sections.

The Archaeology Service is always keen that these results reach the public domain at the earliest opportunity. As well as encouraging formal publication of important results in a relevant journal, and publishing this round up of results, we host an annual archaeology day school. At South Yorkshire Archaeology Day, held in November 2005, the following papers were presented: Dave MacLeod on aerial photography in South Yorkshire; Colin Merrony & Mike Klemperer on investigating the kitchen garden at Brodsworth (see research section); Graham Hague on coke ovens at Deep Pit and the Manor; Sean Bell on excavations along Sheffield's Inner Relief Road (see general section); Mark Douglas on recording historic buildings in Barnsley; Kathleen Cronk on her research on the Roman Ridge; Dan Lee on surveying ancient woodland in Rotherham; and Henry Chapman on the Lindholme trackway on Hatfield Moors.

At South Yorkshire Archaeology Day, held in November 2006, the following

papers were presented: Gavin Robinson on excavations on Roebuck Hill, Jump (see general section); Bill Bevan on the Aggregates Levy Sustainability Fund project 'Romans on the Don'; Ian Roberts on excavations at Laughton-en-le-Morthen (see general section); Ben Chan on excavations in the Crofts, Sheffield - at Tenter Street (see general section); Jenni Chambers on another Aggregates Levy Sustainability Fund project 'The National Ice Age Network'; Simon Johnson on excavations at Cantley in Doncaster (see general section); John Pouncett on the Q-pits of Ecclesall Woods (see research section); and Anna Badcock on recording the last melt at Stocksbridge Steelworks.

The Archaeology Service works closely with other organisations and individuals interested in South Yorkshire's historic environment, particularly through the South Yorkshire Archaeology Advisory & Liaison Panel. In 2005/6, the following people were members of the Liaison Panel: Derek Bayliss of the South Yorkshire Industrial History Society (Chair); Ian Panter, English Heritage's Regional Science Adviser; Anna Marshall of the Portable Antiquities Scheme; Colin Merrony of Sheffield University's Archaeology Department; Peter Robinson of Doncaster Museum; Karl Noble of Rotherham Museum; Gill Woolrich of Sheffield Museum. David Haigh and Archie Sinclair variously represented Barnsley MBC.

In 2006/7, Derek Bayliss of the South Yorkshire Industrial History Society continued to Chair the Liaison Panel and there were just a couple of changes from the previous year: Alison Duce replaced Karl Noble as representative of Rotherham Museum and our new

Regional Science Adviser, Andy Hammon, replaced Ian Panter.

The Archaeology Service also reports to a Joint Committee, made up of representatives from our four constituent local authorities. In 2005/6, the following people were members of this Committee: Councillor Tony Sockett of Doncaster MBC chaired the Committee; Councillor Cynthia Ransome also represented Doncaster MBC. Councillors David Bostwick and Bill Newman represented Barnsley MBC; Councillors Jane Austen and Georgina Boyes represented Rotherham MBC; Councillors Trevor Bagshaw and Mike Pye represented Sheffield CC.

In 2006/7, the following people were members of this Committee: Councillor Michael Stokes of Barnsley MBC chaired the Committee; Councillor Linda Burgess also represented Barnsley MBC. Councillors Cynthia Ransome and Tony Sockett represented Doncaster MBC; Councillors Reg Littleboy and Iain St. John represented Rotherham MBC; Councillors Trevor Bagshaw and Mike Pye represented Sheffield CC.

John Turner, from Sheffield City Council's Committee Secretariat, acted as Secretary to both the Panel and the Joint Committee.

During this period we lost one colleague and gained another. Roy Sykes decided the best way to protect archaeology was to become a planner and started his new career in September 2006. Andy Lines, who had been working on our EH funded characterisation project, started with us in a development control role in January 2007. Two weeks later, Jennifer Marchant arrived to work on the

characterisation project alongside Dan Ratcliffe. Jim McNeil and Louisa Matthews helped keep everything going.

Finally, many thanks go to Dave Sainty of *in*Heritage for helping with the compilation of this Annual Review.

Dinah Saich
South Yorkshire Archaeology Service

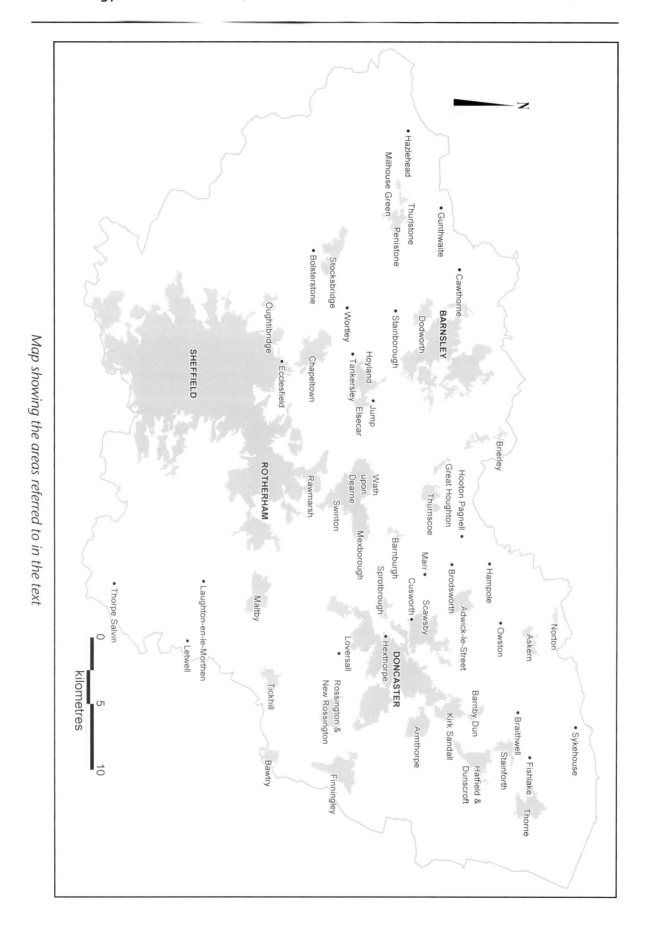

Map showing the areas referred to in the text

RESEARCH PROJECTS

ARCHAEO-ENVIRONMENTAL MODELLING OF HATFIELD AND THORNE MOORS

The archaeological potential of wetlands is well known. Raised mires in particular have previously produced structures including trackways (e.g. Raftery 1990) and bog bodies (e.g. Turner and Scaife 1995). In addition to the exceptional preservation of organic archaeological remains, raised mires also provide source material for the study of the environmental context of sites and their surrounding landscapes. An excellent example of how these different datasets can be combined together usefully is the work at Derryville in central Ireland (Gowen *et al.* 2005).

However, studying mires as archaeological landscapes becomes challenging. Typically, landscape archaeology seeks interpretation through the exploration of relationships between environmental factors (the presence of rivers, hills, slopes etc.) and cultural remains. For raised mires this is problematic because of the dynamic nature of wetland growth and development. It is necessary to reconstruct the environmental context for different periods before the toolkit of landscape archaeology may be applied.

The two largest areas of lowland raised mire in England are Hatfield and Thorne Moors. Until recently, these have been industrial landscapes, drained and cut for the extraction of peat, traditionally for stable litter and fuel, and more recently for horticulture. In 2004 peat extraction finally ceased on these landscapes and their management became the concern of Natural England.

For the last few years, much effort has been focused on the restoration of these landscapes and reconstituting the raised mire landscapes that are so rare yet important for the flora and fauna that make them both Sites of Special Scientific Interest (SSSI). As this process requires the managed re-flooding of both landscapes, this presents something of a challenge for heritage management concerns.

English Heritage has been funding work on Hatfield and Thorne Moors aimed at addressing the broader challenges of the landscape archaeology of raised mire landscapes, using Hatfield and Thorne Moors as case studies. Commencing in 2003, the project has focused on the reconstruction of the dynamic landscape of each of the moors through time, from initial development through to the patterns and processes of wetland spread. Typically, such an undertaking would be resource intensive in terms of extensive borehole survey, radiocarbon dating and palaeoenvironmental analyses. However, this project has been able to make use of existing datasets (including archive data), generated by a range of different methods: archaeology, palaeoecology, Lidar survey etc., at a range of spatial and temporal resolutions (for an example of earlier palaeoenvironmental research on the moors see '*Archaeology in South Yorkshire Number 11*'). It has also embraced statistical techniques for assessing the robustness of these different datasets and for extrapolating information, such as the Bayesian modelling of radiocarbon dates (undertaken by Pete Marshall).

These combined analyses have permitted the generation of spatio-temporal

Section of Neolithic trackway on Hatfield Moors showing birch bark band adjacent to the end platform © Birmingham University

models of both moors that have allowed the application of a landscape archaeology toolkit to our understanding of human activity on the moors. For example, the late Neolithic trackway on Hatfield Moors (see '*Archaeology in South Yorkshire Number 12*') can now be seen to be located at one of the earliest areas of wetland development at a time when much of the rest of the landscape remained peat free (see diagram on page 181 of colour section).

In addition, the project aimed to quantify the surviving peatland resource in volumetric terms, as well as assessing the chronological span that this peat represents. In principle, the earliest and latest peat at a specific location tells us something about the potential for the preservation of cultural remains. For example, if the earliest peat development is in the Bronze Age, and the top of the peat dates to the Iron Age, then it is unlikely that there will be wet-preservation of archaeological remains outside of this chronological envelope.

Modelling using this variety of datasets is providing a valuable insight into the way that we can facilitate a 'landscape archaeology' of these hidden and dynamic environments. Whilst at one level the results of the project will provide quantitative data regarding the potential of the archaeo-environmental resource at different locations across the moors, reconstruction of the moors' changing environments through time will also provide the backdrop for the interpretation and prediction of cultural activity within these landscapes.

Report by Henry Chapman and Benjamin Gearey, Birmingham University

REFERENCES

Gowen, M. O'Neill, J. and Philips, M. (ed.) (2005). *The Lisheen Mine Archaeological Project 1996-1998*. **Co. Wicklow Wordwell Ltd.**

Raftery, B. (1990). *Trackways through Time. Archaeological Investigations on Irish Bog Roads, 1985-1989*. **Dublin: Headline Publishing**

Raftery, B. (1996). *Trackway excavations in the Mountdillon Bogs, Co. Longford 1985-1991*. **Dublin: Crannog Publications, Irish Archaeological Wetland Unit, Department of Archaeology, University College, Dublin**

Turner, R.C. and Scaife R.G. (ed.) (1995). *Bog bodies new discoveries and new perspectives*. **London British Museum Press**

TOTLEY BOLE HILL: GEOPHYSICAL SURVEY OF A LEAD SMELTING SITE

As part of wider investigations into the effect of the lead smelting process on the magnetic characteristics of medieval bole/bale sites, geophysical surveys using both magnetometer and resistivity methods were undertaken over known lead smelting features on Totley Bole Hill. These surveys were undertaken by Alan Powell as part of a doctoral research programme, studying the magnetic response of iron smelting, lead smelting, glass production and charcoal production sites in relation to geophysical survey in order to obtain a better understanding of their magnetic characteristics.

Totley Bole Hill (NGR SK 290 798), located approximately 10km south west of Sheffield city centre, is part of the Blacka Moor Nature Reserve, which is administered by the Sheffield Wildlife Trust. It has been designated as a Scheduled Ancient Monument due to the numerous medieval and post-medieval lead smelting activities known to have taken place here. The Totley Bole Hill area has been surveyed previously by fieldwalking and several lead smelting sites have been noted, in particular a "bole" feature towards the southern end of the hill, which was reported on by Kiernan and van de Noort (1992). Ed Dennison Archaeological Services Ltd. undertook a topographical survey in 2003 that identified more detail of the bole and identified some other sites, believed to be blackwork ovens (Dennison & Richardson 2003). As far as is known,

the geophysical surveys reported on here are the first to have been undertaken on Totley Bole Hill. The geophysical surveys used the site numbers designated in the Dennison and Richardson (2003) survey. The main complex of features (Sites 10 to 15) lies at the southern end of the Bole Hill, with an outlier (Site 22) approximately 110m to the north.

The geophysical surveys were undertaken on several dates during June, July and August 2005. The weather was extremely varied from high winds and rain, hill fog and rain, to dry and sunny: these variations had an adverse effect on the resistivity survey results due to the excessive amount of ground water. The surveys were carried out in two parts, one over the main complex (Sites 10 to 15) and the other over Site 22. The survey base line was initially established within the main complex area but was extended northwards for 110m to link together the Site 22 and main complex survey grids.

Six 5m x 5m grids were laid out specifically over Site 10, the bole reported by Kiernan and van de Noort (1992), in order to identify better any anomalies associated with the bole itself. Both magnetometer and resistivity readings were taken over these six grids at 0.25m resolution (0.25m intervals and 0.25m traverses). In the larger area of the main complex (Sites 10 to 15), a total of sixteen 10m x 10m grids were laid out and magnetometer readings were taken over this area at a resolution of 0.5m (0.5m intervals at 0.5m traverses). Six 10m x 10m grids were laid out over Site 22 and magnetometer readings taken at the same resolution.

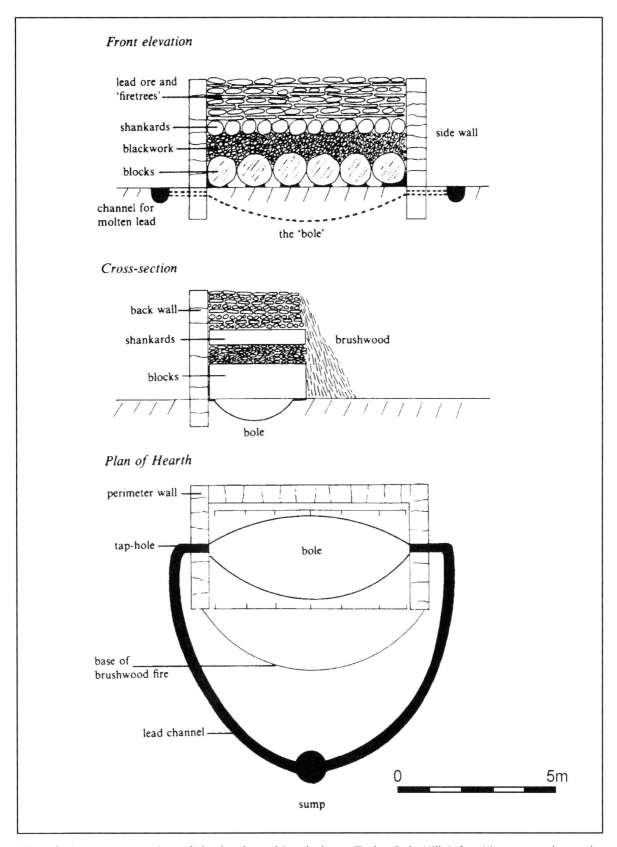

Speculative reconstruction of the lead smelting bole on Totley Bole Hill (after Kiernan and van de Noort 1992) © Alan Powell

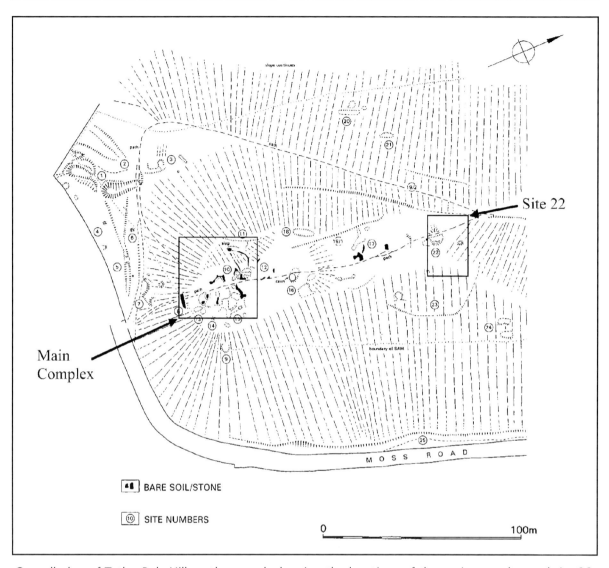

Overall plan of Totley Bole Hill southern end, showing the locations of the main complex and site 22 survey areas (adapted from Dennison & Richardson 2003, Fig. 5) © Alan Powell

The magnetometer surveys revealed considerable activity, larger than that suggested by the Dennison and Richardson (2003) topographical survey, both over the main complex and Site 22. At the main complex, two sub-circular areas of concentrated activity on top of the hill and a large area of (weaker) activity lying on the western downslope of Totley Bole Hill were identified. These areas of concentrated activity do not coincide with the bole identified by Kiernan and van de Noort

(1992), or the features surveyed by Dennison and Richardson (2003), instead they correspond more with a feature lying approximately 5m south. No anomalies in the magnetometer data coincide with the Kiernan and van de Noort (1992) lead channels. This does not mean that these channels do not exist; there simply may not be a sufficiently high magnetic signal from them to stand out against the surrounding background data. There is a sufficient quantity of lead slag

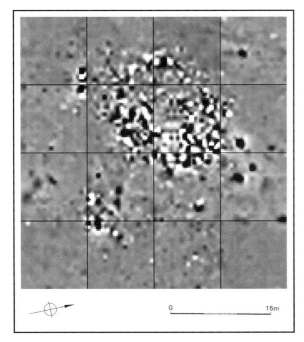

Totley Bole Hill: main complex magnetometer survey plot - clipped range: -20nT (white) to 20nT (black)   © Alan Powell

the patches of bare soil or along the path, it is possible that these two areas of activity are associated with slag heaps. It is also feasible that there could have been a second lead smelting bole here, although there is no supporting topographical evidence such as a sizeable quantity of stones and patches of bare soil as seen at Site 10. Another, extensive area of significant activity spread over the survey area could be a further slag dump, although, if so, it is not obvious as it is buried under a combination of heather, rough grass or a thin layer of grass-covered top soil. Very high positive anomalies in the west of the survey area may be associated with a pipeline; further investigation would be required to determine the cause of these anomalies, which may be masking other weaker anomalies.

remaining in the bare patches of ground on the flat area of the main complex to conclude that there was a significant amount of lead smelting taking place here. A weak rectangular anomaly lying between the two sub-circular areas of activity could be associated with a structure of some kind but there is no obvious supporting topographical evidence. The remaining magnetic anomalies are areas of weak activity that either coincide with topographic features described by Dennison and Richardson (2003) or are possibly responses to geological features.

From the magnetometer survey of Site 22, two areas of activity were identified that correspond to the topographic features west of the path and the areas of slag and bare soil identified by Dennison and Richardson (2003). Due to the large amount of lead slag material that is visible close to both anomalies, either in

The magnetometer surveys conducted at Totley Bole Hill recorded low values of magnetic enhancement at the presumed areas of smelting activity but it was still possible to interpret the extent to which smelting had taken place. Significantly, there was no evidence of thermoremanence anywhere within the areas of the main complex or Site 22; no large clusters of high valued magnetic anomalies were noted (when iron is heated above c770°C, it becomes magnetised as it cools and also fossilises the position of the earth's magnetic field at that time). The possible reasons for these magnetic characteristics are that the affected ground surface and underlying geology have a low iron oxide content, and/or that smelting temperatures were not achieving 700°C or more. Given the quantity of slag remaining on Totley Bole Hill, it seems certain that appropriate smelting temperatures were

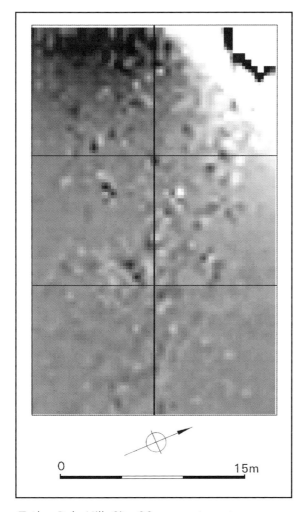

Totley Bole Hill: Site 22 magnetometer survey plot - clipped range: -50nT (white) to 50nT (black)   © Alan Powell

being attained, which suggests that the iron oxide content of the site's geology is indeed low. Unfortunately, the Scheduled Ancient Monument status of Totley Bole Hill prevented acquisition of soil and geological samples for laboratory analysis of magnetic and thermal properties.

The Totley Bole Hill survey has demonstrated that it is feasible to conduct geophysical prospection over archaeological medieval/post-medieval lead smelting sites, and that traces of smelting activities do exist to an extent

that can be identified. However, the survey has shown that thermoremanent magnetism has not been acquired and, consequently, no archaeomagnetic date for the smelting can be obtained.

Acknowledgements

Acknowledgements and gratitude are due to the following for their permissions, co-operation and support: Sheffield Wildlife Trust and English Heritage for access and survey permissions; Dr David Kiernan for his help regarding the lead smelting industry of the Peak District in general and Totley in particular; Ed Dennison of Ed Dennison Archaeological Services for permission to reproduce data from his topographical survey report; the AHRC for its financial support. The author would like to express special thanks to Dr Rob Vernon, Margaret Vernon and Irene Zananiri for their invaluable help with the geophysical survey.

Report by Alan Powell, Cathy Batt & Gerry McDonnell, School of Life Sciences, University of Bradford

REFERENCES

Dennison, E. and Richardson, S. (2003). *Blacka Moor Nature Reserve, Sheffield, South Yorkshire: archaeological survey of Bole Hill.* **Beverley, East Yorkshire: Ed Dennison Archaeological Services Ltd. (unpublished EDAS report 2003/193.R01 for Sheffield Wildlife Trust)**

Kiernan, D. and van de Noort, R. (1992). *Bole smelting in Derbyshire.* In Willies, L. and Cranstone, D. (eds.) (1992) **Boles and Smeltmills. Matlock Bath: Historical Metallurgy Society, 19-21**

DONCASTER ARCHAEOLOGICAL SOCIETY: INVESTIGATIONS AT TICKHILL FRIARY

The present Tickhill Friary is a 16th century house that incorporates substantial remains from the medieval period. Friary Close is a largely Victorian extension to the west that also incorporates several features from earlier medieval buildings. These houses stand on the site of the former Augustinian Friary of Tickhill, which was dissolved in 1538. Friary Close (NGR SK 58619276) is owned by one of the Society's members, Tony Sheridan, who liaised with the other owners and obtained permission for the Society to investigate the site in 2005.

The Friary was an Augustinian foundation from 1265, when a "messuage and land" was donated by John Clarel to Walter, Prior of St Augustine (Yorkshire deeds and fines for 1265 transcribed by the Surtees Society)[1]. Hunter (1828) suggests that this preceding building must also have had a religious purpose and he cites an earlier burial plaque, now lost, within the Friary. By the mid-14th century there were 23 friars although at the surrender to the crown on November 19th 1538 only the prior and 7 brethren were listed, according to the Victoria County History (Page 1913).

The present site occupies some 2 acres and is split by a stream (Paper Mill Dike), flowing roughly west to east across the site, which was diverted to the south sometime in the 19th century. At the southern edge of the site is a limestone cliff, which is possibly where the building

stone for the friary was quarried. The remains of a small building stand on a tiny promontory on top of this cliff, the suggestion being that any quarrying that took place respected this building. All other buildings on the site are to the north of the stream, including elements that seem to be substantial remains of the friary incorporated into the later house. These include two arches and a doorway inside one of the buildings and an early chimney in the exterior west-facing wall of the present house (Pevsner 1967). Pevsner also mentions a 13th century arch in the gardens but an early print[2] depicts a very similar arch in the south wall of the western range, suggesting the arch in the garden has been reset (Magilton & Ryder 1978).

The objectives of the 2005 investigations were:

i) To draw, survey and record any standing masonry thought to be connected with the friary.

ii) To conduct a resistivity survey and a magnetometer survey over as much of the area as possible.

iii) To clear all debris and overgrowth from the ruined building on the promontory, in the hope that it might reveal features attributable to the dovecote mentioned as part of the friary buildings.[3]

Fieldwork was carried out over three days and most of the objectives were addressed in some manner. Work got off to a good start. However, difficulties with the magnetometer survey meant that only one grid was surveyed. The resistivity survey went better and over the three days the Society's volunteers managed to survey most of the grounds and gardens. Recording of standing masonry did not

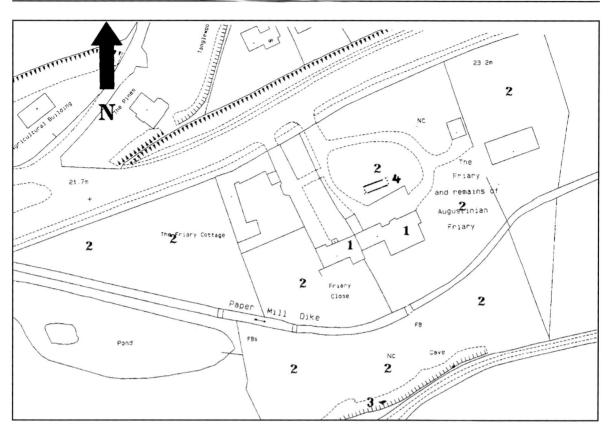

Site plan showing Tickhill Friary (1), geophysical survey areas (2), the promontory building (3), and an indicative outline of the most interesting geophysical results (4)   © Doug Croft

proceed as quickly as hoped, but a measured drawing of the southern façade of the monastic building was produced. An 18th century engraving of a similar view is held in the collection at Doncaster Museum and it is interesting to see that some of the present, apparently early features have been added since then, in the manner of gothic revival.

The results of the 2005 investigations were:

i) The remains of the friary were converted to a dwelling not too long after the dissolution, probably in the 16th century. The roofing slates of the present house are limestone rather than (for this area) the more common and enduring sandstone, which suggests that the roof may well be original to the 16th century

house (Paul Buckland pers.com.). Many medieval features are incorporated within the present buildings, along with Victorian gothic revival features. A print of 1810 shows sash windows in the south face of The Friary that have since been replaced by mullion windows; a very similar arch to that now standing in the gardens is depicted in ruins on the site of the extensions that are now Friary Close.

ii) The resistivity results south and west of the buildings were disappointing as no anomalies of any significance were visible. Even the old course of the stream was not picked up. It is possible that Victorian landscaping, particularly to the south of the stream, or hill wash masked any possible features. The survey to the north of the buildings was more encouraging, with two parallel high resistance features

Society members operating the resistivity meter
© Doug Croft

being picked up some 10m north of and parallel to the northern façade of the main dwelling. These features were about 4m apart and ran for a length of about 9m; less pronounced linear features at either end formed a rectangle. These features may be walls or paths but since they lie under a lawn it is unlikely that they will be excavated in the near future.

iii) The building on the promontory was cleared and a brick floor revealed. The bricks seemed to be late 19th or early 20th century in date, so clearly had no monastic connections. No clear relationship between the building's walls and the adjoining boundary wall, which is thought to be early in date, could be established as they have been much repaired. However, the walls of the building were well constructed and the mortar used in their construction had some gypsum content that dates them later than the 18th century (Paul Buckland pers. com.). Professor Buckland also suggested that the building had the look of a Victorian gazebo or belvedere and there is no denying that it would have afforded an impressive vista before the present trees matured. However, in the future, it may still be worth removing the floor to establish whether there is any evidence for an earlier structure on this site.

Although some of the results were disappointing, the results of the resistivity survey suggest that the medieval remains incorporated into the present buildings may represent the southern range of the friary. This would suggest that the friary was constructed over the former course of the stream, as at Roche Abbey. In this case, a further range of buildings would have existed to the north. A further resistivity survey in drier conditions may produce results worthy of note.

Acknowledgements

Thanks are due to the three owners of the site, which is private property. Thanks are also due to John Burnett and David Hedges for their resistivity survey and to all the volunteers from Doncaster Archaeological Society who worked on the project. I am also indebted to Tony Sheridan for his input to the historical aspects of this report and his efforts in enabling the project.

Report by Doug Croft

REFERENCES

Hunter, J. (1828). *The History and Topography of the Deanery of Doncaster.* London, Nichols

Magilton, J. and Ryder, P.F. *Tickhill Friary.* An unpublished report for Doncaster Museum

Page, W. (ed.) (1913). *Victoria History of the Counties of England. Yorkshire vol. III.* Reprint 1974 London, University of London

Pevsner, N. (1967). *The Buildings of England: Yorkshire, The West Riding.* (2nd ed.) London, Penguin Books

[1] This information is pers.com. from Tony Sheridan and is his reference. Other sources including Hunter (1828) are somewhat vague but give a similar name and date.

[2] A copy of the print is held in the collection at Doncaster Museum.

[3] Hunter (1828 p.245) mentions that an inventory upon transfer from the crown in 1554 includes a dovecote and although the appearance of the ruins does not suggest this, it is worth bearing in mind.

ECCLESALL WOODS, SHEFFIELD

Ecclesall Woods, which lies to the west of Sheffield city centre, has seen a series of archaeological investigations in recent years. Following their survey work on a hilltop enclosure and adjoining field system in 2002, and the rapid assessment of the numerous Q-pits within the woods, (see *'Archaeology in South Yorkshire Number 12'*) the Friends of Ecclesall Woods made a second successful application for funding from the Local Heritage Initiative. This allowed them to carry out further survey work within the woods, under the supervision of a consultant archaeologist.

In August 2005 the survey of a second enclosure was undertaken. This enclosure stands on a low rise to the east of Cow Lane and is formed by an upcast bank with shallow sloping sides. The bank defines an area of about 0.5ha. The form and construction of the enclosure are similar to the field system enclosures recorded previously within the woods. As such, it probably formed part of an irregular field system that may have originated in the Iron Age or Romano-British period.

In December 2005 further work was carried out on the field system recorded in 2002. Reduced ground cover afforded better visibility and earthworks were found to continue to the south and east of those identified earlier. A series of curvilinear and rectilinear enclosures defined by banks of upcast earth and stone were noted. Different alignments suggest that at least two separate

phases of activity are represented. A row of four enclosures was identified, running down the slope from the hilltop enclosure. The spacing of these suggests that a fifth enclosure was originally present and that this has been destroyed or obscured by later activity. A series of smaller structures that may indicate the former positions of buildings were noted; the date of these structures is uncertain.

A number of post-medieval features were noted during both phases of survey, including charcoal burning platforms and Q-pits, three of which were cut into the earthworks of the former field system. A large number of Q-pits (kilns for producing dried wood for the lead industry, thought to have been in use between the late 16th and mid-18th centuries) have been recorded in Ecclesall Woods and other woodlands around Sheffield, but very little is known about how they operated. The last element of this phase of investigation was, therefore, focussed on detailed examination of two example Q-pits.

The Q-pits were investigated in August 2005 and June 2006. Both examples selected were simple typical Q-pits (a variety of Q-pit types have been identified by previous survey work). After the removal of leaf litter and fallen branches, a micro-contour survey was carried out, to better define the form of the features. Two perpendicular profiles across one of the features were then obtained using a gouge auger. Magnetic susceptibility readings were also taken, to look for areas of burning or metalworking. Finally, each Q-pit was divided into quadrants leaving 25cm baulks between them. These

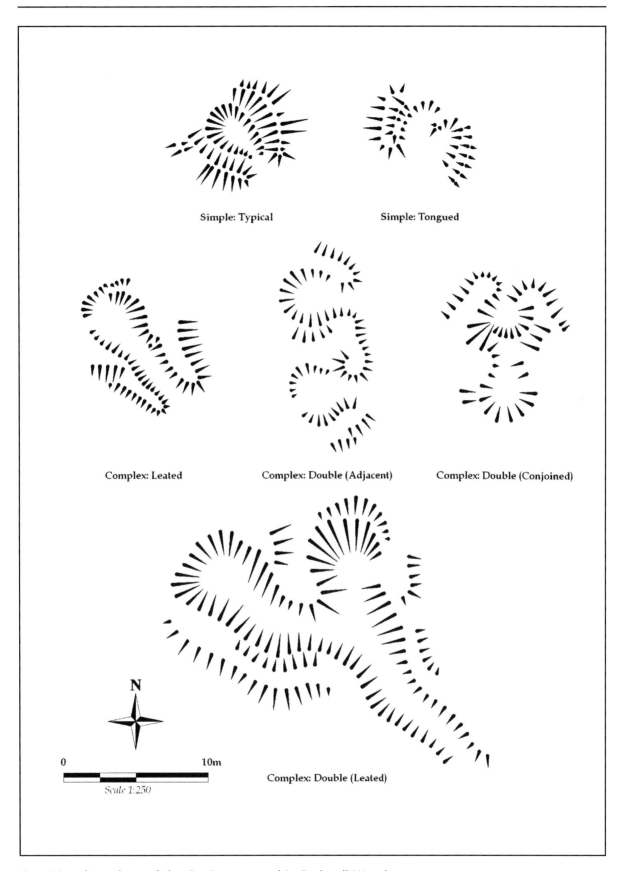

Simple: Typical

Simple: Tongued

Complex: Leated

Complex: Double (Adjacent)

Complex: Double (Conjoined)

Complex: Double (Leated)

0   10m

Scale 1:250

Provisional typology of the Q-pits surveyed in Ecclesall Woods © ASE Ltd.

quadrants were then hand excavated. Although a variety of material was recovered during the excavation, no dating evidence for the construction of the kilns was found.

Both of the Q-pits were found to have comprised rectangular stone-lined pits approximately 2m by 3m in size, cut into the side of a shallow slope. The front edge and sides of the pit were built up to the same height as the back of the pit by the construction of a bank of earth and stone. A stone-lined flue was built at the lowest point of the bank. In both examples, the base of the pit was lower than the flue. The presence of coke and charcoal found near the flue at one of the Q-pits suggests that the feature was later re-used. Similar material found associated with other Q-pits within the woods has led to the suggestion that they were sometimes re-used for coke manufacture (Smylie 1990). The high magnetic susceptibility readings recorded here suggest some sort of metal working, such as iron ore roasting. The magnetic susceptibility readings did not indicate any burning within the rectangular pits or within the flues themselves.

The form of these kilns suggests parallels with unenclosed corn-drying kilns recorded in the north of Britain in the mid-20th century (Scott 1951). In these kilns, the corn to be dried was placed on a series of cross-timbers laid directly over a pit, with a fire lit at the entrance to an adjoining flue. This description matches the archaeological evidence recovered during the Q-pit excavations. Such unenclosed kilns would have been wasteful of heat, but an abundant source of fuel would have been readily available within the

woodland, in the form of brushwood. Brushwood burns unpredictably and some form of blocking would have been required to prevent sparks igniting the drying material; large blocks of gritstone, suitable for this purpose, were recovered during the excavation of both Q-pits.

The auger profile obtained corresponded closely with the excavated sections recorded. It is suggested that augering, combined with magnetic susceptibility survey, would allow a large number of Q-pits to be investigated rapidly. This would help establish whether the excavated examples are representative of the other Q-pits within the woods and suggest priorities for further work.

From reports by Emma Gowans and John Pouncett, ASE Ltd

REFERENCES

Scott, L. (1951). *Corn-drying kilns.* **Antiquity 100, 195-204**

Smylie, W. (1990). *'Q' pits in Ecclesall Woods: Coke Producers' in Whiteley (ed.).* **The Natural History of Ecclesall Woods (Sorby Record, Sheffield: Sorby Natural History Society 27) 25-28**

THE BRODSWORTH PROJECT: INVESTIGATIONS OF THE WALLED KITCHEN GARDEN, BRODSWORTH HALL

This report covers fieldwork conducted in the walled kitchen garden of Brodsworth Hall between August 2003 and September 2005, as part of the ongoing Brodsworth Project (see *'Archaeology in South Yorkshire Number 11'* for an introduction to the project). This report is a summary of the work discussed in the interim report on the fieldwork of 2004 (Klemperer and Merrony, 2004) and geophysical survey of 2003 (Merrony *et al*, 2003) with additional material relating to the fieldwork conducted in 2005.

The walled kitchen garden at Brodsworth Hall was constructed to provide a supply of fruit and vegetables (and possibly cut flowers) to the family and staff that lived and worked in the hall and on the estate. It was functioning as a kitchen garden by at least the end of the 18th century and was further developed at about the time of the demolition of the Old Hall in the 1860s. Despite being aware of a former complex of buildings in the garden area due to photographic and archival records, the potential for archaeological preservation was unknown. To assess the quality of preservation and to explore the information potential of any archaeological remains in the walled garden a geophysical survey was carried out using both resistivity and magnetometry during August 2003. This showed areas of surviving structures in the northern part of the

walled garden, as well as the layout of paths between the planting beds. A low resistance feature running east to west across the centre of the walled garden was also visible on the survey; this was a late 20th century redirection of the stream crossing the site (Cliff Spring Drain) in an attempt to create an ornamental pond. The stream formerly ran in a culvert underneath the northernmost east-west path across the garden and was used to irrigate the planting beds of fruit and vegetables that lay to the south (downslope from it). The survey also showed the extent of the area of buildings lying adjacent to the north wall of the walled garden. Of these structures, the known location of the main heated glasshouse (or stove house) gave the most detail in regards to extent and layout.

Three main trenches were excavated in the walled garden in the summer of 2004, in order to investigate the main buildings near the north wall and the path/culvert. One trench was placed in order to investigate the stove house, which was known to be approximately 54 metres long and to utilise the wall of the walled garden as its 'back' or north wall. The trench was located where the geophysical survey had indicated the entrance porch and central area of the stove house would lie. It was hoped that this area would provide detailed information relating to the development, size, internal structure, heating arrangements and the fabric used in the construction of this important garden building.

The trench located the external (southern) stove house wall as expected. This wall was constructed of roughly finished Magnesian limestone

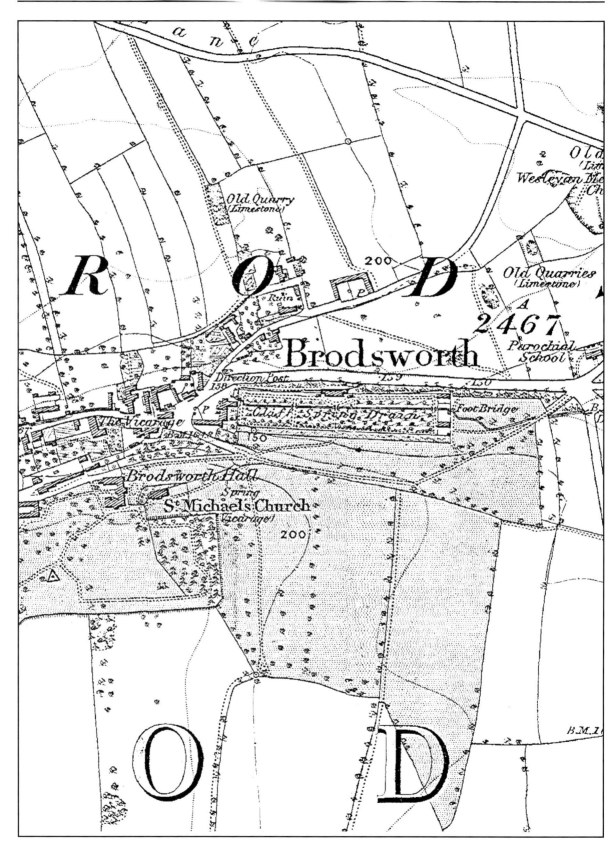

The walled kitchen garden, to the east of Brodsworth Hall, shown on the 6" Ordnance Survey map of 1854

blocks and had 6 slots or perforations along its length; these slots had been blocked at a later date, with brick 'plugs'. To the south of the wall (in the area outside the stove house) the excavation revealed a layer of red clay overlying a layer of Magnesian limestone rubble that contained a drainage pipe from the stove house. It is likely that the limestone rubble layer was acting as a 'soakaway' for this drain and the red clay was presumably laid down to stop the overlying topsoil leaching into the rubble layer. These layers were both associated with redevelopment of the building in the mid 19th century. Below the rubble, a layer of Yorkstone paving from the earliest phase of the stove house was likely to have been used as a standing area for tender plants in pots (for example citrus plants) in the summer months.

The main body and internal features of the stove house were entirely symmetrical, with a network of brick walls and two large water tanks on the left and right of the central axis. The two water tanks were approximately 2m wide and were rendered with a waterproof plaster, with pipes bringing water in from the stove house roof. These tanks presumably provided a source of soft water for the planting beds within the glasshouse (in contrast to the 'hard' or alkali water obtainable from the stream outside, which ran off the underlying limestone). Pipe work from the heating system also survived, running through the 'back' wall of the stove house from the boiler room, which stood just outside the walled garden, immediately to the north. In the centre of the stove house there was evidence for either a conduit for water

or an early heating duct for air, perhaps related to a hot wall forming the north wall of the stove house.

Running parallel to the main external wall was another wall that also had slots in it. This wall lacked the later brick blocking. In the cases of both walls, these slots relate to growing vines in a system where the roots are planted outside the glasshouse and then the trunk is trained through a slot into the inside of the glasshouse. This results in the topgrowth (and fruit) being within the greenhouse to encourage more vigorous growth and ensure ripening of the grapes in the higher interior temperatures. This method is still used today in Britain to grow dessert grapes in unheated glasshouses. It is clear from this 'double wall' that there are at least 2 phases when this structure was used as a vinehouse. The earlier phase was a smaller vinehouse that was then rebuilt and expanded with the external (southern) wall pushed further out and the internal areas remodelled to include the construction of the water tanks. In a later phase, the vinehouse was converted into a stove house for the cultivation of more exotic/tender plants requiring higher temperatures and consequently the slots in the external wall were blocked to enable higher temperatures to be maintained.

The second trench of 2004 was put in at was thought to be the eastern end of the stove house and it was hoped that it would pinpoint the edge of the structure and show its relationship to the surrounding paths and garden. It was also hoped that it would help date the construction sequence of the stove house. However, no substantial structures were uncovered in this trench and the large amount of pottery uncovered did not help with dating of the different phases of construction.

The final trench of 2004 was sited on what was thought to be paths, beds and the location of the culverted watercourse. Excavation showed that the culvert was originally lined with a layer of clay and Magnesian limestone blocks (only surviving on the south facing side). The depth of this feature (1.5m below ground level) suggests that there has been extensive ground remodelling within the walled garden, raising part of it above its pre-1860 level. The site would then be viewed as two tiers with the north being on a slight terrace and the culvert to the south dividing the terrace from a flatter area of planting beds.

The trenches of 2005 were all sited adjacent to the main north wall of the kitchen garden. The first trench was sited to further examine the interior of the stove house. The remainder of the western water tank was uncovered, along with more of the main stove house and vinery structures. At the northern edge of this trench, within 0.40 m of the north wall of the kitchen garden was another wall with slots (running parallel to the stove house's southern wall). This close proximity indicates that the earliest phase of the vinehouse occurred before the north wall of the walled garden was built and that the building was then a free standing structure, very possibly unheated.

In addition there was also evidence for an even earlier structure (or aligned structures) not identified in the previous year. What appeared to be a rectangular

The two 'external' walls on the south front of the stovehouse showing the slots for the trunks of the vines to enter the glasshouse. Note the brick 'blocking' in the wall on the right
© University of Sheffield

planting bed within the stovehouse proved, upon excavation, to be the foundation of either one long freestanding building or an aligned set of freestanding buildings, that stood on the site before the construction of the earliest vinehouse. This structure would have been nearly 18m long, east to west, and almost 2.6m wide, north to south. At the eastern end of the structure the foundations were only around 0.20m deep, but at the western end they were much deeper, at about 1.55m. The discovery of a topsoil layer at the base of the deeper foundations suggests that this building was constructed onto a sloped area – possible evidence of early quarrying. The ground was then raised to a consistent level and the building partially dismantled to form a planting bed within the vinehouse. This planting bed was subsequently also used within the stove house.

These discoveries alter the previous assumption that the walled kitchen garden was constructed before any other buildings in the garden area. It is clear that there was a series of buildings standing on the site before the construction of the walled garden and that the use of the vinehouse's southern wall to form the front wall of the stovehouse was a relatively late phase, in the 19th century. The complex changes made within the stovehouse then occur during the later part of the 19th century, as a result of changes to the heating system, fashions in fruit growing and the management of the kitchen garden.

Excavations in 2005 also examined the Garden Lad's bothy and the fern house. Only the floors and wall bases of both were revealed. The fern house had a very fine tiled floor and was heated by some form of under floor heating, possibly also with a 'hot bed' system.

There remain many unanswered questions about the development of this unexpectedly complex set of structures. Further excavation is required to refine the dating of the various phases and to investigate the previously unrecognised early structure, as well as to explore the large-scale landscape modification that occurred at some point in the early development of the kitchen garden.

Report by J. Hiscock, M. Klemperer and C. Merrony, University of Sheffield

REFERENCES:

Merrony, C. and Klemperer, M. (2004). *The Brodsworth Community Archaeology Project. Interim report on fieldwork undertaken during August and September 2004 on Brodsworth Estate, South Yorkshire.* (**Unpublished report: University of Sheffield**)

Merrony, C., Klemperer, M., Shone, R., Garnham, M. and Cusworth, M. (2003). *Geophysical surveys to evaluate the survival of post-medieval archaeological features in the walled garden, Brodsworth, and adjacent to Elm Farm, Pickburn, South Yorkshire, July/August 2003.* (**Unpublished report: University of Sheffield**)

SOUTH YORKSHIRE INDUSTRIAL HISTORY SOCIETY

The Society encourages interest in all aspects of the industrial history and industrial archaeology of South Yorkshire. It has a Field Recording Group for members who are interested in fieldwork and research. The Group meets informally several times a year to exchange news, compare notes, and arrange research or recording visits. The Society has a programme of talks each winter in Sheffield and Barnsley, and an annual joint meeting with Rotherham Local History Council. In summer it arranges walks and visits. It produces publications, including a journal.

The Society owns four historic industrial sites, which are managed by the South Yorkshire Trades Historical Trust Ltd. Wortley Top Forge (Barnsley) is Britain's only surviving water powered heavy iron forge. It has been restored, mainly by volunteers, and is open to the public, with guided tours, on Sundays and Bank Holidays from Easter Sunday to early November. During 2005-7 work continued on maintaining the Forge and the Society's collections of historic engines and machinery, and on preparing a Conservation Statement and Plan for the Forge.

The Society's site at Rockley (Barnsley), near Rockley Abbey Farm, is an area of woodland containing the ruined stack of a blast furnace of c1700, and the 1813 engine house for a Newcomen atmospheric pumping engine, to drain water from an iron ore mine. There is open access. An annual working party collects litter and controls the vegetation. As it is close to the M1, we registered an interest in the possible impact of the proposals for widening the motorway.

At Hoylandswaine (Barnsley) the Society owns a row of three nail forges, an important monument of the domestic nailmaking trade that existed in a number of South Yorkshire villages. One of them retains its furnace and bellows, and we believe it is the only nail forge, on its original site, in the country to have these. In September 2005, after completing the first stage of conservation work, we opened it to the public for the first time during the national Heritage Open Days, and we have continued to have an open day since then.

The Society's fourth property is the remains of two 1828 steel cementation furnaces at Bower Spring (Sheffield) that now stand next to the final stretch of the city's Inner Relief Road. Their standing brickwork badly needed repair and we applied successfully for a grant from English Heritage to conserve it. The preparatory stages were carried out in 2006-7. In August 2005 ARCUS carried out an excavation of adjoining areas, not belonging to us, which revealed other parts of the works these furnaces belonged to (see report on page 121 of this volume).

Further work was done towards a revised second edition of *Water Power on the Sheffield Rivers*, first published in 1989. Harold Taylor, with Jim Ritchie of the Roggins Group (Silkstone), continued his historical and archaeological research into Barnby

Cementation furnace at Bower Spring, Sheffield, before conservation works © SYAS

canal basin at the head of the Barnsley Canal and its limekilns. He also continued researches into handloom linen weaving in and around Barnsley and the cottages associated with it, and domestic nailmaking around Barnsley and elsewhere in the country. Douglas Oldham continued his research into armour plate forging and rolling by Cammells and Vickers in the late 19th and 20th centuries. Graham Hague looked into bellows manufacture in Sheffield, his interest prompted by the bellows by A Harrop at Hoylandswaine Nail Forge. Derek Bayliss looked into the 'career' of Thomas Needham, one of the villains of the Sheffield Outrages in the 1850s and 60s, following an enquiry from North East Derbyshire Industrial Archaeology Society about Needham's role in an explosion at Damstead Works, Dronfield. He also

looked into the history of Victoria Works, Darnall, an early example (from the 1870s) of a purpose built works for paint manufacture.

The Group collected information about Thrybergh Forge, Rotherham, a 17th century water powered steel forge that was associated with the beginnings of steel manufacture in the area, and later one of the works of the famous 18th century Rotherham ironmasters, the Walkers. We made a number of interesting visits to current archaeological excavations on industrial sites, by courtesy of the archaeological contractors, and were often able to offer information or suggestions.

The Group monitored planning applications for historic industrial sites, and advised Albert Kirton, who represents the Society on Sheffield's Conservation Advisory Group. The Sheffield sites that we were concerned with included Hancock & Lant, between Blonk Street and the river, where there is a crucible furnace stack; Low Matlock rolling mills in the Loxley valley; the horse tram stables in Albert Road, Heeley; the works of Williams Bros. in Green Lane, Kelham Island, which included a crucible steel melting shop; and Whirlow Wheel on the Limb Brook, an unusual example of a cutlery grinding wheel latterly powered by a water turbine, which was partly demolished as unsafe during this period. Important cases in Barnsley included the 1936 works of CEAG Lamps, where we supported a suggestion that one of the stone carvings of miners' safety lamps on the roofline should be preserved; the Beatson Clark glassworks at Stairfoot; the former Hoyle Mill at Thurlstone; and the railway coal drops at Penistone. In Doncaster we had contact with the Don Gorge Heritage Forum.

For the 2005 Sheffield Environment Weeks we led a walk round Malin Bridge, Hillsborough and Owlerton, looking at the intermingling of workshops and housing in the late 19th century suburbs. In 2006 we led walks along the line of the Inner Relief Road extension between Shalesmoor and the Wicker (in a memorable downpour), and down the river Porter from Hunters Bar to the city centre. Our contribution to the Rotherham Walking Festival in 2005 was a walk from Braithwell to Thrybergh Country Park via the Ruddle Mill and Micklebring, where on a reconnaissance for the walk we identified slight traces of ruddle pits. In 2006 we led a walk from Treeton to Norwood locks on the Chesterfield Canal. In February 2007 we helped the Shire Brook Valley Heritage Group with a public walk in the valley, between Woodhouse and Hackenthorpe, to look at its water powered sites, which include Nether Sickle Wheel, a small grinding wheel excavated in 1988.

2005 was the tercentenary of the birth of Thomas Boulsover, the inventor of Old Sheffield Plate. With the profits he bought Whiteley Wood Hall, and we marked the occasion by a walk round Whiteley Wood including, by courtesy of the Guides, a visit to the stables and gardens of the now demolished Hall. Our 2005-6 lecture programme included a talk about Old Sheffield Plate by Trevor Brighton.

The same year was the bicentenary of the birth of the early railway engineer Joseph Locke, who was compared with Isambard Kingdom Brunel and Robert Stephenson by his contemporaries but is less well known today. He was born in Attercliffe and grew up in Barnsley. The Woodhead line between Sheffield and Manchester (now closed), with its unprecedented summit tunnel over three miles long, was one of the many railways he built. Barnsley Council took the lead in planning a celebration of the occasion, with the Friends of Locke Park, the Railway & Canal Historical Society and ourselves. Our contributions included talks about Locke by Graham Hague in Barnsley and Sheffield; a contribution by Derek Bayliss to a video that was distributed to all Barnsley schools; and a walk along the trackbed of the Woodhead railway, now part of the Trans-Pennine Trail, from Penistone to the eastern end of the tunnel at Dunford Bridge, looking at examples of Locke's engineering.

Report by Derek Bayliss

GENERAL PROJECTS

TOLL BAR WASTE WATER TREATMENT WORKS, ADWICK-LE-STREET, DONCASTER

The construction of a new sewer from Edward Road pumping station was preceded by the preparation of a desk-based assessment in March 2005, on behalf of Yorkshire Water Services Ltd. The archaeological potential of this area is considered to be low, given its generally low-lying nature. However, this area contains deposits associated with the Devensian period Lake Humber, which could include peat deposits with significant palaeoenvironmental potential relating to the late glacial period.

Grid Reference SE 546 088 to SE 564 087

**From a report by Mary Lakin,
Northern Archaeological Associates**

ADWICK SCHOOL, WOODLANDS, ADWICK-LE-STREET, DONCASTER

Proposed construction of a new school building, in the grounds of the current school, led to preparation of a desk-based assessment and monitoring of geotechnical test pitting in October 2006, on behalf of Doncaster Metropolitan Borough Council. The site lies in an area with significant archaeological evidence for activity in the Iron Age/Romano-British period.

However, no archaeological features were observed in the test pits.

Centred at Grid Reference SE 535 083

From a report by Mark Stenton, ARCUS

STATION CAR PARK, ADWICK-LE-STREET, DONCASTER

A desk-based assessment was prepared in July 2006 for South Yorkshire Passenger Transport Executive, in advance of a proposed extension to the car park. The area was historically part of Adwick Common, which was enclosed in the 18th century. It has remained undeveloped but, given the limited number of archaeological finds recorded in the near vicinity, may be considered to have a low archaeological potential.

Grid Reference SE 545 085

**From a report by Greg Speed and Oliver Cooper,
Northern Archaeological Associates**

MOTOR TRAINING CENTRE, RANDS LANE, ARMTHORPE, DONCASTER

Proposed development led to a geophysical survey (magnetometer) and trial trenching in May and June 2005, for Mowlem Plc. The site lies to the west of West Moor Park, an area where an extensive late prehistoric/Romano-British landscape has been identified (see overleaf). The geophysical survey results were inconclusive as the site was found to have seen some dumping and disturbance. Subsequent trial trenching confirmed recent disturbance over part of the site. One linear, a pit and a possible post-hole were identified but these were too few to develop an interpretation regarding their relationship to the surrounding archaeological landscape.

Centred at Grid Reference SE 636 053

From reports by A Webb and Marina Rose,
Archaeological Services WYAS

RANDS LANE CEMETERY, ARMTHORPE, DONCASTER

Six trial trenches were excavated in July 2005 for Armthorpe Parish Council, ahead of a proposed extension to the cemetery. The site lies to the west of West Moor Park, an area where an extensive late prehistoric/Romano-British landscape has been identified (see below). No archaeological features were revealed, but this is possibly because of the land's previous use as allotments.

Grid Reference SE 637 054

From a report by Paul Major,
Archaeological Services WYAS

WEST MOOR PARK, ARMTHORPE, DONCASTER

Following earlier archaeological investigations (see 'Archaeology in South Yorkshire 1999/2001', 'Number 11' and

A substantial portion of a South Yorkshire grey ware vessel from a ditch at West Moor Park, Armthorpe © AS - WYAS

'Number 12') further investigation of the West Moor Park site (known as West Moor Park II) was carried out between August and October 2006, on behalf of Priority Sites Ltd. Initial trial trenches were followed by more detailed excavation of three areas. Features identified included ditches and gullies from trackways and enclosures, and discrete elements comprising pits, post-holes, ovens or corn driers and slots that may represent foundations for windbreaks or shelters. The remains appeared to represent small-scale industrial activity, such as grain parching, malting, bread making or large-scale meat cooking, rather than an occupation site. Some features originated in the pre-Roman Iron Age (probably the 1st century AD), but the site was principally in use in the 2nd and 3rd centuries AD.

Centred at Grid Reference SE 637 050

From a report by Adrian Chadwick,
Caroline Powell and Jane Richardson,
Archaeological Services WYAS

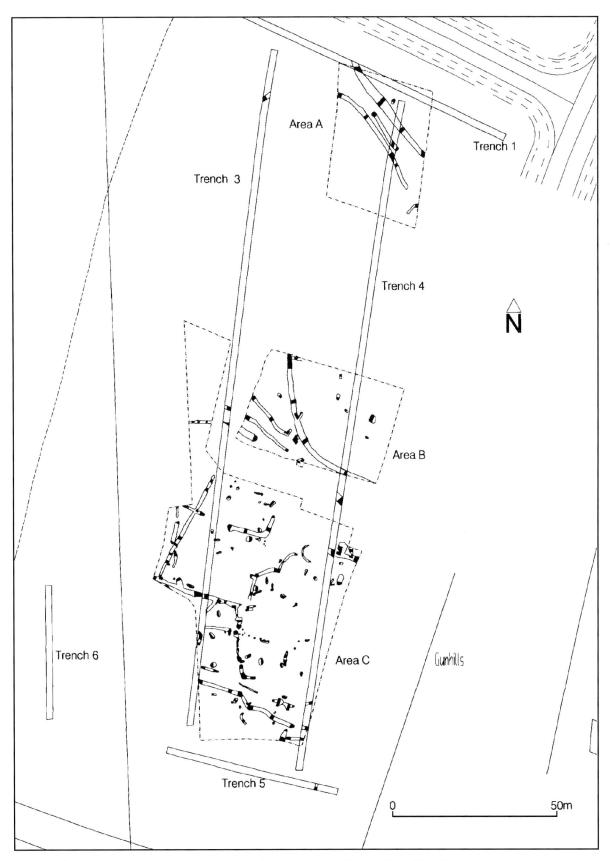

Area A

Trench 1

Trench 3

Trench 4

N

Area B

Trench 6

Area C

Gunhills

Trench 5

0   50m

A plan showing the features and excavated sections from West Moor Park II, Armthorpe   © AS - WYAS

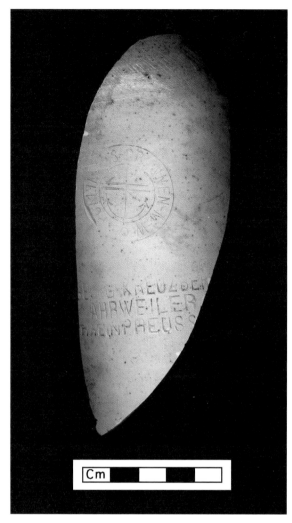

A piece of German Stoneware mineral bottle recovered from Mere Lane, Armthorpe. The piece probably dates from around 1852-1900   © AS - WYAS

MERE LANE, ARMTHORPE, DONCASTER

Trial trenching in August 2006 and archaeological excavation in September 2006 were carried out for Urban i Ltd, in advance of the construction of three apartment blocks. The site lies close to the historic core of the settlement, which is medieval in origin - the church of St Mary is early Norman in date.

Initial investigation revealed two pits and a post-hole of late medieval date, a post-medieval ditch and pits, and the remains of 19th century cottages. More detailed excavation revealed a possible late medieval land surface that had been truncated by an early post-medieval agricultural building with an internal pebble floor and external cobbled yard. A small pottery assemblage was recovered that included sherds of Cistercian ware dating between c.1460 and 1600 AD, and late medieval/early post-medieval Purple Glazed ware, suggesting activity on and around the site from the 14th century onwards.

Grid Reference SE 623 050

From reports by Bernie McCluskey and Martin Lightfoot, Archaeological Services WYAS

LAND OFF MARKET PLACE, ASKERN, DONCASTER

Proposed redevelopment of a site formerly occupied by the Swan Hotel led to a trial trench evaluation in January 2006, for Britannia Developments Ltd. The site lies close to the historic core of the settlement, which has medieval origins and was developed as a spa town in the late 19th century, but no archaeological remains of significance were revealed. Much of the area was found to have been disturbed by demolition of the hotel buildings.

Grid Reference SE 561 136

From a report by Marina Rose, Archaeological Services WYAS

A modern rock carving on former quarry face, Barnburgh Cliff © ARCUS

CLIFF PLANTATION & STABLES WOOD, BARNBURGH, DONCASTER

A desk-based assessment and woodland survey was carried out in May 2006 for Barnburgh and Harlington Parish Council, to support the development of a management plan. The study area is located immediately south of Barnburgh Cliff, which is known to be an area of prehistoric and Romano-British settlement.

The area south of the bridleway was enclosed in 1819 and is named as Cliff Plantation in 1839. Tree planting, and replanting between 1906 and 1930, may have disturbed any subsurface deposits of archaeological interest. The area north of the bridleway was not included in the plantation until 1933. Prior to this, this area was an active quarry. Further work would be required to establish whether any of the fissures present in the rock face are natural features, which may have archaeological potential, or whether they all relate to quarrying.

The remains of Cliff Cottages lie on the edge of Stables Wood. These had been constructed by the time of the 1839 tithe map and were probably linked to the adjoining quarries. The wood itself was recorded as 'ancient' in 1819 and there is evidence that the wood was actively managed by coppicing – at least in the early 20th century.

Centred at Grid Reference SE 495 039

From a report by Mark Stenton, Chris Breeden and Helen Holderness, ARCUS

SCHOOL HOUSE, CHURCH LANE, BARNBURGH, DONCASTER

A watching brief was maintained on groundworks for a new house in February 2006, for Oxford Properties Ltd. Although the site lies within the historic core of the village, close to St Peter's church, which dates to the early Norman period, no archaeological features or finds were found.

Grid Reference SE 483 032

From a report by M Cusworth, Dearne Valley Archaeological Services Ltd.

One of the mid-nineteenth century buildings at Ivy House Farm   © CS Archaeology

IVY HOUSE FARM, BARNBURGH, DONCASTER

A desk-based assessment was prepared in July 2006 for Wortley Construction Ltd, to inform a planning application for redevelopment. The farm lies within the historic core of Barnburgh village and is first shown on the 1839 tithe map, although some of the standing buildings on site suggest earlier origins. Overall, the collection of farm buildings charts the development of agricultural techniques and intensification during the 19th and early 20th centuries. The farmstead's development is on model farm lines but came very late, towards the end of the period of model farm construction. This is probably linked to the expansion of the surrounding coal industry triggering a late 19th century expansion of the local agricultural industry.

Grid Reference SE 484 033

From a report by Chris Scurfield, CS Archaeology

GREEN FARM, BARNBURGH, DONCASTER

Proposed conversion and demolition of farm buildings led to the preparation of a desk-based assessment and building appraisal for Chris Carr Associates. The farm buildings range in date from the 17th to the 19th centuries. The farmhouse, which dates to the late 17th century, is listed grade II. The central section of the farmhouse was the earliest structure noted; it contains re-used medieval timbers in the roof space. The assessment noted potential for buried features to the rear and northeast of the farmhouse.

Grid Reference SE 484 032

From a report by Mark Douglas and Oliver Jessop, ARCUS

STATION ROAD MALTINGS, BARNBY DUN, DONCASTER

A desk-based assessment and building appraisal was prepared for Wright Investments in November 2005 in advance of redevelopment. The maltings had been grade II listed but the building was de-listed in 2004 due to partial destruction by fire in 1999. The Station Road maltings were erected c.1900, as was the terrace of workers' housing situated nearby. The building still contains evidence for the main stages of the malting process (controlled germination of cereals and the termination of this process by the application of heat, for brewing): barley storage, steeping, controlled germination, kilning and malt storage.

Grid Reference SE 618 082

From a report by AC Swann, Archaeological Services WYAS

The timber clad grain hoist at The Maltings, Barnby Dun   © AS - WYAS

GRUMBLEHURST, THORPE MARSH NEAR BARNBY DUN, DONCASTER

The site of a proposed borrow pit, to provide material to reform a flood defence bank, was investigated in June 2004, for the Environment Agency. The trial trench revealed no archaeological deposits or finds.

Grid Reference SE 597 087

From a report by Sean Bell, ARCUS

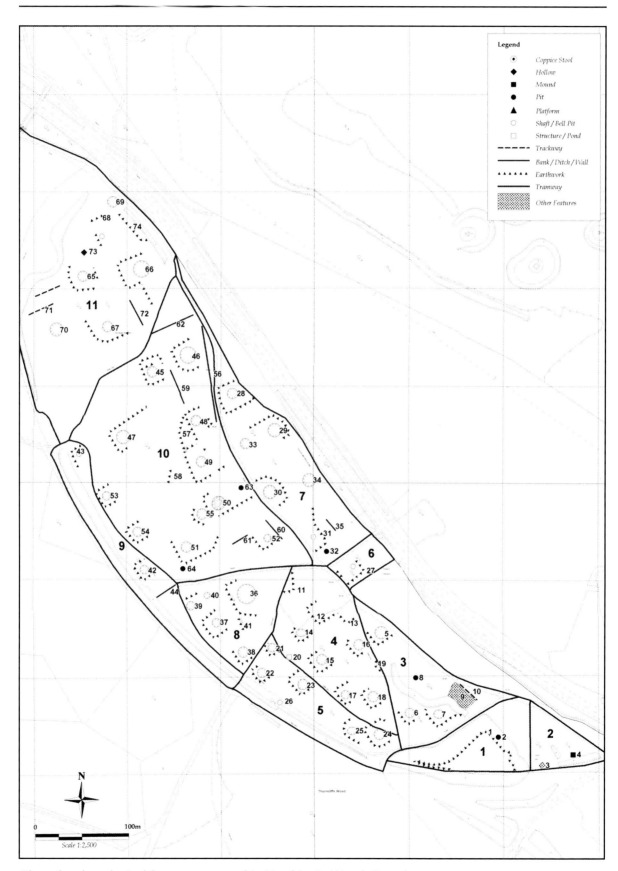

Plan of archaeological features surveyed in Newbiggin Wood, Barnsley   © ASE-Ltd

WOODLAND SURVEY: CLIFFE WOOD, NEWBIGGIN WOOD AND BELL BANK WOOD & WOOLEY BANK WOOD, BARNSLEY

Following earlier desk-top assessments, walk-over surveys of these woodlands were carried out between September and December 2005, for Barnsley MBC. The work formed part of the *Fuelling a Revolution Project: the Woods that Founded the Steel Country* (see 'Archaeology in South Yorkshire 1999/2001, 'Number 11' and 'Number 12').

Seventy seven archaeological sites were identified in Cliffe Wood, all of which were post-medieval in date. They include a possible charcoal burning platform, mine shafts, and an area of open grassland that corresponds to the former course of the Aire and Calder Navigation, built in 1799. The Cudworth to Barnsley branch of the Midland railway also crossed the site and demolition rubble from two former viaducts was noted.

Seventy four archaeological sites were identified in Newbiggin Wood, all of which were post-medieval in date. These include the remains of the hamlet of New Biggin and an extensive area of mining comprising thirty shaft mounds, three shafts and two bell pits. Other features included quarry pits, a possible Q-pit, and the remains of a tramway, which used to link Newbiggin Colliery with the Manchester, Sheffield & Lincolnshire railway, via Tankersley Colliery.

Thirty five archaeological sites were identified in Bell Bank and Woolley Bank

Woods, all of which were again post-medieval in date. These included two well-defined bell pits, quarry pits, a disused mine shaft and the remains of a tramway.

Centred at Grid References SE 362 068 (Cliffe Wood), SE 343 985 (Newbiggin Wood), SE 348 029 (Bell Bank Wood), SE 353 032 (Woolley Bank Wood)

From reports by Emma Gowans and John Pouncett, ASE Ltd

WILLOWBANK AND DEARNE VALLEY PARK, BARNSLEY

A desk-based assessment was prepared for Barnsley MBC in August 2005, to assess the archaeological potential of this area and to provide an understanding of the area's wider historic landscape. The information gathered is to be used for educational purposes and will identify features that warrant on-site interpretation.

Although no evidence of prehistoric or Romano-British activity has been found within this area, the results of fieldwork along the Dearne valley further to the east suggest the valley was farmed and settled by the late Iron Age. There is also little direct archaeological evidence for medieval activity in this area, other than the remains of the former Monk Bretton Priory, which dates from the 12th to the late 15th centuries, and the associated Priory Mill, which is possibly 13th century in origin. However, it is likely that the valley was heavily cultivated at this time; the villages of Barugh and Darton, which lie on either side of the river, are both entered in the Domesday Book.

The character of the landscape in this area has been heavily influenced by industrial activity from the late 18th century onwards. The linen industry was important locally and this area contains the remains of one linen works, at Old Mill, and the remains of associated bleach works, at Old Mill, Green Foot and Hoyle Mill. By the mid-19th century there were numerous collieries and smaller coal pits working throughout the area. The colliery sites have now mostly been cleared, but their former spoil heaps continue to be a feature in the landscape. Infrastructure associated with the 18th and 19th century industrial landscape also survives, such as short lengths of the Barnsley canal and the pillars that supported its aqueduct, and the courses of a number of railway lines.

Centred at Grid Reference SE 346 075

From a report by Mitchell Pollington, Archaeological Services WYAS

TRANSPORT INTERCHANGE, BARNSLEY

Two trial trenches were excavated in the current bus station between December 2005 and January 2006, for Laing O'Rourke. An earlier desk-based assessment (see *'Archaeology in South Yorkshire Number 12'*) had confirmed that this area was developed in the late 19th century, with a series of buildings associated with the nearby railway. One

trench targeted the former Carriage Works, but no archaeological remains were identified; this area appeared to have been levelled previously. The second trench targeted a building of unknown purpose and identified a stone and brick surface, but no associated finds. A section of a former railway viaduct, on the east side of Midland Street, was also photographically recorded, prior to its demolition. The stone-built viaduct was constructed for a line to the new Court House Station in the 1870s.

Centred at Grid Reference SE 346 064

From a report by Daniel Lee, Archaeological Services WYAS

MANDELA SQUARE, BARNSLEY

A watching brief during geotechnical test pitting was carried out here in May and June 2005, for Estell Warren Ltd. An earlier desk-based assessment (see *'Archaeology in South Yorkshire Number 12'*) identified that this proposed redevelopment site, off Regent Street, lies on the edge of Barnsley's historic core and didn't get developed until the early 19th century. The remains of demolished properties of this date and associated yard surfaces were found; no evidence for medieval activity was recovered.

Grid Reference SE 346 064

From a report by Marina Rose, Archaeological Services WYAS

The nineteenth century coal railway tunnel at the junction of Old Mill Lane and Burton Road   © ARCUS

BARNSLEY CITY ACADEMY, WORSBOROUGH BANK END, BARNSLEY

Proposals to develop a new academic centre led to the preparation of a desk-based assessment in April 2005, for Cundall Johnston and Partners. The site remained as fields until the mid 20th century, when a series of terraces were constructed to form playing fields for the residents of the growing settlements of Kendray and Worsbrough Dale. The extent of groundworks for these suggest this site can be considered to have a low archaeological potential.

Grid Reference SE 361 047

From a report by Robin Taylor-Wilson, Pre-Construct Archaeology

BURTON ROAD BUS CORRIDOR, BARNSLEY

Plans to develop a quality bus corridor led to the preparation of a desk-based assessment in February 2007, for Barnsley MBC. The proposed route runs southeast from Burton Road, through the Dearne Valley Park. This area remained as fields until the late 19th century, when it was developed for industrial use. By the time of the 1894 Ordnance Survey, the site was occupied by the Old Mill Gas Works and the Barnsley Coal Railway extension line crossed the north of the site, continuing via a tunnel under Burton Road/Old Mill Lane. The Gas Works buildings were demolished by 1973 and the site was subsequently used as a depot. The industrial archaeological impact of the

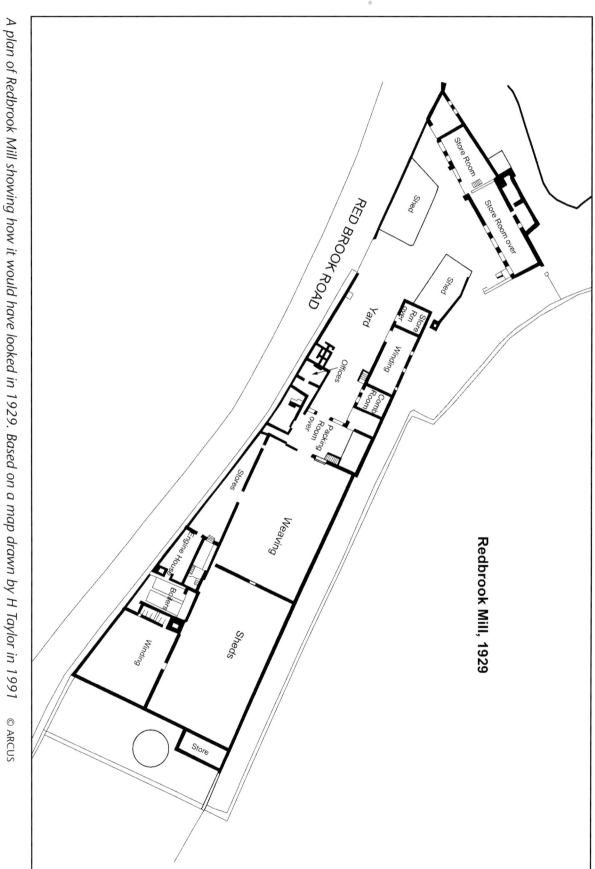

A plan of Redbrook Mill showing how it would have looked in 1929. Based on a map drawn by H Taylor in 1991   © ARCUS

Redbrook Mill, 1929

RED BROOK ROAD

Store Room

Store Room over

Shed

Shed

Store Rm over

Winding

Offices

Yard

Comb Room

Packing Room over

Stores

Weaving

Engine House

Boilers

Winding

Sheds

Store

scheme will depend on the extent of the demolition of the works and, therefore, the extent of below-ground survival.

Centred at Grid Reference SE 352 074

From a report by Mark Stenton, ARCUS

REDBROOK MILL, BARNSLEY

Proposals to develop the site of Redbrook Mill for residential use led to the production of a desk-based assessment in July 2005 and an evaluation in January 2006, for Redbrook Mill Developments. The mill is the site of a late 18th century bleachworks and 19th century linen mill, which remained in use until the late 20th century. A site visit found few visible features of early date. Linen production ceased in 1957, despite major redevelopment of the site; this and subsequent developments removed many earlier structures. The original bleachery building was demolished in the 1970s.

Excavation of five evaluation trenches showed that few elements from the original bleachery survived, although some early sandstone and brick walls from this phase were revealed. Elsewhere, elements of the 19th century linen mill were recorded, including the cobbled floor of the weaving room, the backfilled cellars of a winding room and two wheel pits within the former engine house. The evaluation, therefore, confirmed the

presence of relatively well-preserved sub-surface archaeology.

Grid Reference SE 321 076

From reports by Mark Stenton and Helen Holderness, ARCUS

WESTGATE, BARNSLEY

A watching brief was carried out during soil stripping in April and May 2006, for Osprey Commercial Properties Ltd. An earlier desk-based assessment (see *'Archaeology in South Yorkshire Number 12'*) had indicated that redevelopment here could impact on remains of the former Barnsley Canal, which ran down the eastern edge of the site. The canal was established in 1799 and closed in 1953, after which this stretch was infilled.

The watching brief revealed remains of a dry dock and part of the main canal wall, to its west. The canal wall was constructed of substantial sandstone blocks, in place standing up to 2m in height. Where the wall met the dry dock there was an L-shaped gatepost, the internal corner having been carved out to accommodate the wooden lock gate. This gatepost was mirrored on the eastern side of the dry dock, although the canal wall on this side had been lost to later disturbance. Most of the dry dock wall had also been constructed from sandstone blocks, except in the northwest corner where wooden sleepers had been used – perhaps to act as a fender for incoming barges. The concave floor of the dock was constructed from sandstone setts, except at the northern end, where wooden planks had been laid to form a small pad.

Grid Reference SE 346 072

From a report by Michael Klemperer and Richard Jackson, ARCUS

WILBROOK RISE, BARNSLEY

A watching brief took place here during groundworks carried out between November 2004 and September 2005, for Scott Wilson Kirkpatrick & Company. An earlier desk-based assessment had suggested that, although it lies within the grounds of the 12th – 13th century Gawber Hall, the site had low archaeological potential, as a result of later mining and quarrying (see *'Archaeology in South Yorkshire Number 11'*). The watching brief confirmed this; no archaeological features or finds were identified.

Grid Reference SE 323 076

From a report by Marina Rose, Archaeological Services WYAS

LOW LAITHES FARM, ARDSLEY, BARNSLEY

Building recording of this farm complex was carried out between May and July 2006, on behalf of the Hesley Group, in advance of residential conversion. Agricultural intensification led to the development of 'model farms' in the 18th and 19th centuries across the country, where a range of buildings

Detail shot showing dove nest-boxes in the dovecote at Low Laithes Farm   © CS Archaeology

would surround a central rectangular courtyard. Low Laithes Farm follows this pattern and probably dates in origin from the late 18th century. The farmhouse and a cart shed/dovecote are the oldest standing structures, pre-dating 1840. Other buildings, such as the barn, cart shed and possible carriage house, reflect the development of the farm in the earlier 19th century. This investment in the farm continued in the later 19th century, with the construction of the stables and the dairy. The 20th century saw partial demolition of some of these structures and much rebuilding.

Grid Reference SE 389 049

From a report by Chris Scurfield, CS Archaeology

THE COURTYARD, HIGH STREET, BAWTRY, DONCASTER

A proposed development of office and retail units, within the town's historic core, led to evaluation of the site in May 2006, for Leonard Tomlinson Ltd. Two trial trenches were excavated, but no deposits of archaeological significance were recorded – perhaps as a result of modern disturbance.

Grid Reference SK 651 928

From a report by Linda Hamilton, Pre-Construct Archaeology

LAND NEAR RIVER IDLE, BAWTRY, DONCASTER

An archaeological watching brief was carried out in August 2005 during soil stripping. A large quantity of 3rd and 4th century Roman pottery sherds and coins were discovered. The pottery has a high proportion (c30%) of bowls/dishes and beakers, typical of a higher status urban site or villa. However, a high proportion of the pottery showed evidence for burning or sooting and contained some unusual forms, including part of a facepot, with moulded eye and nose, and possible tazze or incense burners. This has led to the suggestion that the finds indicate the presence of a late Roman shrine.

In April 2006 a geophysical survey (magnetometer) was carried out over the surrounding area but this did not identify anomalies typical of archaeological activity except in the immediate vicinity of the original findspot.

From reports by T S Harrison, A Webb, Dave Berg and Paul Major, Archaeological Services WYAS

BRIDGE LANE HOUSE, BAWTRY, DONCASTER

Planned construction of new houses led to an archaeological evaluation in July 2006, for Lewis Holdings Ltd; the site lies near the River Idle, on the edge of the town's historic core. Three trial trenches were excavated, which revealed a number of features relating to the medieval settlement of Bawtry. Features relating to water management included a channel and possible pond. Other features included post-holes and a timber-lined (barrel) pit. These features appear to have gone out of use in the late medieval period. Demolition rubble and the remains of a wall, not shown on maps from 1850 onwards, indicated later activity.

Two distinct groups of pottery were recovered from across the site: late medieval pottery, including Humberwares and Coal Measures Wares; and post-medieval wares, predominantly from the late 18th/early 19th century. Waterlogging of some deposits ensured good organic preservation; five fragments of leather recovered were identified as being parts of medieval/late medieval shoes.

Grid Reference SK 653 928

From reports by Richard O'Neill, ARCUS

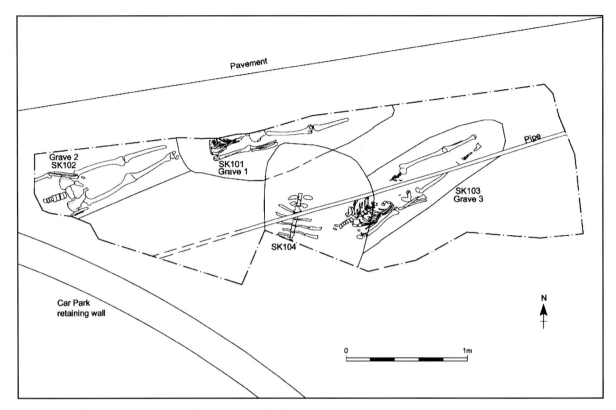

A trench plan showing burials from Bawtry Hall, Bawtry   © ARCUS

BAWTRY HALL, BAWTRY, DONCASTER

Further archaeological investigations were carried out here between October 2005 and July 2006, for Bett Homes (Yorkshire) Limited (for earlier work see *'Archaeology in South Yorkshire Number 11'* and *'Number 12'*). Building recording of a gate lodge and five agricultural buildings was carried out; all are late 18th to mid 19th century in origin, and all have been subject to alteration in recent years. Excavation of two areas thought to have potential for medieval remains revealed no features pre-dating the late post-medieval period; the small amount of medieval pottery recovered was residual in these later features.

Ground works for a widened access road exposed two burials, which led to detailed recording, followed by a watching brief during further works. The burials lie adjacent to the former chapel of St Mary Magdalene, part of a medieval hospital established by the 13th century. Only one further burial was observed during the watching brief, suggesting that the graveyard was always small. Documentary evidence records the chapel as a resting place for members of the Morton family, wealthy local benefactors; it is not known if the graveyard was also used for former residents of the hospital.

Centred at Grid Reference SK 650 929

From reports by Oliver Jessop, Mark Douglas, Dr Ben Chan, Richard O'Neill and Richard Jackson, ARCUS

MORE HALL FARM, BOLSTERSTONE, SHEFFIELD

A proposal to convert the farm from agricultural use to residential use led to an archaeological assessment and building appraisal on behalf of N&V Horton in January 2005, not previously reported. The buildings of More Hall Farm comprise two ranges of buildings around an open yard. The earliest structure identified was the barn, which contains three re-used cruck timber trusses. The remainder of the buildings appear to have developed with expansion of the farm in the early part of the 19th century, and their design reflects the trend towards improved agricultural efficiency at the end of the 18th century.

Grid Reference SK 292 958

From a report by Mark Douglas, ARCUS

MALTKILN FARM, BRAITHWELL, DONCASTER

A proposal for residential redevelopment led to preparation of a desk-based assessment and buildings appraisal in April 2005, for Modern Homes. The site lies within the historic core of the village of Braithwell, which has medieval origins. However, many of the standing buildings are modern; only the farmhouse and barn to its west can be identified on the tithe map of 1839. Earthworks on land to the west of the farm complex were tested by a trial trench evaluation later in April and were found to be geological in

A cruck truss at More Hall Farm, Bolsterstone
© ARCUS

origin. A subsequent watching brief during demolition of the buildings identified no features or finds of archaeological interest.

Grid Reference SK 530 945

From reports by C Clay and R D Gardner, Pre-Construct Archaeology (Lincoln)

ST PAUL'S SCHOOL, BRIERLEY, BARNSLEY

Proposed demolition of the former school building, in advance of redevelopment, led to a photographic survey being carried out in July 2006, for WBH Homes. Whilst a school building is shown on Ordnance Survey maps from 1850, the current school building relates to a building first shown on the 1893 map. The present building shows three phases of construction, with most relating to a reorganisation of the internal space in the early 20th century – reflected in a date stone of 1916 in the front extension. The layout from this phase comprises a central corridor, with entrance doors at either end, with two classrooms on either side.

This mirror-image arrangement is typical of school buildings of this date and was designed to separate boys and girls. Map evidence shows that the playground was also split into two separate areas.

Grid Reference SE 411 109

From a report by Tegwen Roberts, ARCUS

CHURCH STREET, BRIERLEY, BARNSLEY

Proposed development on land off Church Street led to a trial trench evaluation in September 2006, for Richard Ryder Partnership. The site is within the core of the village of Brierley, which is mentioned in the Domesday Book as Breselai – meaning 'clearing among the briar', and which has a layout typical of medieval linear settlements. Two post-holes and a gully were identified towards the rear of the plot. Sherds of 11th–13th century shell-tempered pottery were recovered from one of the post-holes, suggesting that the structure they formed part of was early medieval in date.

Grid Reference SE 413 110

From a report by Bernard McCluskey, Archaeological Services WYAS

WOOLGREAVES FARM, CAWTHORNE, BARNSLEY

Building recording of the farmhouse and adjoining barn, which are both listed, was carried out in September 2003 for Matthew Whitehead; the farm buildings are to be converted to residential use. Farmhouse and barn both appear late 17th century in date, and a Latin dedication inscription on a stone lintel of the farmhouse gives 1672 as the date of construction. These buildings were linked together, soon after, by a long range containing good quality residential rooms either side of an access cartway. Later, possibly at the start of the 20th century, these rooms were changed into agricultural implement stores and stables.

Grid Reference SE 145 159

From a report by C G Lee, Archaeological Services WYAS

RED HOUSE, CHURCH STREET, CAWTHORNE, BARNSLEY

A proposal to construct a new dwelling within the walled garden of Red House led to archaeological work here in March 2007, on behalf of Mr and Mrs Russum. Red House is a grade II listed building that was built during the late 18th century. Part of the garden wall was recorded prior to its demolition and trial trenches investigated the site. These revealed a garden path and three ditches, which are all probably post-medieval in date. A watching brief during later groundworks observed exposure of a stone lined well that may be an original garden feature.

Grid Reference SE 284 080

From a report by Chris Scurfield, CS Archaeology

HESLEY WOOD, CHAPELTOWN, SHEFFIELD

A desk-based assessment was prepared in August 2005 for Carl Bro Group Ltd, to inform a planning application for site redevelopment. No archaeologically significant find spots or features were identified within the proposal area and the scheme is considered to have a low archaeological impact.

Grid Reference SK 362 962

From a report by Mark Stenton, ARCUS

CUSWORTH HALL AND PARK, CUSWORTH, DONCASTER

Further fieldwork was carried out between August 2005 and April 2006, for Doncaster MBC, as part of the restoration scheme for the hall and park (see *'Archaeology in South Yorkshire 1999/2001'*, *'Number 11'* and *'Number 12'*). The hall was built in 1740-45 by George Platt, for William Wrightson, and was altered in 1749-53 by James Paine. Building recording identified examples of historic wallpaper in four rooms during the restoration works. A watching brief on the excavation of service trenches around the hall was also carried out. One service trench cut through a former brick drain that contained a sealed midden of 18th century ceramics, glass and bone. Of these, the glassware represented the most significant find, comprising glass from

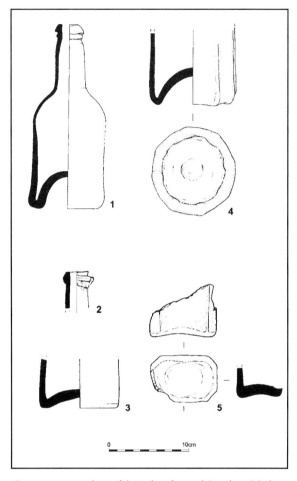

Some examples of bottles found in the 18th century midden at Cusworth Hall © ARCUS

mid 18th century wine bottles, a proportion being from relatively rare moulded types.

Centred at Grid Reference SE 546 038

From reports by Mark Douglas and Oliver Jessop, ARCUS

DODWORTH BYPASS, BARNSLEY

Following an earlier desk-based assessment (reported in *'Archaeology in South Yorkshire Number 11'*), which suggested this road scheme would affect an area of low archaeological potential, a watching brief on initial construction works was carried out for Barnsley MBC. Observation of the site topsoil strip, in April 2005, revealed a modern field boundary and evidence of earlier ridge and furrow ploughing. No other archaeological features were identified.

Centred at Grid Reference SE 315 060

From a report by Bernie McCluskey, Archaeological Services WYAS

CAPITOL PARK, DODWORTH, BARNSLEY

A series of archaeological works were undertaken here between May 2005 and January 2006, following an earlier desk-based assessment and geophysical survey, which suggested the site had good archaeological potential (see *'Archaeology in South Yorkshire Number 12'*). The work was undertaken for Sterling Capitol Estates Ltd.

Nine trial trenches were excavated, targeting a range of geophysical anomalies. A series of pit-like anomalies, thought to represent small-scale coal extraction, were revealed to be the result of natural coal outcrops. Most of the trenches revealed little of archaeological interest, but one trench revealed a large boundary ditch with post voids, suggesting it originally held a substantial fence or palisade. To ensure this feature was properly understood, a larger area around it was then stripped and recorded. Further ditches, gullies and pits were identified. No dating

evidence was found, but a quantity of daub was recovered (80 fragments in total, of which 79 came from the boundary ditch), suggesting they are of prehistoric date.

Three areas were then subject to detailed excavation and a watching brief maintained on construction works elsewhere on the site. This work identified further stretches of the boundary ditch and additional pits and gullies. A fire-pit containing a thick layer of charcoal was sampled for radiocarbon dating. These findings are of particular importance because of the apparent lack of prehistoric/Romano-British cropmark sites on the coal measures west of Barnsley. The features discovered at Capitol Park suggest that late prehistoric settlement was present, implying that the absence of cropmarks reflects infilling of cut features with a subsoil that is not nutrient rich enough to generate observable variation in crop growth.

Building surveys and watching briefs were conducted prior to and during demolition of Lane Head Farm North (SE 316 061) and Lane Head Farm South (SE 316 060). Demolition of the former revealed the remains of a timber framed building comprising a single storey post and truss structure; dendrochronological dating gives a felling date for the timbers of 1627. Distortions of the timbers indicate that the framing was prepared while the timbers were still green, giving a construction date within a few weeks or months of felling. The buildings of Lane Head Farm South have their origins as a small cottage in the late 18th century, since when it has been expanded and developed. A survey of 1806 describes the property as 'cottage – weaver's shop and chamber'. No cellar

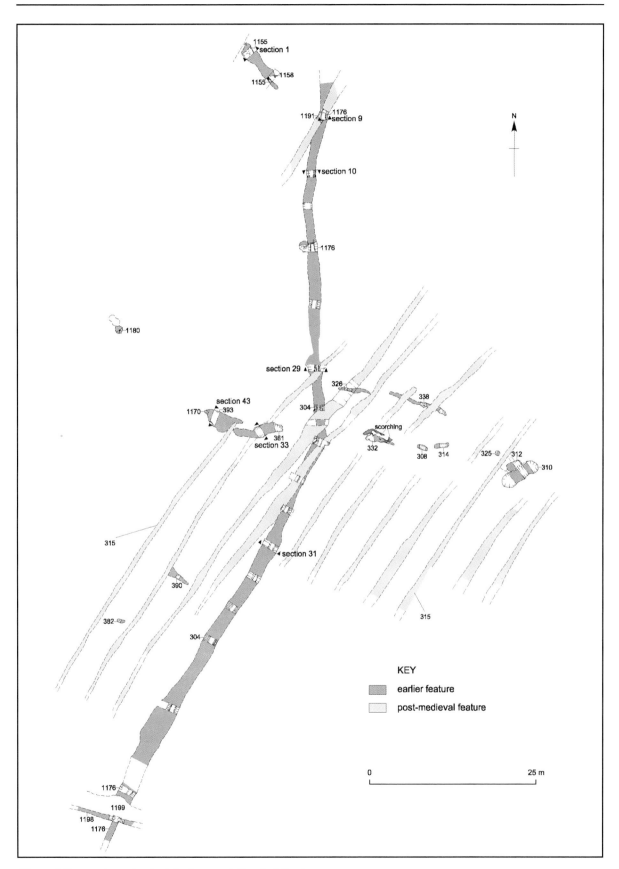

Plan of the archaeological features at Capitol Park   © NAA

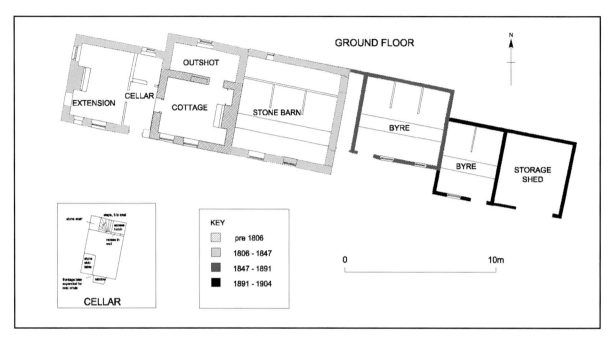

Phased plan of the range of buildings at Lane Head Farm South   © NAA

was found, suggesting that the weaver's workshop was above ground, unlike the below ground workshops often associated with weaver's cottages in the local area.

Centred at Grid Reference SE 317 060

**From reports by Gavin Robinson
and Penny Middleton,
Northern Archaeological Associates**

NUTWELL WATER TREATMENT WORKS PIPELINE, DONCASTER

A desk-based assessment for the route of a series of new water mains to connect with Nutwell WTW was prepared in August 2005, on behalf of Yorkshire Water. The assessment identified 103 known archaeological sites close to the proposed works, with the pipeline due to cross several areas of late prehistoric/Romano-British field systems, identified from cropmarks.

A series of geophysical surveys (magnetometer) were carried out at six locations along the route. Anomalies with archaeological potential were observed in two of the locations, suggesting buried pits and field boundaries. Subsequent trial trenching and archaeological monitoring during soil stripping confirmed the presence of boundary ditches and trackways, some of which were not visible as cropmarks. Some ditches displayed evidence of deep siltation prior to being re-cut to re-define the boundaries. The features are likely to be part of the wider landscape of Iron Age/Romano-British field systems known in the area.

Grid Reference SE 631 031 (Nutwell WTW)

**From reports by Oliver Cooper, Greg Speed
and Jonathan Tabor, Northern Archaeological
Associates; GSB Prospection Ltd (geophysics)**

LAND AT RIDGEWOOD SCHOOL, SCAWSBY, DONCASTER

A proposal for construction of a new school block led to a desk-based assessment and a watching brief on geotechnical pitting in October 2006, for Doncaster MBC. The school lies to the east of the site of a probable deserted medieval village and this was probably agricultural land until the construction of the school in the 1960s. The test pits demonstrated that the school's construction included formation of a level platform that would have impacted on any earlier archaeological features present, at least on the northern part of the site.

Centred at Grid Reference SE 541 049

From a report by Mark Stenton, ARCUS

BARNSLEY ROAD PLAYING FIELD, SCAWSBY, DONCASTER

A watching brief took place in September 2005 during soil stripping for construction of a games area. The work was done for Brodsworth Parish Council. The site lies in an area where Roman period burials have been recorded. However, the groundworks carried out were very limited in nature and no archaeological features or finds were observed.

Grid Reference SE 549 048

From a report by Daniel Lee, Archaeological Services WYAS

BAWTRY ROAD BUS CORRIDOR, DONCASTER

Following an earlier assessment (see *'Archaeology in South Yorkshire Number 12'*), monitoring of construction ground works took place in September 2006. The route lies in an area of known Romano-British activity, but no archaeological remains were observed.

Centred at Grid Reference SE 595 026

From a report by Katherine Baker, ARCUS

DONCASTER RACECOURSE, DONCASTER

Further investigation comprising a geophysical survey (magnetometer) was carried out in August 2006 on the Bloodstock Sales site adjoining the racecourse (for earlier work see *'Archaeology in South Yorkshire Number 12'*). Magnetic anomalies of potential archaeological origin included two parallel anomalies to the east of the stable block that could mark the boundary of an enclosure. A number of trial trenches were excavated in August 2006, focusing on the possible archaeological anomalies identified. The majority of features discovered were dateable to the 19th and 20th centuries; where features contained no definite dating evidence, sedimentary and cartographic evidence still implies post-medieval dates.

In November 2006 building recording and trial trenching took place in advance of work for a new hotel and apartments. Three early 20th century buildings were recorded but these were thought to be of limited archaeological/historical interest. No archaeological deposits were revealed during the evaluation.

Grid References centred on SE 601 034 (Bloodstock Sales site), SE 600 030 (proposed hotel site)

From a report by F S M Prince, Bartlett-Clark Consultancy (geophysics), and L Craddock-Bennett, Suzanne Reeve and K H Crooks, Archaeological Investigations Ltd. (evaluation/building recording)

Excavation of a substantial ditch section, High Fisher Gate © SYAS

HIGH FISHER GATE, DONCASTER

A desk-based assessment was prepared for Urban i Ltd in May 2006, to inform a planning application for site redevelopment. The assessment concluded that redevelopment here has a high potential to impact on sub-surface archaeology. The defences of the Roman fort and the Anglo-Saxon *burh* are both projected to run across the site. Historic maps suggest that the site was occupied by medieval burgage plots and contained a number of post-medieval structures and yards. The close proximity of the churchyard of St Mary Magdalene also raises the possibility of human remains being present.

Four evaluation trenches were excavated in November 2006, in and adjacent to the modern building on the site. These revealed two ditches: one very large ditch corresponding to the likely position of the Anglo-Saxon *burh*

defences; a more truncated ditch coinciding with the postulated line of the early defences of the Roman fort (see page 182 in the colour section).

Centred at Grid Reference SE 575 035

From reports by Louise Ford, Adrian Chadwick and Martin Lightfoot, Archaeological Services WYAS

GREYFRIARS ROAD, DONCASTER

Construction of a new electricity substation led to a trial trench evaluation and a watching brief during groundworks between March 2005 and March 2006. The archaeological works were carried out for Doncaster MBC and Yorkshire Electricity Distribution Ltd. The evaluation revealed evidence for medieval occupation of the area between the 12th and 16th centuries, probably associated with the nearby Grey Friars Franciscan Friary. Auger testing highlighted the potential for earlier archaeological deposits to survive buried below layers of alluvium; these were not investigated.

Features recorded included a wall foundation, beam slots and a pebble floor. Finds recovered included medieval pottery sherds, roof tiles, cereal grain, and animal/fish remains. In addition, a quantity of casting debris associated with copper-working was recovered, mostly from one pit. No mould or crucible fragments were recovered, however, suggesting that the debris came from a casting workshop located elsewhere. The pottery found in association dates this activity to the 13th to 14th centuries.

Grid Reference SE 571 036

From reports by Bernard McCluskey and Andrew Walsh, Archaeological Services WYAS

LAND OFF PRIORY WALK, DONCASTER

Following earlier archaeological works (see *'Archaeology in South Yorkshire Number 12'*) a watching brief was carried out during excavation of foundation footings in April 2005, for Lazarus Properties Ltd. The footings were shallow and did not penetrate below 19th/20th century garden soils. As a result, no archaeologically significant features or finds were found.

Grid Reference SE 575 032

From a report by Bernard McCluskey, Archaeological Services WYAS

PRIORY SCHOOL, CANTLEY, DONCASTER

Following earlier archaeological assessment and evaluation (see *'Archaeology in South Yorkshire Number 11'* and *'Number 12'*) detailed excavation of four areas was carried out for Persimmon Homes (South Yorkshire) Ltd. The site lies in the vicinity of a number of known Roman pottery kilns and evidence for pottery production was revealed, in the form of pottery wasters and kiln waste, but no kilns were identified.

Exposed features indicated four phases of occupation during the Roman period. The first phase included the partial remains of a sub-rectangular enclosure dated to between AD70 and AD120 by the pottery (including large sherds from a flanged mortarium, or mixing bowl, and the rims and bodies of two neckless jars). The second phase saw apparent expansion of the site by the addition of a further enclosure and a droveway with attached field systems, sometime from the mid to late 2nd century AD. Pottery from this period included a fragment of a South Yorkshire white slipped mortarium and a Dressel 20 amphora sherd, used to carry olive oil from the Roman province of Baetica in southern Spain.

From the late 2nd to early 3rd centuries AD the northern part of the site was marked by features attributable to settlement associated with the nearby Roman pottery industry. The second phase enclosure was re-modelled and enlarged and small discrete features including probable domestic ovens were added. Sherds from a total of 34 waster vessels were found in this phase, most of

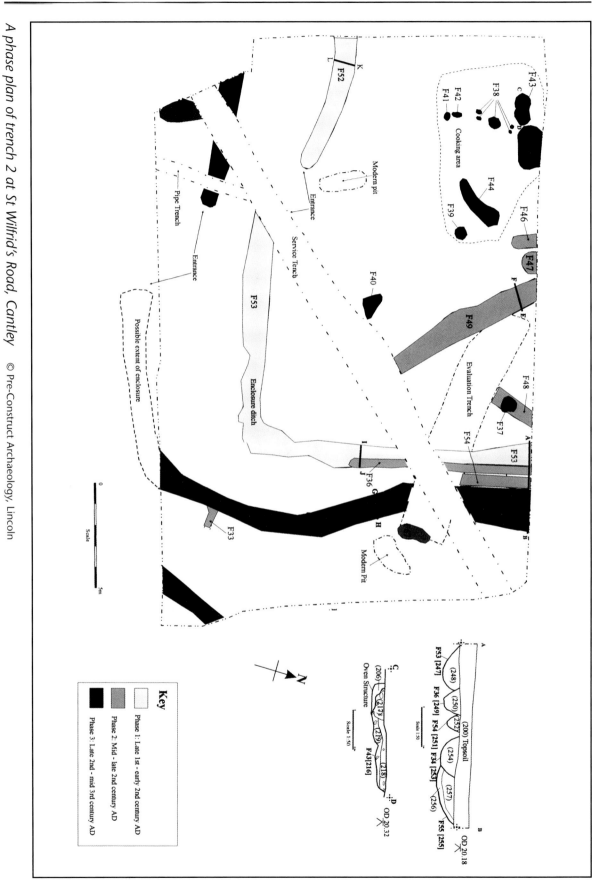

A phase plan of trench 2 at St Wilfrid's Road, Cantley   © Pre-Construct Archaeology, Lincoln

them jars or deep bowls. Two nearly complete vessels found alone in one pit may represent deliberate placement as a ritual act, perhaps encouraging future successful kiln firings. A single ditch dug between the late 3rd and early 4th centuries AD, which may indicate an eastward migration of a former land boundary, marked the final phase. Pottery from this included a complete Dales ware jar that shows clear signs of use in the form of sooting and a near complete long-necked beaker of unusual form, with round thumb indentions around the shoulder and rather oval indentations around the middle. These pots may also have been deliberately placed in an act of structured deposition, associated with a ritual termination of occupation.

Centred at Grid Reference SE 613 013

**From a report by Mike Daley,
Pre-Construct Archaeology (Lincoln)**

GOODISON BOULEVARD, BESSACARR, DONCASTER

Following an earlier geophysical survey (see *'Archaeology in South Yorkshire Number 12'*), a number of trial trenches were excavated here between May and June 2005, for Bellway Homes. A scatter of undated post-holes and pits with charcoal in their upper fills were identified, but no finds were recovered making dating difficult. It seems likely that most of the anomalies identified by the geophysical survey were caused by the natural sand and gravel geology.

Centred at Grid Reference SE 619 008

From a report by Dr Ben Chan, ARCUS

EARL OF DONCASTER HOTEL, BENNETTHORPE ROAD, DONCASTER

A watching brief was carried out in December 2006 for Graham Rhodan during groundworks associated with the construction of an extension to the hotel. The site lies within an area of archaeological significance, lying close to the Roman road that runs south from Doncaster. However, the limited groundworks revealed no features or finds of archaeological interest.

Grid Reference SE 585 028

**From a report by Linda Hamilton,
Pre-Construct Archaeology (Lincoln)**

1 AND 1B CHURCH LANE, BESSACARR, DONCASTER

A desk-based assessment was prepared in May 2006 for Church Lane Development Ltd, to inform a planning application for a housing development. The site is adjacent to the Roman road running south from Doncaster and close to the known sites of a number of Roman kilns. However, a large part of the proposal area was quarried for gravel in the 19th century, making the survival of archaeological remains unlikely.

Grid Reference SE 613 008

**From a report by R D Gardner,
Pre-Construct Archaeology (Lincoln)**

115 BAWTRY ROAD, BESSACARR, DONCASTER

An evaluation trench was excavated in November 2005, for Lewis Holdings Ltd, to inform a planning application to build an apartment block. The site is adjacent to the Roman road running south from Doncaster and close to the known sites of a number of Roman kilns. However, the work revealed no features or finds of interest.

Grid Reference SE 610 011

From a report by Helen Holderness, ARCUS

161 BAWTRY ROAD, BESSACARR, DONCASTER

A desk-based assessment was prepared in April 2005, to inform a planning application for residential development. The work was done for Wright Investments. The site is adjacent to the Roman road running south from Doncaster and close to the known sites of a number of Roman kilns, but recent development activity will have reduced the site's archaeological potential.

Grid Reference SE 614 008

From a report by Rowan May, ARCUS

CATESBY BUSINESS PARK, BALBY CARR, DONCASTER

Further investigation of this large development site was carried out in several phases between July 2005 and October 2006 (see '*Archaeology in South Yorkshire Number 11*' and '*Number 12*' for earlier work); the work revealed further evidence for the late prehistoric/Romano-British landscape previously identified.

Evaluation trenches were excavated in July 2005, for BDL Management Ltd, on the prospective site of a hotel (at SE 583 005). This identified two ditches that appeared to be of a relatively early date, which may represent a continuation of the late prehistoric/Romano-British field systems known in the immediate area. The remains of a wooden fence line were also exposed, and the discovery of Romano-British wooden structures on an adjacent site could indicate a similar age for this structure. Investigation of the adjoining plot to the east (at SE 584 005), for Cloverleaf Pubs Ltd, took the form of a topsoil strip of the site and recording of the features revealed. This showed that the area had been heavily disturbed by modern activity and where natural ground was encountered no archaeological features were observed. Subsequent evaluation of a small plot to the north (at SE 585 008), for the Catesby Property Group, similarly revealed only modern disturbance.

In July-August 2005 soil stripping and recording of land to the east of the Iron Age/Romano-British settlement identified in 2003 was carried out for the Catesby Property Group (at SE 583 004). Further remains of Iron Age settlement were identified in the form of five roundhouses and a series of enclosures that may be of later date. Radiocarbon dates from two of the roundhouses give a date of approximately 400-200 BC, suggesting that this settlement may be the

Photograph of the isolated ring ditch at First Point, Balby Carr   © AOC

predecessor of the one found further to the east. The enclosure ditches are thought likely to be part of a later field system, of late Iron Age/Romano-British date. Articulated sheep or goat bones found in a ditch terminal may represent a special deposit at the entranceway of an enclosure.

Evaluation trial trenching in May and June 2006, for Bucknall Austin, of a large area of land to the north west (centred at SE 582 006) revealed no archaeological features except the foundations of a recently demolished farmhouse of 19th/early 20th century date. Evaluation of further land, on the western side of the development site (centred at SE 577 005), was carried out in September 2006 for the Catesby Property Group. The trial trenching revealed a ring ditch and

two possible enclosure ditches. Excavation of a sample slot across one of the ditches recovered a piece of daub, suggesting prehistoric occupation nearby. Further excavation took pace in October 2006, revealing a 'D' shaped enclosure with an entrance to the east, containing the ring ditch of a probable roundhouse with an entrance to the northeast. Radiocarbon dating of recovered charcoal fragments showed that the enclosure ditch and roundhouse were contemporary and dated to the end of the first millennium BC, with the isolated ring ditch being a little later, at approximately AD80-AD320.

From reports by Richard O'Neill and Neil Dransfield, ARCUS; Marina Rose, Archaeological Services WYAS; Mike Roy and Donald Wilson, AOC Archaeology Group

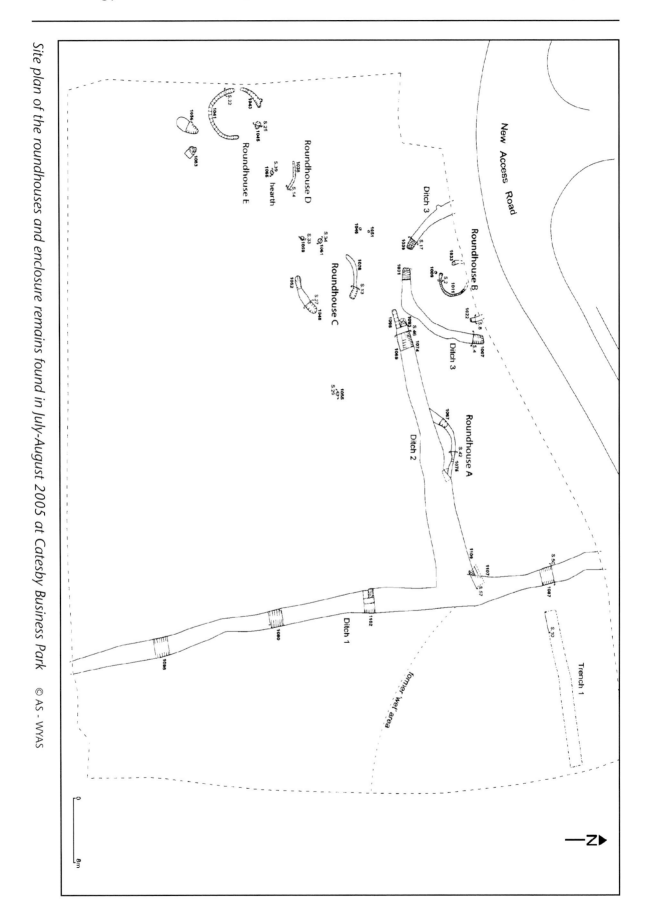

Site plan of the roundhouses and enclosure remains found in July-August 2005 at Catesby Business Park   © AS - WYAS

115 CHURCH STREET, ECCLESFIELD, SHEFFIELD

A watching brief was carried out in May 2005, during demolition and excavation of new foundation trenches, for Mr B Charlesworth. Ecclesfield has Anglo-Saxon roots and was an important place during the medieval period. This site is adjacent to the 'Willow Garth' medieval moated site and associated fishpond. The foundation trenches exposed naturally silted depressions containing 18th century ceramic material. These depressions could represent cut features but equally could be natural features utilised for later disposal of domestic waste.

Grid Reference SK 354 944

From a report by Owen Raybould, ARCUS

EDLINGTON SCHOOL, NEW EDLINGTON, DONCASTER

Following an earlier desk-based assessment (see *'Archaeology in South Yorkshire Number 12'*), a series of trial trenches were excavated in September 2005. The work was carried out for Andrew Martin Associates in relation to proposals to build a new school in the grounds of the existing school. The site lies close to a known Romano-British settlement, but no archaeological features or finds were identified.

Centred at Grid Reference SK 542 977

From a report by Anna Badcock, ARCUS

ST PETER'S CHURCH, OLD EDLINGTON, DONCASTER

A watching brief was carried out in September 2005 for the Churches Conservation Trust during the laying of new services and a pathway. The church, which is grade I listed, dates back to the 12th century. Uncovered limestone slabs were probably associated with a burial vault. Less easy to interpret were limestone wall footings found near the porch. These may form part of another burial chamber (see plan overleaf).

Grid Reference SK 532 972

**From a report by Ed Dennison
and Shaun Richardson,
Ed Dennison Archaeological Services Ltd**

WESLEYAN REFORM CHURCH, ELSECAR, BARNSLEY

A photographic survey of the church was prepared in May 2005, in advance of proposed demolition as part of a scheme for redevelopment. The work was carried out for Trent Architecture and Design. The datestone in the front gable of the building gives a construction date and reads 'Mount Zion, hitherto the Lord helped us, 1859'. A side extension has a further three datestones, bearing the names of different individuals and the date September 1st 1913. The building retains most of its original layout, but not many original features. The main chapel was on the first floor, above

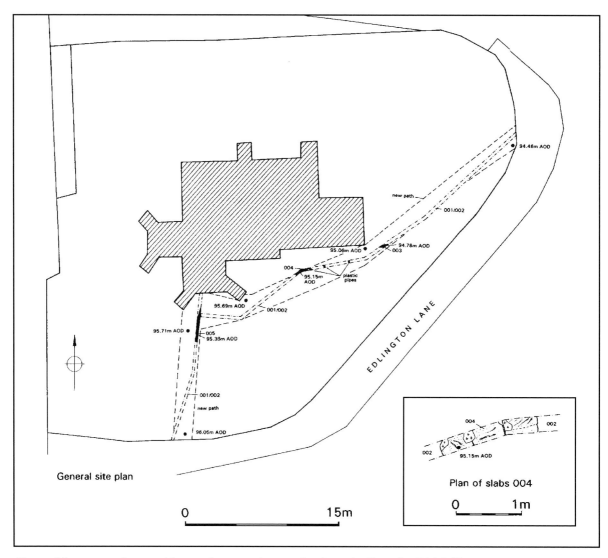

Plan of features observed in service trenches at St. Peter's Church, Old Edlington
© Ed Dennison Archaeological Services Ltd

meeting rooms and offices on the ground floor. There were stained glass windows on all sides of the chapel. Those on the south wall, where the altar was sited, being quite elaborate with memorials dating from 1915-1939; those on the side and rear walls were simpler in design, but probably also date from this period.

Grid Reference SE 384 012

From a report by Tegwen Roberts, ARCUS

ELSECAR MAIN COLLIERY SITE, ELSECAR, BARNSLEY

Plans to redevelop the former Elsecar Main Colliery site led to the preparation of a desk-based assessment in May 2005, for H J Banks and Company Ltd. Maps from the mid-19th century show the area as fields and woodland. The first development here was the construction of the railway line serving

*Concrete cap marking the location of a shaft,
Elsecar Main Colliery*   © ARCUS

Simon Wood Colliery, which was built along the eastern boundary of the site in the late 19th century. The first shaft of Elsecar Main Colliery was begun in July 1905; the Parkgate coal seam was reached on 20th September 1906, at a depth of 314 metres, and work began on shaft no.2 soon afterwards. The development of Elsecar Main influenced the development of the surrounding area; the owner, Earl Fitzwilliam, constructed nearby Elsecar model village, between 1910 and 1912, to accommodate workers and their families.

The coal industry was nationalised in 1947 and suggestions of intensification of extraction, or of increased mechanisation, can be seen on subsequent Ordnance Survey maps – with the construction of new buildings and conveyor belts to load the trains transporting coal from the site. By the late 1970s, production was diminishing and the last full coal train left the colliery on 5th June 1981; the colliery closed in October 1983. The buildings were demolished in April 1985 and few structural remains now survive on the site, except the concrete and brick bases of some buildings, and concrete caps marking the locations of the former mine shafts.

Centred at Grid Reference SE 390 003

From a report by Mark Stenton, ARCUS

ROBIN HOOD AIRPORT BUSINESS PARK, RAIL STATION & ACCESS ROUTE, FINNINGLEY, DONCASTER

A variety of archaeological works took place between January 2006 and October 2006, in relation to proposed development around Robin Hood airport, on behalf of Peel Investments (North) Ltd. An evaluation of land previously occupied by housing for RAF Finningley (SK 655 998) revealed no archaeological evidence. A geophysical survey (magnetometer) was carried out along a proposed access route off Hurst Lane (centred on SK 649 989) in April 2006. This identified an area of former ridge and furrow cultivation and some possible archaeological anomalies. Further geophysical survey (magnetometer) was carried out on the site of a proposed business park off Hayfield Lane (centred on SK 654 999) in June 2006. This work identified a linear anomaly, possibly representing an infilled ditch or gulley. Subsequently, both these areas were tested by trial trenching. Little of archaeological interest was found; some possible remnant furrows were identified on the Hurst Lane site and a ditch of unknown date was identified at Hayfield Lane.

From reports by Marina Rose, Archaeological Services WYAS; Sam Roberts, Archaeological Services Durham University; William Munford, Pre-Construct Archaeology

ST CUTHBERT'S CHURCH, FISHLAKE, DONCASTER

A watching brief was carried out for the Parochial Church Council in July 2006 during repairs to the roof of the south aisle. The church is grade I listed and is predominantly of 14th and 15th century date, although it includes some earlier elements. The repair work revealed windows that predate those of the clerestory of the south aisle and hence are earlier than the 15th century. Their narrow form may date them to the early 13th century, possibly indicating the position of an earlier clerestory.

Grid Reference SE 656 131

From a report by Ed Dennison, Ed Dennison Archaeological Services Ltd

WEST HAIGH WOOD AND HOUGHTON COMMON, GREAT HOUGHTON, BARNSLEY

A desk-based assessment and walk-over survey of these woodlands were carried out between September and December

One of a series of post-medieval pits identified in West Haigh Wood   © ASE Ltd

2005, for Barnsley MBC. The work formed part of the Wildspace! Local Nature Reserves Project. West Haigh Wood is shown as woodland on historic maps, whereas Houghton Common is shown as an area of heathland or scrub, suggesting the woodland here is secondary regeneration. The assessment identified a number of sites within the woodlands, including a medieval enclosure within West Haigh Wood and a post-medieval quarry, pond and guidepost on Houghton Common. A total of 146 archaeological sites were identified during the subsequent survey. As well as the known medieval enclosure, several other possible enclosures were identified, which could be medieval in date, or could date from the Iron Age/Romano-British period. Other features included an area of former ridge and furrow cultivation, charcoal burning platforms and saw pits.

Centred at Grid References SE 424 086 (West Haigh Wood) and SE 430 086 (Houghton Common)

From reports by Emma Gowans and John Pouncett, ASE Ltd

LILYDENE AVENUE, GRIMETHORPE, BARNSLEY

A geophysical survey (magnetometer) and trial trench evaluation were carried out here between May and August 2005, for Ben Bailey Homes Ltd. An earlier desk-based assessment had indicated that the site lies in an area of known cropmarks, indicating Iron Age and/or Romano-British activity in the vicinity, as well as being partly within the grounds of the 17th century Grimethorpe Hall (see *'Archaeology in South Yorkshire Number 12'*). The geophysical survey identified no clear archaeological anomalies and the excavated trial trenches revealed only two shallow ditches. No dating evidence was recovered from these features, but they lie on a different alignment to nearby modern boundaries, suggesting that they represent an earlier phase of land division.

Centred at Grid Reference SE 410 095

From reports by Alistair Webb and James Gidman, Archaeological Services WYAS

MILL FARM, GUNTHWAITE, BARNSLEY

A proposal to convert farm buildings to holiday cottages led to a photographic record of the complex, which contains the remains of a former corn mill. The work was carried out in July 2006 on behalf of Mr Robert Nicholson. The corn mill originated in the 17th century and was in use until the 1950s, when new owners let it fall into disuse. The 17th to 19th century structures on the site are Grade II listed and consist of the mill and its associated cast iron (pitch-back) waterwheel, and a range of ancillary buildings. The 17th century mill is the oldest building in the complex and still contains much of its milling gear intact, including two and a half of the original four pairs of millstones. Interestingly, the roof of the mill was found to have been made with reused oak timbers that came from an earlier timber framed building. Documentary evidence does indicate that there was a mill on the Gunthwaite estate from the 13th century, but it has been suggested that this stood further to the west, directly south of Gunthwaite Hall.

Grid Reference SE 249 062

From a report by Mark Douglas, ARCUS

HAZEL LANE QUARRY, HAMPOLE, DONCASTER

A series of archaeological investigations have taken place in advance of mineral extraction here over recent years, for Catplant Ltd. (see *'Archaeology in South Yorkshire Number 11'* and *'Number 12'*). Further archaeological works in February and March 2006 comprised monitoring of soil stripping and excavation of the features revealed. Three ditches, two gullies and twelve pits were observed; two of the ditches probably represent the boundary of an enclosure. Finds were sparse. The ten

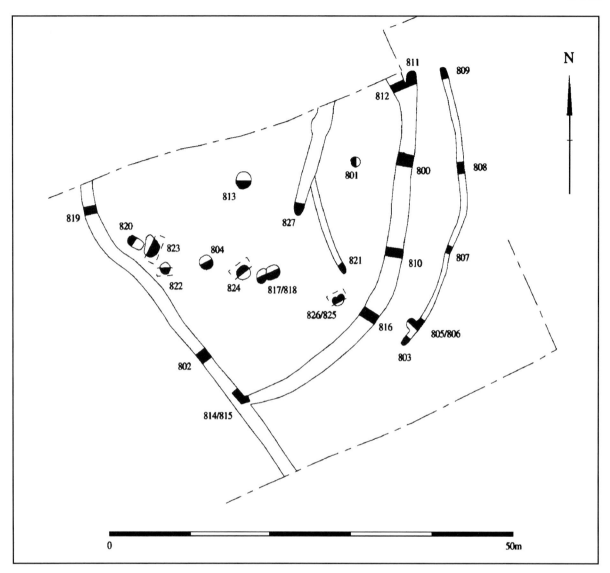

A plan showing the ditches, gullies and pits excavated at Hazel Lane Quarry
© Thames Valley Archaeological Services

sherds of Romano-British pottery that were recovered, all of a black shell tempered ware, included one rim sherd that is suggestive of a 2nd century date.

Centred at Grid Reference SE 498 117

**From a report by Andy Taylor
and Stephen Hammond,
Thames Valley Archaeological Services**

LAND AT OLD MILL FIELD, HATFIELD, DONCASTER

A geophysical survey (magnetometer) was carried out in May 2006 for Mr John Grayson on land where it is proposed to create a fishing pond and access road. The site lies close to a findspot of Roman pottery and cropmarks indicative of Romano-British settlement have been recorded nearby. However, the underlying geology of the site – sand and gravel – produced a very noisy response, making the identification of any archaeological anomalies difficult.

Grid Reference SE 670 088

From a report by J Gidman and A Webb, Archaeological Services WYAS

BOOTHAM LANE, DUNSCROFT, NEAR HATFIELD, DONCASTER

A watching brief was maintained on foundation excavations for a commercial development in September 2006, for Dantom Homes Developments Ltd. The Cistercian monks of Roche Abbey are known to have owned a smallholding, possibly a grange, at Dunscroft, whose location is unknown. No archaeological features or finds were observed during these works.

Grid Reference SE 655 103

From a report by Richard Jackson, ARCUS

CROW HEAD, HAZLEHEAD, BARNSLEY

An archaeological watching brief was undertaken in September 2005 for H J Banks & Company Ltd in connection with a proposed reclamation scheme. During the 19th and 20th centuries the site was the location of two collieries, an iron works and a number of clay pits. Stripping of the site compound,

excavation of two ditches and the removal of a spoil deposit in the centre of the site was observed. No archaeological features or finds were observed during these works.

Grid Reference SE 180 040

From a report by Andrew Walsh, Archaeological Services WYAS

HEXTHORPE MANOR, HEXTHORPE, DONCASTER

In May 2006 a desk-based assessment was prepared on behalf of Ferrey and Mennim architects, to inform a planning application for residential development. The current house, known as Hexthorpe Manor, was probably built in the mid 18th century on the site of the medieval manor house. The proposal area lies within walled gardens associated with the house. It is likely that these have remained relatively undisturbed since the 18th century, giving the site good potential for sub-surface archaeological remains from the medieval period.

Grid reference SE 559 021

From a report by Chris Fenton-Thomas, On-Site Archaeology

MAPPLEYARD FARM, HOOTON PAGNELL, DONCASTER

A proposal for conversion of redundant farm buildings, including a grade II listed barn, led to the completion of an

The eastern elevation of the Bull House at Mappleyard Farm © ARCUS

archaeological assessment and building appraisal in July 2005 for Chris Carr Associates. The structures comprise two ranges of 18th/19th century buildings arranged around two courtyards. The earliest structure is a large 18th century threshing barn, with characteristic triangular vents. Of particular note is a prestigious Bull House, built between 1840 and 1848, with opposing doorways and an external opening mechanism for the rear door, to facilitate safe stock handling.

Grid Reference SE 485 084

From a report by Oliver Jessop, ARCUS

LAND OFF HAWSHAW LANE, HOYLAND, BARNSLEY

Following an earlier desk-based assessment (see *'Archaeology in South Yorkshire Number 12'*) a geophysical survey (magnetometer) of this proposed development site was carried

out in August 2005. No definite archaeological anomalies were detected.

Grid Reference SE 364 011

From a report by N Barker, Met Surveys

ROEBUCK HILL, JUMP, BARNSLEY

Trial trench evaluation and excavation took place here between January and June 2006, following an earlier desk-based assessment and geophysical survey (see *'Archaeology in South Yorkshire Number 12'*), which suggested the site had good archaeological potential. The work was carried out for Persimmon Homes.

Three distinct phases of activity were identified. The earliest was associated with a multi-period flint scatter comprising 538 struck pieces including: cores, blades and bladelets, microliths, a single leaf-shaped arrowhead and a few scrapers, as well as a large quantity of debitage, e.g. chips and spalls. The assemblage contains a lack of finished tools and a small number of cores, which implies a sequence of minor flint knapping episodes – possibly at a temporary occupation site, such as a hunting camp. The multi-period nature of the lithics, ranging from mesolithic through to early Bronze Age, suggests the site was revisited many times.

The second phase was associated with an Iron Age/Romano-British farmstead represented by an enclosure with boundary ditches and pits. Artefacts

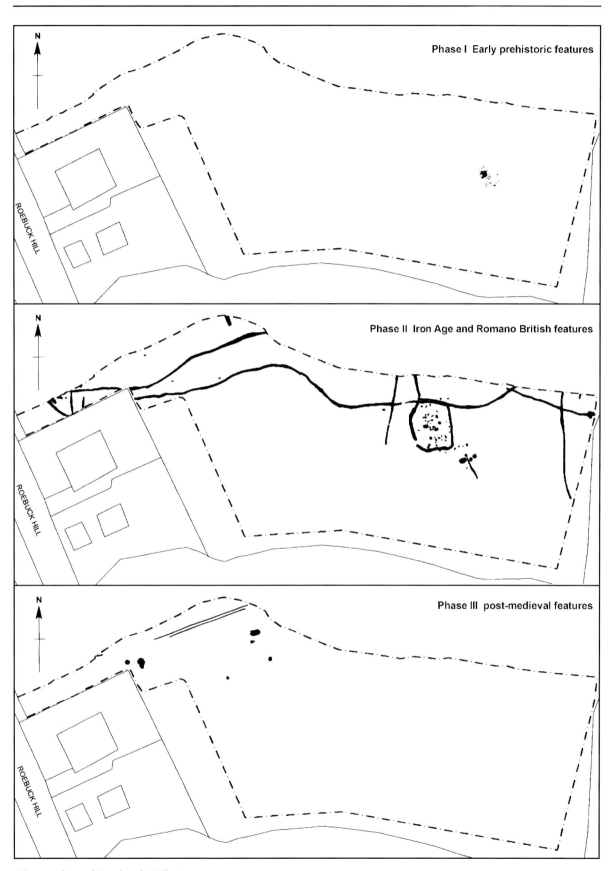

Phase plan of Roebuck Hill, Jump   © NAA

The 1807 enclosure map for Kirk Sandall showing St. Oswald's Church and the application boundary   © AS - WYAS

recovered from these features included fragments of very late Iron Age/early Romano-British pottery, burnt animal bone, pieces of quernstone and a number of triangular baked-clay loom weights. A cluster of post holes in the centre of the enclosure has been tentatively identified as the remains of a rectangular building. Post holes forming a ring that crosses the enclosure ditch have been tentatively identified as an earlier roundhouse.

The third phase was associated with post-medieval industrial activity. Two roughly circular fire-pits, with remnant stone linings and flues were recorded. Nearby pits containing pieces of clinker are interpreted as dumps of fire waste. Associated pottery dates this industrial activity from at least the 16th to the18th century.

Grid Reference SE 379 016

From reports by Gavin Robinson, Northern Archaeological Associates

GROVE ROAD, KIRK SANDALL, DONCASTER

A desk-based assessment was prepared in May 2006 for Urban i Ltd, in relation to a proposal to develop land here. The site lies adjacent to St Oswald's church, which dates back to the 12th century. Earthworks in a field south west of the church and within the site may represent former settlement remains; Kirk Sandall is considered a shrunken medieval village. Other elements within the site with potential archaeological significance include a school building that dates from at least the 17th century, and a grade II listed barn and cart shed dating from 1824.

Centred at Grid Reference SE 610 080

**From a report by Louise Ford,
Archaeological Services WYAS**

DONCASTER ROAD, KIRK SANDALL, DONCASTER

A geophysical survey (magnetometer) was carried out in August 2005 on behalf of ARCUS on land to the north west of the site of an earlier evaluation (see *'Archaeology in South Yorkshire Number 11'*). Although the site lies in an area where cropmark evidence for earlier enclosures is known, no certain anomalies of archaeological origin were identified.

Grid Reference SE 610 072

From a report by N Barker, Met Surveys

ALL SAINT'S CHURCH, LAUGHTON-EN-LE-MORTHEN, ROTHERHAM

A watching brief during excavation of a drain was carried out in August 2005 on behalf of All Saints' Laughton PCC. The church is listed grade I and is mostly late 14th century in date, but includes a 12th century chancel and has a Saxon north doorway. The groundworks were limited and no archaeologically significant features or finds were observed.

Grid Reference SK 517 881

**From a report by Bryan Antoni,
York Archaeological Trust**

RECTORY HOUSE FARM, LAUGHTON-EN-LE-MORTHEN, ROTHERHAM

Following an earlier desk-based assessment (see *'Archaeology in South Yorkshire Number 12'*), a series of eight trial trenches were excavated across the site, in September 2005. The two trenches closest to the High Street frontage were found to contain archaeological features and this area was the focus for excavation between October and December 2005. The work was carried out for Rectory Farm (Laughton) Ltd.

The excavations revealed extensive archaeological remains dating from the Anglo-Saxon period onwards. A series of ditches sub-divided the excavated area, which may reflect former tenement boundaries running off the main village street. Within the various site subdivisions were a range of pits, post-holes and the remains of three kilns, one of which was a wattle and daub construction of Anglo-Saxon date, whilst a second was a medieval drying

The stone built kiln from Phase 2 at Rectory House Farm © AS - WYAS

kiln made of stone. The artefact assemblage contained a significant group of Anglo-Saxon wares from Lincoln, as well as other notable pre-Conquest diagnostic artefacts. Elements of the medieval assemblage, notably window glass, a possible distilling vessel and some of the metalwork, are suggestive of high status occupancy in the near vicinity. The findings confirm Laughton's pre-Conquest origins and demonstrate its continued importance post-Conquest.

Four main phases of activity were identified (see plan on page 183 of colour section), based on the pottery recovered and on archaeomagnetic and radiocarbon dating:

Phase 1 - 10th to 12th century

Phase 2 - 13th to 14th century

Phase 3 - 14th to16th century

Phase 4 - 17th to 20th century

Features from Phase 1 include a wattle and daub clay-lined kiln, last used for drying oats, that has been dated to between AD1050 and AD1180 (95% confidence) using archaeomagnetic dating. Associated artefacts, in particular the pottery, imply pre-

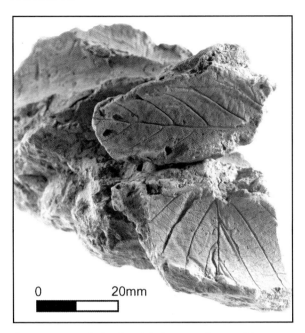

Remnants of daub with impressions of leaves, from the wattle structure of the Phase 1 kiln at Rectory House Farm   © AS - WYAS

Conquest occupation, possibly as early as the mid-9th century AD. Anglo-Saxon wattle and daub corn drying kilns are known from elsewhere in the country, for example Hereford, but this is the first known example in South Yorkshire.

The greatest number of features relate to Phase 2. The nature of these tends to support the suggestion that this was a working area to the rear of domestic properties along the High Street. Post-holes and two beam slots may indicate the presence of an open-sided timber agricultural structure within one tenement. Two large pits may have been used for rubbish disposal. A large stone-built kiln lacked evidence for high temperatures, which might suggest that it was used for drying crops or other foods, rather than for baking. A second, smaller kiln was lined with a single course of limestone at its bowl end and had been sealed by a charcoal deposit;

this was radiocarbon dated to AD 1180-1280.

Phase 3 was the least well-represented period of activity on the site, with only three features definitely identified for this period - two shallow linear features and a possible post-hole.

Features from Phase 4 were all associated with activity after the site became part of Rectory House Farm, and comprised two animal burials, two short linear features, post-holes, a large irregular pit and a well.

Grid Reference SK 518 882

From a report by Marina Rose and Ian Roberts, Archaeological Services WYAS

LANGOLD FARM, LETWELL, ROTHERHAM

Building recording was carried out in August 2006 for Lewis Holdings Ltd, in advance of proposed conversion of the farm buildings into residential dwellings. The group of farm buildings at Langold are listed grade II* and include a barn, stables, coach/cart houses and workers accommodation. The U-shaped south range of buildings, consisting of a barn with flanking stable wings, dates from the mid 18th century and is a fine example of the Palladian Revival style of architecture. Their design shows typical classical influences with a triumphal-arched entrance, pyramidical hipped roofs, deep projecting cornices, and pediments. Their design reflects the high status of the former house at Langold, which was demolished in the 19th century.

Grid Reference SK 572 864

**From a report by J Prudhoe,
Archaeological Services WYAS**

QUARRY FARM, LOVERSALL, DONCASTER

An archaeological watching brief was carried out in February 2007 for B and M Chappell during topsoil stripping for a fishing pond. The site lies within an area known to contain evidence for a late Iron Age agricultural landscape. However, no archaeological deposits were observed.

Grid Reference SK 569 991

**From a report by R D Gardner,
Pre-Construct Archaeology (Lincoln)**

WATER MILL, STONE, NEAR MALTBY, ROTHERHAM

Planned alterations that could result in loss of original features within these Grade II listed buildings led to building recording in February 2006, for Bryton Developments. The building comprises two mills, one of 17th century and later date, and one of 18th century date. The later mill contains earlier stonework within the wheelhouse. This may be *in situ* medieval work and represent remains of a mill belonging to Roche Abbey, but built outside its precinct, in the Augustinian fashion. It is perhaps more likely that it represents reused stone from nearby Roche Abbey (two mason's marks are visible, which have been noted on the abbey ruins). Both mills contained hurst frames, which were used to provide a stable

Rectified photographic elevations of the barn at Langold Farm　　© AS - WYAS

Internal view of the wheelhouse at Water Mill, Stone, showing re-used ashlar blocks
© AS - WYAS

support for transferral of power from the water wheel to the millstones. These were probably built in the 19th century, but re-using timbers from earlier frames. One of the hurst frames was complete and supported a French burr stone.

Grid Reference SK 554 896

**From a report by A C Swann,
Archaeological Services WYAS**

MARR LODGE WINDFARM, MARR, DONCASTER

A proposal to build a windfarm led to a desk-based assessment and geophysical survey in October 2006 on behalf of Banks Developments Ltd. Cropmark evidence in the immediate vicinity shows a series of features likely to relate to late prehistoric/Romano-British enclosures. The continuity of these features across the proposal area was confirmed by the geophysical survey (magnetometer), which produced

evidence of linear anomalies across the site, indicating infilled ditches from field systems, enclosures and trackways (see geophysics plot overleaf).

Centred at Grid Reference SE 505 043

From reports by Arcus Renewable Energy Consultants (assessment) and A Webb, Archaeological Services WYAS (geophysics)

THE EMBANKMENT, LEACH LANE, MEXBOROUGH, DONCASTER

Development proposals led to preparation of a desk-based assessment in September 2006, for Coda Studios. The two proposal sites lie on the outskirts of the historic town and adjoin the Mexborough New Cut of the Sheffield & South Yorkshire Navigation, which was built in the first half of the 18th century. This area is first shown as partly developed in the 19th century; the 1839 tithe award records a number of cottages, a wharf on the canal and a boatyard situated here.

Historic maps also show a winding hole on the canal, since infilled, used by narrow boats to turn. The construction of modern buildings will, however, have caused disturbance, reducing the potential for buried features to survive.

Centred at Grid Reference SK 474 996

From a report by Margaret Bennett-Samuels, John Samuels Archaeological Consultants

Geophysics plot for part of Marr windfarm. The features shown include possible field boundaries and ridge and furrow cultivation   © AS - WYAS

SECTOR 3

N

LAND OFF PASTURES ROAD, MEXBOROUGH, DONCASTER

Proposals for construction of an industrial development led to preparation of a desk-based assessment, a geophysical survey (magnetometer), and trial trench evaluation between October 2005 and April 2006, for Ben Bailey Homes Ltd. Aerial photographs show cropmarks of a probable Iron Age/Romano-British trackway running across part of the site, possibly being contemporary with an adjoining field system. Earlier prehistoric activity is also suggested as Mesolithic/Neolithic flint artefacts consisting of scrapers, retouched flakes and retouched blades have been found on the site.

The geophysical survey identified three probable enclosures in the north east of the site, and part of the trackway to their west. A subsequent trial trench evaluation confirmed the existence of infilled ditches forming two or three enclosures. The upper fills of two ditches contained a total of ten Neolithic/Bronze Age flints and an unfinished blade, which could indicate a prehistoric origin for the features, whilst the presence of heat-affected rock from one ditch fill may suggest occupation.

Other evaluation trenches were targeted on the probable trackway. This varied in form between two parallel ditches approximately 3m apart, and a hollow-way with flanking ditches. Several sherds of Roman pottery were recovered from one of the hollow-way fills, implying a Roman date for the siltation of the feature; it is probable that the trackway's origins are prehistoric.

Centred at Grid Reference SE 493 005

From reports by Mitchell Pollington, Alistair Webb and David Williams, Archaeological Services WYAS

ECKLAND BRIDGE WORKS, MILLHOUSE GREEN, BARNSLEY

A series of archaeological works took place here between December 2005 and February 2007, in advance of proposed demolition and redevelopment. The work was carried out for Cala Homes (Yorkshire) Ltd. The Eckland Bridge Works lie on a stretch of the River Don that has been heavily exploited by various industrial mills. The Thurlstone Paper Mill formerly stood on this site and part of its 18th century mill race survives. William Hoyland's umbrella works was constructed here in 1875 and a number of buildings from that phase of use still survive. The mill played an important role in the development of the settlement at Millhouse Green.

A photographic record of the building complex was made. Three buildings from the late 19th century umbrella works were identified, but their original functions could not be established. Continual use of the buildings had led to extensive internal and external alteration. A fire in the 1980s had led to the demolition of other historic structures and the erection of modern steel buildings.

The overgrown mill race or goit at the Eckland Bridge Works © NAA

Twelve trial trenches were also excavated, to test the survival of earlier archaeological remains in the open space around the mill complex. The only archaeological features identified were six stone-lined drains and a series of post and stake holes. All the features identified were post-medieval in date.

Centred at Grid Reference SE 222 031

From reports by Jonathan Tabor, Northern Archaeological Associates (assessment); Sanne Roberts (building recording), Scott Wilson Ltd; Nathan Flavell (evaluation), Northamptonshire Archaeology.

NORTON PRIORY FARM, NORTON, DONCASTER

Following earlier building recording (see 'Archaeology in South Yorkshire Number 12'), a series of trial trenches were excavated in and around the farm buildings, in August 2006. The work was carried out for C and E Metcalfe, in relation to a proposal to convert the buildings to residential use; the site lies

within a Scheduled Ancient Monument – the site of the medieval Norton Priory. The majority of the trenches were archaeologically sterile. The one feature of interest noted was part of a substantial stone built wall, which pre-dates the earliest mapping of the area.

Grid Reference SE 545 158

From a report by Helen Holderness, ARCUS

LAND OFF NORTON COMMON ROAD, NORTON, DONCASTER

A desk-based assessment was prepared in February 2007 for Kevin Tyree, to inform a planning application for creation of a large fishpond. The site was common land until enclosure in 1814, since when it has been used for agriculture and allotments. Cropmarks in the immediate vicinity may indicate potential for sub-surface remains from the late prehistoric/Romano-British periods.

Centred at Grid Reference SE 559 152

From a report by Rowan May, ARCUS

LAND OFF LOW ROAD, OUGHTIBRIDGE, SHEFFIELD

A watching brief was carried out in June 2005 for Cala Homes (Yorkshire) Ltd during groundworks in connection with a new housing development. The site was the location of Upper Middlewood

Forge from at least 1761. The site stayed in industrial use until the 1920s, but the forge is shown as 'disused' on the 1934 Ordnance Survey map. It is thought that the buildings were demolished shortly afterwards, and the site levelled up. A watching brief during the site strip revealed no archaeological features or finds; any industrial remains are thought likely to survive at a deeper depth.

Grid Reference SK 308 932

**From a report by Claire Coulter,
On Site Archaeology Ltd**

LAND AT OWSTON HALL, OWSTON, DONCASTER

Owston Hall dates to the early 18th century and was extended in 1794-5. Proposals to build an extension led to excavation of two evaluation trenches in July 2005, for Peter Edwards. No structural remains were found, but a ditch identified in the second trench raises some possibility of early activity - it does not appear on estate plans from the 1760s onwards.

Grid Reference SE 550 111

From a report by Helen Holderness, ARCUS

LAND OFF MARKET STREET & ST MARY'S STREET, PENISTONE, BARNSLEY

A desk-based assessment was prepared in August 2006, for Spawforths, ahead of the proposed demolition of existing buildings, including the cattle market, and construction of a supermarket. The site lies on the western edge of the historic town core and much of it remained as fields until the construction of the market in 1910. The market was traditionally held outside the church gates, but the sale of livestock in the street was banned at the end of the 19th century and new premises had to be found. There is a stone building within the current market site, which appears to pre-date the markets' construction; this may be a remnant of the farm known as Backfields, which is shown on the 1893 Ordnance Survey map. The only other feature of interest noted was the façade of the 19th century jail or lockup, which forms part of the retaining wall along the northern edge of the site.

Centred at Grid Reference SE 243 032

**From a report by R D Gardner,
Pre-Construct Archaeology (Lincoln)**

LAND OFF SHEFFIELD ROAD, PENISTONE, BARNSLEY

Proposals for residential redevelopment led to the preparation of a desk-based assessment in March and April 2005, for McInerney Homes Yorkshire Ltd. Historic maps show the site as fields with a long thin shape, suggestive of enclosed strip fields. These would have formed part of Penistone's open field system of farming. The site is bordered to the north by the river Don and to the east by the Penistone Green beck. Such a situation would often make a site attractive to early settlement, but the steepness of this site suggests it is unlikely to have seen much earlier activity, giving the site a low archaeological potential.

Grid Reference SE 254 032

From a report by Laura Broughton, Scott Wilson Ltd

NEW VICARAGE, SHREWSBURY ROAD, PENISTONE, BARNSLEY

A proposal to replace the 19th century vicarage led to an evaluation for the Wakefield Diocese in July 2006. Two trial trenches were excavated on the new plot, which lies to the east of the historic core of Penistone. No features or finds of archaeological interest were revealed by the work.

Grid Reference SE 247 032

From a report by Chris Scurfield, CS Archaeology

PENISTONE SAW MILL, PENISTONE, BARNSLEY

A photographic survey of this building was carried out in July 2005, for Clayton Roberts Architect and Design Partnership, ahead of partial demolition and redevelopment of the site. The earliest part of the complex is a pair of cottages in the northwest corner, which were probably built in the early 18th century, on what was Penistone Green. Some original features survive within

these buildings, including sash windows with wooden shutters. The site developed rapidly through the second half of the 19th century, with the addition of workshop ranges and offices around an open yard (see phase plan on page 184 of the colour section). By 1901, this open area had been covered, completing the development of the site. Three large saw pits are sited within this former yard area

Grid Reference SE 245 028

From a report by Tegwen Roberts, ARCUS

ST JOHN THE BAPTIST CHURCH, PENISTONE, BARNSLEY

A watching brief was carried out in February 2007 during excavation of a new drainage system. The work was on behalf of the Parochial Church Council. Despite running for 26 metres at depths of nearly 2 metres, the trench encountered little archaeology. Only a small amount of disarticulated bone and two *in situ* burials were observed; these were left undisturbed.

Grid Reference SE 246 033

From a report by Ed Dennison, Ed Dennison Archaeological Services

RAWMARSH RECTORY, RAWMARSH, ROTHERHAM

Plans to convert St Mary's Rectory to flats led to a watching brief during geotechnical test pitting and a subsequent trial trench evaluation between September and December 2005; the work was undertaken for Globe Architects. The site lies within the historic core of Rawmarsh, opposite the parish church; the rectory building is Georgian in date, but earlier occupation evidence could be expected here.

The test pitting revealed a possible buried stone wall, which was further examined by a trial trench. The stone feature was confirmed to be a stone-capped drain, the fill of which contained a quantity of pottery, which had washed in. The recovered material included biscuit fired wares (probably Creamwares) and a number of stilt and rod fragments (kiln furniture). Such finds are indicative of pottery production in the 18th and 19th centuries; Rawmarsh is known to have had a thriving pottery industry in this period and it is likely waste material was brought in from a nearby pottery for levelling during the construction of the present rectory building.

Grid Reference SK 436 959

From reports by Tim Poyner and Helen Holderness, ARCUS

ROSSINGTON ALL SAINTS SCHOOL, NEW ROSSINGTON, DONCASTER

A scheme of archaeological works took place between November 2005 and March 2007 for David Morley Architects, in respect of demolition

and rebuilding of the school buildings. A desk-based assessment noted aerial photographic evidence from the surrounding area suggesting that the site lies within part of an Iron Age/Romano-British field system. A geophysical survey (magnetometer) found no evidence of any archaeological anomalies; this was thought to be possibly due to later landscaping masking features. However, evaluation trenches similarly found no evidence for any archaeological remains and this result was replicated by a watching brief during topsoil stripping, when no finds or features of interest were revealed.

Grid Reference SK 620 972

From reports by Mitchell Pollington, Antony Brown, Alistair Webb, Bernard McCluskey and David Williams, Archaeological Services WYAS

LAND AT LITTLE MOOR, NEW ROSSINGTON, DONCASTER

A desk-based assessment was prepared in September 2006 for Planning Prospects in relation to proposals for a rail interchange, warehousing and business park on land to the west of Rossington. The area of the proposal site that lies to the west of the railway line contains significant numbers of cropmarks typical of Iron Age/Romano-British enclosures and field boundaries. Lack of intrusive development later in the history of this area gives it a high potential for the survival of sub-surface

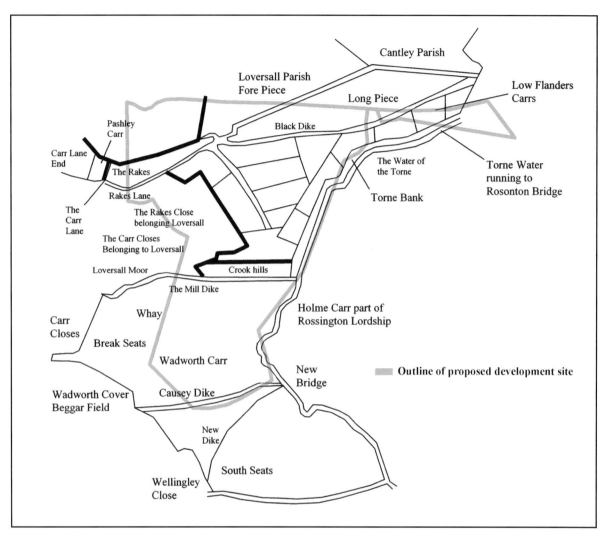

*Interpretation of a 1616 plan drawn up to show the drainage of Potteric Carr and Loversall lordship.
The development area has been superimposed on the map*   © Pre-Construct Archaeology, Lincoln

archaeology. The potential of the remainder of the site is less clear, although it is known to contain former palaeochannels, suggesting that it will have at least palaeoenvironmental significance.

Centred at Grid Reference SK 596 988

**From a report by R D Gardner,
Pre-Construct Archaeology (Lincoln)**

FINNINGLEY AND ROSSINGTON REGENERATION ROUTE, DONCASTER

Following an assessment into the potential archaeological impact of three possible routes to link the M18 to Finningley airport, a watching brief was carried out during geotechnical test pitting. The work was carried out for Golder Associates (UK) Ltd in May and

June 2005. The test pits were largely devoid of archaeology but did reveal three linear features, two of which are adjacent to areas of known Romano-British activity.

Grid Reference SK 652 989 (airport)

From a report by Antony Brown, Archaeological Services WYAS

GUEST AND CHRIMES, DON STREET, ROTHERHAM

Proposed redevelopment at the former Guest and Chrimes iron and brass foundry led to further archaeological works between May and November 2006, for the Evans Property Group (for earlier investigations, see *'Archaeology in South Yorkshire Number 11'*). A further desk-based assessment confirmed that the earliest known archaeological remains that could be expected would be the Holmes Tail Goit, which dates to at least to the early 17th century, when iron working is recorded at Holmes, but which may have originated as a natural watercourse. A watching brief during geotechnical test pitting reinforced the findings of the desk-based study; excavations revealed a retaining wall, thought to be from the Holmes Tail Goit, and organic-rich soils typical of watercourse deposits.

Subsequently, evaluation trenches found evidence for the original and culverted course of the goit, the south side of the early-19th century canal basin on the Don Navigation, and brick footings and floor surfaces that appear to relate to the earliest phase of the foundry works. No

Ongoing evaluation at Guest and Chrimes
© SYAS

evidence for revetment of the edge of the canal basin was discovered, suggesting that the basin served merely as a turning bay, rather than a loading point. The remains identified from the foundry are thought to represent the remains of small workshops and the boiler house chimney. Parts of two crucibles containing copper rich deposits were recovered from a large pit found on the edge of the foundry complex.

A building appraisal identified a core group of standing buildings that relate to the mid/late 19th century foundry complex, surrounded by a variety of later 20th century buildings. More detailed recording is recommended for both the 19th century buildings and the early 20th century buildings identified, as these are all important for understanding the development of the site's layout and function.

Centred at Grid Reference SK 425 925

From reports by Under Construction Archaeology (desk-based assessment); Richard Jackson (watching brief) and Alex Rose-Deacon & Oliver Jessop (building appraisal), ARCUS; Adrian Burrow, Northamptonshire Archaeology (evaluation)

SPEED'S BUILDING, 18 HIGH STREET AND 14-15 VICARAGE LANE, ROTHERHAM

Works comprising a second phase of evaluation trenching and a watching brief during groundworks took place here between June 2004 and May 2005, for Phoenix Enterprises (for earlier investigations, see *'Archaeology in South Yorkshire Number 12'*). A 12th century ditch was identified, sealed by occupation layers from the 13th/14th century. The late medieval oven, previously identified, was further recorded; carbonised plant remains from the oven fills suggest cereal drying and processing in its early stages of use, possibly indicative of brewing. A floor and walls of 15th to 16th century date probably indicate a contemporary domestic structure. Subsequent 16th – 17th century layers, and an associated pit, were found to contain charcoal and coal fragments, suggesting the presence of some industrial activity close by. Slag and hammerscale recovered indicates that metalworking – particularly welding

– was occurring in the close vicinity of the site from the medieval through to the post-medieval period.

Grid Reference SK 428 928

From a report by Bernard McCluskey, Archaeological Services WYAS

OLD COACH HOUSE, SNAIL HILL, ROTHERHAM

A photographic record of this building was made, as part of an application to demolish the building, which was in danger of collapse. The building lies within the Rotherham town centre Conservation Area. The recording was carried out in June 2005 on behalf of D C Peat Farms Ltd.

Grid Reference SK 429 927

From a report by David Michelmore, Consultancy and Conservation for Historic Buildings

WESTGATE, ROTHERHAM

Evaluation trenches were excavated on two former car parks south of the town centre, between October 2005 and March 2006; the work formed part of the ongoing Rotherham Westgate Demonstrator project and was carried out for Rotherham MBC (for earlier investigations, see *'Archaeology in South Yorkshire Number 12'*). At one site (site 5), structural evidence was found relating to the public baths that occupied the site from the late 19th

A mid to late nineteenth century clay pipe with embossed Velocipede, or bone shaker bicycle (c1863+), recovered from below the old Market Hall site, Rotherham Westgate
© ARCUS

century to the late 20th century; no evidence for the former Rotherham Old Pottery, known to have stood here, was identified. At the other site (site 3), remains of two phases of the 19th century Market Hall were identified. The Market Hall was originally built in 1879 and was then rebuilt after a fire in 1888. An earlier sandstone wall, re-used as foundations for the later market buildings, was also identified.

During August 2006 these features were further investigated. The earlier sandstone wall was found to survive to a height of over 5m. Originally a freestanding structure, it had been

buried by deposition of material prior to the construction of the market buildings, suggesting that the slope down from Westgate may originally have been much more pronounced. The wall may have been part of a building to the immediate east of the Rotherham Old Pottery, shown on a 1774 map of the town.

Grid References SK 427 928 (Site 3) and SK 426 927 (Site 5)

From reports by Neil Dransfield and Richard O'Neill, ARCUS

PHOENIX PARK, ICKLES, ROTHERHAM

A series of archaeological investigations took place here between April 2005 and September 2006, on behalf of St Paul's Developments. The proposed redevelopment site contains the site of the Ickles corn mill, which was probably established in the 13th century and was part of the estate of Roche Abbey until its dissolution in the mid 16th century. It is probable that the later corn mill, shown on 19th century maps and demolished in the 1970s, occupied the same site as the earlier one.

Three evaluation trenches were excavated on the site of the former mill and the line of the mill goit and structural remains of the later mill were identified. Ancillary buildings to the north of the mill were also identified; notable quantities of animal bone and pottery were recovered from this area. This material predominantly dates from between

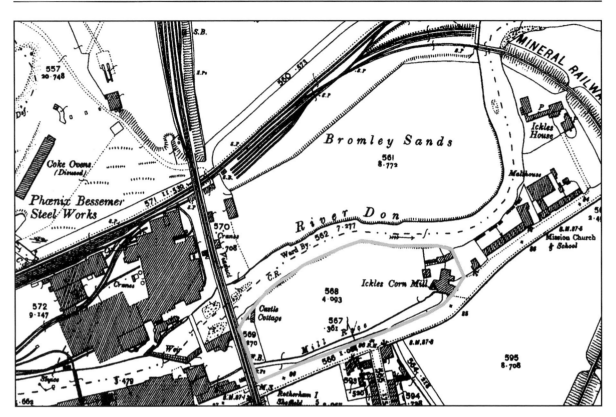

1901 Ordnance Survey map showing Ickles Corn Mill lying within the area proposed for development
© ARCUS

1740 and 1840 and indicates a moderately well to do domestic setting. One sherd of residual medieval pottery was also recovered.

More detailed excavation was subsequently carried out, to record the identified remains prior to redevelopment. The work examined the Ickles Mill building and associated wheel-pit, the course of the Ickles goit and a later diversion, as well as housing at the eastern end of the area. These features all appeared to relate to the late 18th or early 19th century, rather than any earlier phases.

Grid Reference SK 420 919

From reports by Rowan May and Sean Bell, ARCUS

LAND OFF FITZWILLIAM ROAD, EASTWOOD, ROTHERHAM

A desk-based assessment was prepared for the South Yorkshire Fire and Rescue Service, as part of a proposal to develop land at the rear of Eastwood Fire Station with new buildings to house support staff. Eastwood was first mentioned in a document of 1279 and the name suggests this area was still largely woodland at that date. By the 18th century the site was part of a large system of fields surrounding Rotherham town centre. This area was developed in the 19th century and in 1899 a chapel, for the parish of Eastwood, was constructed in the southwest corner of the current site. By 1974 a large bakery had been constructed within the proposal site. After its closure, the current fire station was built in 1990.

In July 2006 a watching brief was carried out for Ove Arup and Partners, during the excavation of geotechnical test pits. A considerable quantity of recent dump material was discovered, indicating that the site had been built up as part of previous development. This made ground contained a number of glass bottles made by Beatson Clark and other local manufacturers. No other finds or features of archaeological interest were observed.

Grid Reference SK 446 940

From reports by Rowan May and Chris Swales, ARCUS

LAND OFF COKE HILL, ROTHERHAM

A desk-based assessment was prepared in February 2007 for Bond Bryan Architects, to inform a proposal to construct offices for Voluntary Action Rotherham. The site lies on the edge of what was West Gate Green and does not appear to have been developed until the end of the 19th century, when terraced houses were built here. Prior to this the land was in agricultural use, although there is the possibility that there was earlier activity along the edge of the green that is not recorded on any historic maps. However, the construction of terraced houses in the 19th century is likely to have impacted on any such earlier features.

Grid Reference SK 427 924

From a report by Rowan May, ARCUS

LAND OFF MEADOWHALL ROAD, KIMBERWORTH, ROTHERHAM

A desk-based assessment was prepared in November 2005 to inform a planning application for demolition of an existing cottage and construction of a house. The first known use of the site was as a sandstone quarry, which is shown on the 1840 OS map. By 1892, the site is shown as a disused colliery. The colliery was active again by the time the 1905 OS map was surveyed and is named as Jordan Colliery; the colliery was then worked until 1913. Earthworks and standing structures on the site are thought likely to relate to this colliery use.

Grid Reference SK 399 923

From a report by Jill Stephenson, Hallam Environmental Consultants

LAND OFF DROPPINGWELL ROAD, KIMBERWORTH, ROTHERHAM

A desk-based assessment was prepared in October 2005 to inform a planning application to develop the site; the work was done on behalf of Malcolm Watkinson. The proposal area is partly a mix of scrub, fields and a disused sports field. Historic maps suggest that much of the area was enclosed from Kimberworth Middle Common at the end of the 18th century. As it had not seen previous development, a geophysical survey (magnetometer) was undertaken in

April 2006, to help establish the site's archaeological potential. No anomalies of probable archaeological origin were identified, suggesting the site has a low potential to contain archaeological remains.

Centred at Grid Reference SK 393 930

From reports by Paula Ware and Kelly Hunter, MAP Archaeological Consultancy Ltd (desk-based assessment) and T S Harrison and A Webb, Archaeological Services WYAS (geophysics)

CANKLOW WOODS, ROTHERHAM

Following earlier archaeological survey work (see '*Archaeology in South Yorkshire Number 11*'), a watching brief was maintained during excavation of foundations for woodland furniture between October and November 2005; the work was carried out for Rotherham Metropolitan Borough Council.

The watching brief was focused on works within the area of known prehistoric/Romano-British enclosures and terraces, which are scheduled as an Ancient Monument (SAM SY382). No archaeological features or finds were observed.

Centred at Grid Reference SK 431 905

From a report by Daniel Lee, Archaeological Services WYAS

HAIL MARY HILL WOOD, FALCONER WOOD AND BASSINGTHORPE SPRING, ROTHERHAM

A desk-based assessment covering these woodlands was prepared in April 2005, for Rotherham Metropolitan Borough Council. The assessment was required as part of proposals for managing and restoring the woodlands, for the benefit of the community.

Hail Mary Hill and Falconer Wood lie between the parishes of Treeton and Orgreave; they were established by the 16th century and may have originated as part of the medieval woodland mentioned in Domesday Book. Archaeological material discovered here includes a Mesolithic flint scatter and pieces of Roman pottery, indicating some earlier activity.

Bassingthorpe Spring lies to the southwest of Greasbrough; it is first mentioned in a list of spring (or coppiced) woods belonging to the 7th Earl of Shrewsbury, indicating the woodland was being managed at that time (1598-1616). Coal mining was carried out here from the mid 18th century; wagon-ways linked the coal pits in the wood to the Don Navigation, two miles away. Originally the tracks had wooden rails, but these were replaced by metal ones in 1766; the tracks were removed in the 1830s. The main wagon-way was reutilised as a mineral railway between 1854 and 1890. Earthwork evidence for the wagon-ways and coal pits is known to survive within the wood. Two derelict

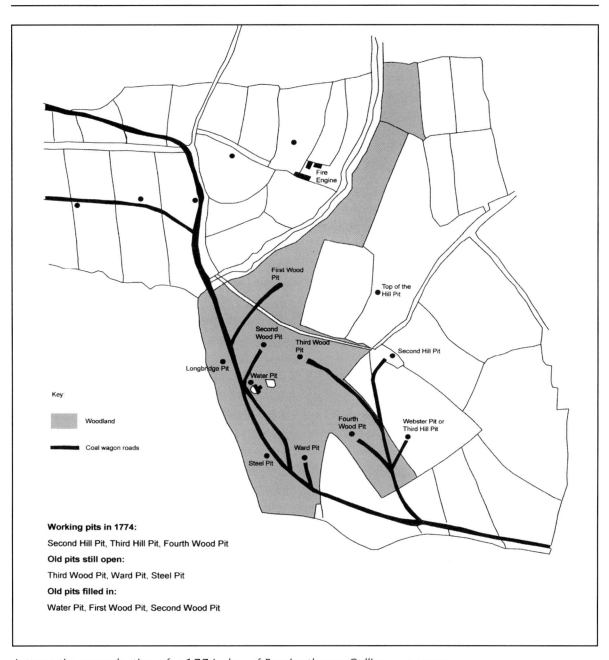

Key:

▨ Woodland

▬ Coal wagon roads

Working pits in 1774:

Second Hill Pit, Third Hill Pit, Fourth Wood Pit

Old pits still open:

Third Wood Pit, Ward Pit, Steel Pit

Old pits filled in:

Water Pit, First Wood Pit, Second Wood Pit

Interpretive reproduction of a 1774 plan of Bassingthorpe Colliery   © ARCUS

cottages, possibly originally a single building shown on a map of 1774, are also present.

Centred at Grid References SK 440 868 (Hail Mary Hill and Falconer Wood) and SK 412 944 (Bassingthorpe Spring)

From a report by Rowan May, ARCUS

TEMPLEBOROUGH ROLLING MILL, ROTHERHAM

A proposal to redevelop the site of the former rolling mill led to a trial trench evaluation in May and June 2006; the work was carried out for Jaguar Estates.

A section through one of the Roman ditches at Templeborough   © ARCUS

This was the site of Templeborough Roman fort and its associated vicus (civilian settlement) and earlier observation of geotechnical testpits had suggested that Roman deposits survived on the site, despite extensive later disturbance (see '*Archaeology in South Yorkshire Number 12*'). The excavated trenches confirmed that remains survived in places across the site, reflecting changes in the site's original topography. In formerly low-lying areas, features were found buried beneath modern dumping, which had raised the ground surface; in other areas, truncated Roman features were found immediately below the modern surface, where areas of formerly higher ground had been levelled down. Well-preserved areas contained evidence for the former vicus; truncated areas revealed remnants of the former defensive ditches around the southern corner of the fort.

The earliest pottery recovered dates from the Flavian-Trajanic period in the late 1st century – early 2nd century and included neckless everted-rim jars and rusticated jars. A small quantity of later pottery was also recovered, including a Dales ware jar and a Nene valley colour coated beaker of late 2nd – 3rd century date. No other later pottery was recovered, although occupation is known to have continued at Templeborough until the early 4th century. A number of pottery wasters were recovered, confirming that there was pottery production on the site.

Between November 2006 and January 2007, detailed excavation took place of an area of land between the former rolling mill and Sheffield Road, where archaeological remains had been shown to survive at a very shallow depth; where remains survived at a deeper level, these would be left undisturbed by the proposed redevelopment. Three lines of defensive ditches were identified around the southern corner of the fort. All of these ditches had been recut. With one exception, these recuts were sufficiently offset from the original ditches to suggest they took place after a period of fort abandonment. Finds recovered indicate two main phases of recutting (and fort occupation), spanning the mid 1st to mid 2nd centuries AD. A substantial sandstone wall and burnt sandstone surface to the east of the fort represents part of the vicus. Nearly half of the pottery recovered during the excavation came from this area of the site and these finds indicate a late 1st century date for the establishment of the vicus. Two of the jars recovered are unusual in that they appear to be facepots: one has an applied strip for hair and incised decoration for eyes, nose and beard; the other has applied eyes and hair and

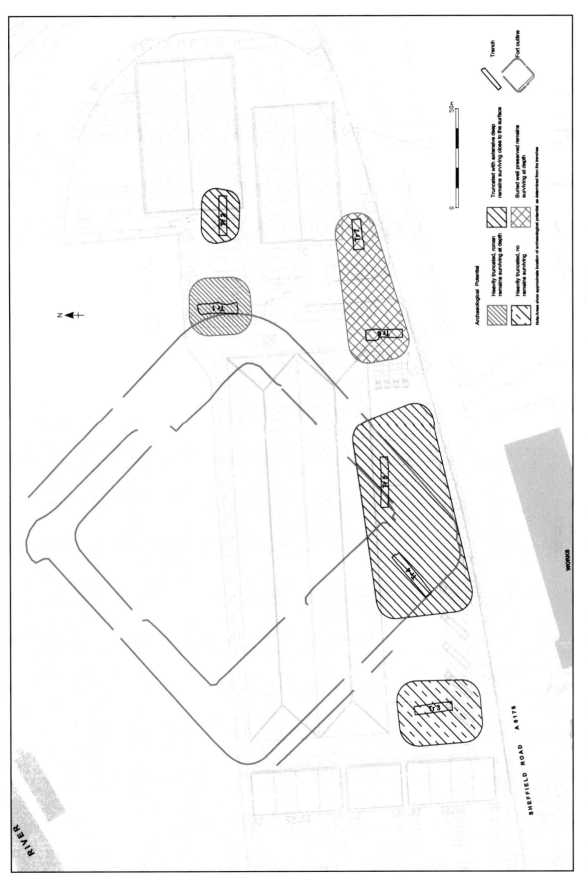

A schematic plan of Templeborough showing areas where Roman remains are most, or least, likely to survive   © ARCUS

incised decoration for nose and beard. The fabric of the second jar suggests a local source.

Centred at Grid Reference SK 414 915

From reports by Dr Ben Chan and Michael McCoy, ARCUS

WOODLAND SITES IN THE RIVELIN AND LOXLEY VALLEYS, SHEFFIELD

A desk-based assessment was prepared in February 2006 for Sheffield CC to inform management proposals for several woodlands in the area:

Acorn Hill and Little Matlock Wood – this is an area of historic woodland, a remnant of Stannington Wood, a wooded common recorded in the 1637 survey of Sheffield Manor. The main potential identified for these woods consists of features associated with 19th/20th century clay, coal and ganister extraction. Surface features include sleepers and a trackway that may be associated with this mining, and features relating to the water-powered industry in the valley.

Bole Hill Wood – this area was subject to quarrying in the 19th century, during which time several Neolithic polished stone axes were found. Allied to the proximity of Bronze Age burials to the southwest of the area, this could indicate potential for further prehistoric remains within the wood.

Walkley Bank Plantation – surface evidence for disused routeways could relate to the nearby medieval Racker Way packhorse route.

Reaps Wood, Tofts Wood and Jackey Bank Allotments – Reaps Wood is the only one of these areas that appears to have been woodland historically, being shown as such on a survey of 1728. The highest archaeological potential for these areas relates to Tofts Wood, which lies close to the site of two Bronze Age cremation burials and the find site of a Neolithic polished axe. This could indicate potential for further prehistoric remains within the wood.

Clough Fields Wood – few features were identified in this wood, other than possible allotment plots and associated paths.

Den Bank Wood and Millstone Edge Rough – features relating to millstone quarrying were observed at the latter site, along with a substantial hollow way that may represent an access route to the quarry face.

Blackbrook Wood – this was part of an area known as 'the Coppice' in the 17th century and may have remained wooded from at least that time.

Roscoe Plantation – this area contains evidence for a dam, sluice, goit and wheel pit associated with the former Roscoe Wheel.

Rivelin Glen – the western part of this area is another remnant of 'the Coppice'. The whole area contains well-documented remains of former water-powered wheels, all constructed in the 18th century, except Rivelin Corn Mill, which was first recorded in 1632, and

Hind Wheel, which was first recorded in 1581. The visible wheel remains consist mainly of water-management features, although some structural remains can be seen.

Centred at Grid Reference SK 310 876

From a report by Rowan May and Chris Breeden, ARCUS

STORRS BRIDGE, LOXLEY VALLEY, SHEFFIELD

A proposed residential redevelopment led to a desk-based assessment and watching brief during geotechnical test-pitting being carried out between May and July 2006 for Bovis Homes Ltd. The proposal area is the location of several post-medieval industrial sites and is considered as having good potential for the survival of sub-surface remains relating to:

Rowel Bridge Wheel – first recorded in an indenture for 1718. The dam was enlarged in 1794 and served 28 troughs and employed 40 men. One wheel was enlarged in 1811 to provide 25 troughs for grinding penknives, table knives, razors and saws. It was demolished in the mid 20th century.

Loxley Old Wheel – first recorded in a rental document of 1690. In 1794 the wheel had 27 troughs and a workforce of 33. By 1811 the Loxley Plane Wheel had two tilt hammers, two forge hammers and seven tool troughs. The wheel buildings were demolished in the 1960s and the tail goit infilled in the 1980s.

Storrs Bridge Forge – first recorded in 1720 when a lease was taken out to build a cutler's wheel. By 1811 it consisted of one forge, two tilt-hammers and a grinding wheel. In the 20th century the works were demolished though elements of the dam, overflow and tail goit survive.

Storrs Fire Clay Works – this works combined extraction of pot clay with manufacture of fire-bricks. A number of clay shafts are evident on the 1855/6 Ordnance Survey map and by 1864 the Clay Works was established. The Works expanded through the late 19th/early 20th century and by 1923 incorporated 23 kilns and a tramway. Large scale modernisation took place in the 1950s and the site only finally closed in 1997. A watching brief during test-pitting located the remains of a demolished beehive kiln.

Storrs Bridge Fire Brick Works – established after 1855, this refractory works lost part of its semi-constructed buildings in the Sheffield Flood of 1864. By 1892/3 the Works comprised a large building with two kilns and a tramway. Expansion continued in the early 20th century until decline in the 1970s and 1980s and by 2004 the original buildings had been replaced.

Claremont House – built between 1894 and 1903 the house and stable block appear on Ordnance Survey maps standing in formally laid-out gardens. In 2002 the house was used as a social club but then fell into a state of disrepair.

The site as a whole is considered as having good potential for survival of

Malin Bridge Corn Mill photographed in 2003   © SYAS

sub-surface remains pertinent to the industrial heritage of the Loxley Valley.

Centred at Grid Reference SK 294 898

From a report by Paula Ware and Anne Finney, MAP Archaeological Consultancy Ltd

MALIN BRIDGE CORN MILL, LOXLEY ROAD, SHEFFIELD

Following an earlier desk-based assessment (see '*Archaeology in South Yorkshire Number 11*'), evaluation trial trenches were excavated on land adjoining the mill in March 2007, for Bagley UK Ltd. The evaluation revealed evidence of 19th century levelling and a late 19th/early 20th century brick floor

and wall footings presumed to relate to an ancillary mill building. No finds of interest were recovered.

Grid Reference SK 325 893

From a report by Mark Peachey, Archaeological Project Services

BRADFIELD ROAD COMBINED SEWER OVERFLOW, HILLSBOROUGH, SHEFFIELD

Archaeological monitoring was carried out for Earth-Tech Morrison during groundworks associated with construction of a sewage outflow. Extensive post-medieval remains were encountered, mainly associated with the former Upper Owlerton Wheel. This former grinding wheel was in use from at least 1783, was converted to a wire mill c.1864 and continued in use until the early 20th century. Exposed features included the northeast wall of the building and two stone culverts. Numerous fragments of grinding wheels were recovered, along with sherds of post-medieval pottery and fragments of clay tobacco pipe stems. A thick layer of silt observed in several places is thought likely to relate to the Sheffield Flood of 1864.

Grid Reference SK 334 897

From a report by John Buglass, Northern Archaeological Associates

REDMIRES CAMP PLANTATION, SHEFFIELD

A desk-based assessment was prepared and a walkover survey was carried out for Sheffield CC, between November 2006 and February 2007, to inform future management of the woodland. The present plantation was created in 1958; previously the site had a history of different uses. Redmires Camp was constructed here in 1915 to house the newly formed Sheffield City Battalion, formed in response to an appeal for volunteers made three days after the outbreak of WW1 by Field Marshal Lord Kitchener. Towards the end of the war, the camp was used for German Prisoners of War. It was used as a smallpox hospital during the epidemic of 1925-27 and the converted buildings were used to house convalescent patients from nearby Lodge Moor

Hospital in the 1930s. Lodge Moor Camp was built in 1939 to the north east of the earlier camp. The footings of this Prisoner of War camp, which housed both Italian and German PoWs, still survive. Projections based on the number of accommodation huts identified during the survey suggest that the main compound could have accommodated approximately 5,300 PoWs (see interpretive plan on page 185 of the colour section). It is known that this permanent accommodation was increased by the use of bell tents, shown on an aerial photograph taken in June 1945. It is estimated that this temporary accommodation could have housed an additional 2,700 PoWs.

Centred at Grid Reference SK 277 859

From a report by ASE Ltd

WHIRLOW WHEEL, SHEFFIELD

Whirlow Wheel is first recorded as a corn mill in the 16th century and this use appears to have continued into the 18th century. In 1803 a grinding wheel was installed and the adjacent reservoir enlarged. Numerous repairs and refurbishments are recorded in the 19th century and in 1901 the then tenant replaced the water wheel with a turbine. However, by 1935 the structure was considered too dilapidated to be let for manufacturing and the wheel building was sold to Sheffield Corporation, who used it as a store. The recent collapse of much of the roof structure and resultant damage to the east wall led to a decision to demolish the building on grounds of safety. Before this demolition took place a photographic record of the remains was made in October 2006, for Sheffield CC.

The main building was found to be a single storey structure with Venetian windows high in each gable. The adjoining wheel pit was two-storey, with a substantial retaining wall running from the wheel pit towards the Limb Brook to the north. On the higher ground to the west, the remains of the former pentrough, which brought water from the adjacent reservoir to the water wheel, could still be traced. It is likely that the retaining wall and an associated rebuild of the north wall of the wheel-pit date to 1803, when the dam is known to have been heightened.

Grid Reference SK 311 825

From a report by Stephen Duckworth, ARCUS

SHEFFIELD UNIVERSITY STUDENT VILLAGE, BROOMHILL, SHEFFIELD

Following earlier assessment (see *'Archaeology in South Yorkshire Number 12'*) further archaeological investigation was carried out, on behalf of Bovis Lend Lease Ltd. Between December 2005 and May 2006 a photographic record was made of the student halls of residence to be demolished. The earliest buildings on the site were originally part of large 19th century houses that were bought by the University in the 20th century to provide student accommodation. Despite later alteration these still retained some historic features from their original use. Other buildings represent purpose built

Photograph of the Sorby Hall of Residence reception area © ARCUS

construction in the 20th century in response to the expansion of the University.

Geophysical survey of an area known as the Paddock was carried out in December 2005. Two areas of magnetic disturbance identified relate to slight earthworks that might indicate sub-surface structural remains. Thirty one evaluation trenches and nine test pits were then excavated at various locations across the site, between December 2005 and February 2006. These revealed that the majority of the site had been disturbed by modern groundworks. The exceptions to this were two trenches close to Endcliffe Vale Road where features were found that relate to Endcliffe Vale House and development of the area in the 19th century.

Centred at Grid Reference SK 328 862

From reports by Lucy Dawson, Oliver Jessop and Sean Bell (building recording and evaluation), ARCUS; M Whittingham, Met Surveys (geophysics)

LAND OFF POMONA STREET, SHEFFIELD

Excavation of an evaluation trench was carried out in January 2007 on behalf of Rapidelevation Ltd, in relation to proposed residential development of the site. The site was undeveloped until the mid 19th century when it formed part of a large area of allotments. By the 1890s the land was gardens for an adjoining row of terraces. Two parallel walls delimiting the plots of the gardens were revealed during the excavation. Artefacts recovered from this phase of activity include fragments of clay tobacco pipe, mid/late 19th century pottery and unglazed fired clay balls that were probably used for the game of 'knurr and spell'.

Grid Reference SK 344 862

From reports by Richard O'Neill, ARCUS

CLOUGH LODGE, 74 EDMUND ROAD, SHEFFIELD

A planning application that incorporated demolition of 'Clough Lodge' led to a building appraisal in January 2006 on behalf of Mike Griffiths and Associates. The Lodge was built in the early 19th century as the entrance lodge to Clough House. The lodge had been divided from the house by the time of the 1894 OS map, by the construction of Shoreham Street. By 1953 the plot containing the lodge had been further developed with workshops and garages. At the time of the appraisal, the lodge building was in a poor state of repair, having been fire damaged, with internal fittings already stripped out.

Grid Reference SK 355 863

From a report by Guy Hopkinson, Archaeoscope

FORMER BED NIGHTCLUB, LONDON ROAD, SHEFFIELD

Proposed part-demolition and redevelopment of the site led to a scheme of archaeological investigation, on behalf of Mike Griffiths & Associates. A desk-based assessment identified that the site lay within the hamlet of Little Sheffield in the 18th and 19th centuries. Map evidence from 1817 showed buildings within a walled yard here. As Sheffield expanded in the first half of the 19th century, these buildings were demolished and the site was occupied by back-to-back housing and small commercial units. These were in turn replaced by the Lansdowne Picture Theatre in 1914, which was later used as a dance hall and then nightclub. Three evaluation trenches were excavated following the demolition of the rear of the nightclub building. These identified a series of walls associated with the late 18th/early 19th century structures depicted on the 1817 map, as well as with the 19th century back-to-back houses. No evidence was found that could identify the function of the earlier buildings.

Grid Reference SK 349 862

From reports by C Fern, Fern Archaeology (desk-based assessment) and A Dickson, A D Archaeology (evaluation and watching brief)

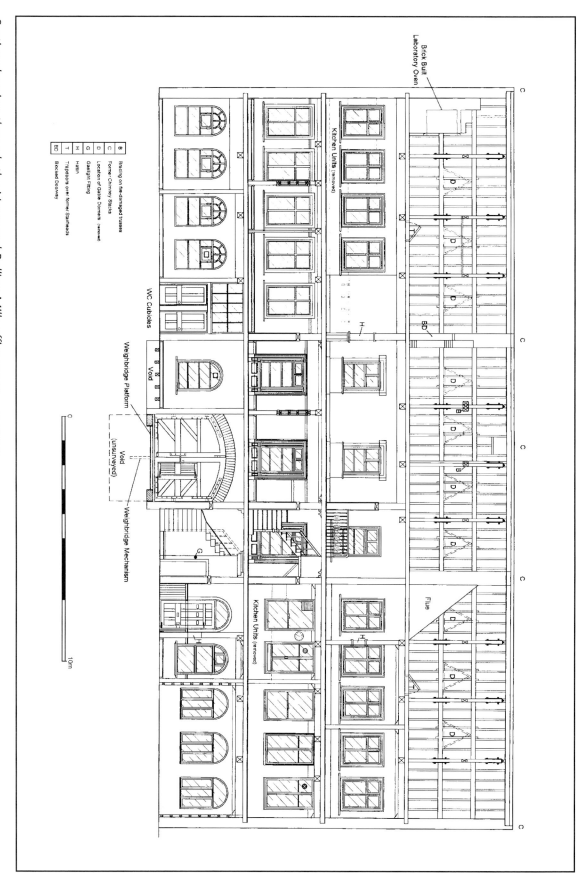

Section drawing through the Neepsend Rolling Mills office range   © ARCUS

FORMER STANLEY TOOL WORKS, RUTLAND ROAD, SHEFFIELD

A desk-based assessment was prepared in April 2006 for ECUS Ltd, to inform a planning application for residential and retail redevelopment. The site remained undeveloped until the second half of the 19th century when back-to-back and terraced housing, a beerhouse, mission hall and new road were constructed. By 1903 J A Chapman's Industry Tool Works had expanded into the site but buildings associated with these works were demolished and replaced following takeover by Stanley in 1936. Surviving 19th century buildings elsewhere on the site were cleared in the mid 20th century.

Centred at Grid Reference SK 353 888

From a report by Mark Stenton, ARCUS

NEEPSEND ROLLING MILLS, SHEFFIELD

Further research comprising building recording of the office range associated with the former Rolling Mills was carried out between December 2004 and June 2005 for Harrison Construction Ltd (for earlier work see *'Archaeology in South Yorkshire Number 11'* and *'Number 12'*). The office range probably dates from the 1870s or earlier and comprises a three storey red brick building with a central cart passage. Much of the building originally served as offices and stockrooms, with the attic space originally being accessed via stairwells

and being lit by dormer windows (probably removed in the mid 20th century). The presence of a substantial oven built against the west gable in the attic could indicate this space was used as a laboratory test area.

Grid Reference SK 349 884

From a report by Tegwen Roberts, Stephen Duckworth and Oliver Jessop, ARCUS

THE LANCASTER COMPLEX, BALL STREET, SHEFFIELD

Further archaeological works comprising a watching brief during groundworks and recording of standing buildings was carried out between December 2004 and June 2006 for Harrison Construction Ltd (for earlier work see *'Archaeology in South Yorkshire Number 12'*). Features exposed during groundworks include a vaulted concrete chamber and an external wall from the early factory buildings. The concrete chamber contained chemical toilets and has been interpreted as a World War II air raid shelter. An assemblage of grinding wheels was also recovered. These would have been used to grind/sharpen blades and files and displayed extensive wear.

The building recording established that the buildings on the corner of Ball Street, a pair of dwellings and the former Cardigan Tavern, were built in a single phase between 1855 and 1859. They appear to have been built as part of a phase of speculative building during the urbanisation of Neepsend at this time; the use of a curved frontage on a corner site, such as here, is a particular

Some of the grinding wheels observed during the watching brief at the Lancaster Complex   © ARCUS

feature of Sheffield vernacular building and was once a common sight in former industrial quarters.

Grid Reference SK 349 883

From reports by Lucy Dawson, Stephen Duckworth and Oliver Jessop, ARCUS

45 MOWBRAY STREET, SHEFFIELD

Following an earlier desk-based assessment (see '*Archaeology in South Yorkshire Number 12*') the footprint for the new building was stripped, and features of archaeological interest recorded, in March 2007 for Nu Build Construction (Leeds) Ltd. The cellar of a mid 19th century crucible furnace, with one row of melting holes, was identified.

Eight melting holes were visible, but more could have originally been present as not all of the furnace structure survived. The remains examined were fairly well preserved: the cellar retained some original vaulting; the brick and stone piers between the ashpits were numbered, presumably to assist the operation of the furnace; and some melting holes still contained the fire bars that would have supported the crucibles. Elsewhere on the site a mid 19th century grinding trough with an intact grinding wheel was also revealed. Changing production practices were indicated by a large red brick structure, interpreted as part of an early 20th century gas conversion furnace, which replaced the crucible furnace.

Grid Reference SK 352 882

From a report by Helen Holderness, ARCUS

The crucible cellar discovered at 17-39 Mowbray Street   © ARCUS

17-39 MOWBRAY STREET, SHEFFIELD

Further archaeological works comprising evaluation, excavation and building recording were carried out between February and October 2005 for Riverdale Construction Ltd (for earlier work see *'Archaeology in South Yorkshire Number 12'*). Trial trenches exposed the very well preserved remains of a mid 19th century crucible furnace (with two rows of six melting holes) and of a late 19th/early 20th century grinding shop with grinding troughs. As well as excavation of the surface features, building recording of the intact crucible cellars was undertaken (see plan on page 186 of the colour section).

A wooden post, cast-iron mould and 'plug and bonnet' in one of the cellars was testament to the manufacture of crucibles. The 'plug' was used to shape the interior of a crucible and the 'bonnet' used to manufacture its tapered top. Once the crucible had been shaped the mould would be knocked onto the wooden post to allow removal of the shaped crucible, ready for drying. In the same room, a low metal trough, nearly 3m long and 2m wide, contained traces of grey clay. This is likely to have been a 'puddling pit' for the preparation of clay for crucible manufacture.

Grid Reference SK 353 882

From a report by Steve Baker and Ben Chan, ARCUS

CALEDONIA WORKS, 41 MOWBRAY STREET, SHEFFIELD

A desk-based assessment was prepared in March 2006 for Riverdale Construction Ltd, to inform a proposal for redevelopment. The site is likely to have been open ground until the mid 19th century, when Mowbray Street was constructed. The area quickly developed into a manufacturing/business quarter. By 1879 an iron foundry is recorded on the site; the 1895 edition OS map describes this as the Union Foundry. By 1939 the site was occupied by William Turner & Son Ltd, steel manufacturers, and was renamed the Caledonia Works. The standing buildings are the remains of the 19th century courtyard works, but they have been largely gutted and most evidence for original use removed.

Grid Reference SK 353 882

From a report by Dan Slatcher, John Samuels Archaeological Consultants

LAUREL WORKS, NURSERY STREET, SHEFFIELD

Proposed demolition of standing buildings and construction of residential units was preceded by a desk-based assessment, prepared in April and May 2006 for Building Link Design. The site lay within the Duke of Norfolk's nursery in the late 18th century, but from the mid 19th century it was developed for residential and retail use. In 1913 the site was used for the East End Branch of the Sheffield Children's Hospital, which had formerly been located on The Wicker. The branch closed in 1931, after which the present works building was constructed. However, the standing buildings appear to incorporate a late 19th century or early 20th century brick-built building, which may warrant further investigation.

Grid Reference SK 356 880

From a report by CG Cumberpatch, Freelance Archaeologist

FORMER BICKERTON GARAGE, INFIRMARY ROAD, SHEFFIELD

A proposal to demolish existing warehousing and build apartments led to preparation of a desk-based assessment in March 2006, for Coda Studios Ltd. During the medieval period the site was part of the common grazing ground of Shalesmoor and remained undeveloped until the mid 19th century when back-to-back and terraced housing was built. All 19th century buildings were cleared in the early 20th century and survival of sub-surface remains will be dependent upon the extent of intrusive works associated with construction of the garage in the 1950s.

Grid Reference SK 347 881

From a report by Mark Stenton, ARCUS

LAND AT ROSCOE ROAD, SHEFFIELD

A desk-based assessment and building appraisal was carried out between August 2005 and August 2006 on behalf of the Opal Property Group, to inform a planning application for redevelopment. The site appears to have been undeveloped prior to the early 19th century when a fender and stove grate works was constructed at the northern end. The remainder of the site was developed between 1823 and 1850, predominantly as metal trade works but with a few areas of back-to-back housing. The stove grate works had been demolished by 1890 and replaced by terraced housing. The terraced housing was demolished in the mid 20th century, presumably as part of a wider clearance programme.

Many works buildings survived the clearance episode. These include the Grade II listed Titanic Works, which contains a former crucible furnace, with chimney stacks at either end of the furnace building. The building appraisal identified other 19th century buildings including those of the former Hoyle Street Works, which may have contained cementation furnaces as well as a further crucible furnace, and former houses converted into industrial use. There are also areas where more recent developments appear not to have intruded at depth, offering potential for survival of sub-surface archaeology.

Centred at Grid Reference SK 348 881

From reports by Rowan May and Stephen Duckworth, ARCUS

The Don Brewery wall revealed during work at Cornish Square, Sheffield © ARCUS

CORNISH STREET GARAGE, SHEFFIELD

Further works comprising excavation and a watching brief during demolition and groundworks were carried out between January and May 2005 for Harrison Construction Ltd (for the earlier assessment see '*Archaeology in South Yorkshire Number 12*'). The two excavated trenches revealed remains of the 19th century Don Brewery, including a boiler/engine house, as well as contemporary back-to-back housing. The watching brief during the demolition of standing structures revealed a large sandstone wall that had clearly formed part of the original brewery building. In a second phase of the watching brief, the removal of brick vaulted cellars on the southern part of the site was observed. The vaulting sprang from a series of iron girders that were held up by evenly spaced iron columns. Two main cellars were recorded, but it was clear that a further two cellars had been backfilled during previous development, suggesting that they originally covered most of the site.

Grid Reference SK 348 882

From a report by Dr Ben Chan, ARCUS

DAISY SPRING WORKS, GREEN LANE, SHEFFIELD

Following an earlier desk-based assessment (see '*Archaeology in South Yorkshire Number 12*'), evaluation and a watching brief were carried out between September and November 2005 for Harrison Construction Ltd. The trenches excavated uncovered the remains of a cobbled lane (formerly Dun Lane), footings that probably relate to the former Gardener's Rest public house, and cellars from 19th century housing. Evidence for the latter was also found during a watching brief on later soil stripping. Artefacts recovered included 18th/19th century ceramics and tobacco clay pipe fragments.

Grid Reference SK 349 881

From a report by Helen Holderness, ARCUS

LAND AT DUN FIELDS, SHEFFIELD

A desk-based assessment was prepared in August 2006, for Hepher Dixon, to inform a planning application for redevelopment. The site was not developed until the 1820s, when back-to-back housing and industrial workshops were constructed. By the mid 19th century, the southern end of the site formed part of the Shalesmoor Foundry, which was established early in the 19th century. By 1890, the whole site had been redeveloped as the Shalesmoor Foundry (steel & iron). The present building dates from this period and, although altered, warrants more detailed recording. There is also some potential for sub-surface domestic and industrial remains.

Grid Reference SK 349 880

From reports by Leonora O'Brien and Isabel Mason, Scott Wilson

LAND AT ACORN STREET, SHEFFIELD

A desk-based assessment was prepared in August 2006, for Hepher Dixon, to inform a planning application for redevelopment. The first phase of development was the construction of the Cannon Brewery, established by William Stones, which was probably built in 1825. Terraced housing was also constructed along the Acorn Street frontage. By 1890 the brewery site had been taken over by the Acorn Street Foundry (iron). This works later became a steel spring works and has had various uses in the late 20th century. The terraced housing was cleared sometime after 1935 but elements of the earlier industrial buildings survive within the present structure. The site also has some potential for sub-surface domestic and industrial remains.

Grid Reference SK 350 880

From reports by Leonora O'Brien and Isabel Mason, Scott Wilson

KUTRITE SCISSOR WORKS, ALMA STREET / RUSSELL STREET, SHEFFIELD

A desk-based assessment was prepared in April 2006 for H J Banks and Co Ltd, ahead of proposed mixed-use redevelopment. This site adjoins the Richardson's Cutlery Works site, which was subject to an earlier assessment (see *'Archaeology in South Yorkshire Number 12'*). The site was open land until the 19th century, when workshops and possibly back-to-back houses were built. By mid-century these had been replaced by, or incorporated into, the Russell Works, thought to have been a steel works. The present Kutrite Scissor Works are modern brick built buildings, but there remains potential for sub-surface archaeology relating to earlier uses of the site.

Grid Reference SK 351 880

From a report by Jenny Emmett, Charlotte Dawson and Helen Martin-Bacon, Wardell Armstrong

CORNISH STEEL WORKS, GREEN LANE, SHEFFIELD

A desk-based assessment was prepared in March 2006 for Coda Studios Ltd, to inform a planning application for residential and retail redevelopment. The site was part of common pasture or meadowland until the 19th century but had been fully developed with back-to-back housing and shops by 1853. These 19th century buildings were demolished during the 1930s and by 1951 the site

had been redeveloped as the Cornish Steel Works. The present buildings date from this period.

Grid Reference SK 350 881

From a report by Mark Stenton, ARCUS

CORNWALL WORKS, GREEN LANE, SHEFFIELD

Archaeological building recording was carried out in October 2005 for Axis Architecture prior to partial demolition and conversion of the buildings on this site. The complex comprises three ranges of buildings dating from the late 19th century to the mid 20th century, representing the development of a Sheffield flatware company through time.

Grid Reference SK 351 881

From a report by Mark Douglas, ARCUS

LAND OFF BOWLING GREEN STREET, SHEFFIELD

A desk-based assessment was prepared in September 2006 for Axis Architecture, to inform a planning application for residential redevelopment. The proposal area was part of an area of common pasture that was enclosed by the late 18th century. It remained open land until the early 19th century when it was developed as terraced and back-to-back housing. The Sheffield Flood of 1864 affected the area, but the properties here seem to have survived, only to be demolished during the early 20th century as part of a wider clearance programme. By 1963 a cutlery works occupied the eastern part of the site until it too was demolished, early in the 21st century. Survival of below-ground remains associated with the 19th century housing will be dependent upon the degree of intrusive works by later development.

Grid Reference SK 351 880

From a report by Mark Stenton, ARCUS

KELHAM RIVERSIDE (UNION WHEEL), ALMA STREET, SHEFFIELD

Further archaeological works comprising building recording and excavation at the site of the former Union Grinding Wheel were carried out between April and June 2005 (for earlier work see '*Archaeology in South Yorkshire Number 12*'). This work was carried out for the UNITE Group. Two ranges of brick-built structures relating to the adjoining Alma (file) Works were recorded prior to demolition. These contained a number of features relating to their industrial use, including a former boiler/engine house and evidence of line shafting. The west range of these buildings appears on the first edition Ordnance Survey map of 1853, whilst the south range first appears on the 1890 map.

Sub-surface survival of features associated with the Union Grinding Wheel, constructed in 1817 and demolished in the 1950s, was variable. The walls of the building were found to coincide with the floor plan shown on the 1853 Ordnance Survey map. Stone footings in a repetitive pattern against either side of a central wall were probably line-shaft supports, for the power-transmission system. Sub-floor pits between these footings were likely to have contained rotating drums that allowed power to be transferred into the individual grinding workshops via leather belts. Ten workshops (out of a total of 22 on the ground floor, originally) were investigated, with two of the better-preserved being subject to full excavation. The deposits within the drum pits proved to be the most valuable in yielding evidence for changing practices during the life of the building. The laminated nature of these fills suggests gradual accumulation over a considerable period of time. The pottery collected from earlier fills is dominated by late 18th to early 19th century material; the later fills consistently include mid to late 19th century pottery. The clay pipe assemblage recovered from these later fills includes some examples as late as the 1930s, which is consistent with archive evidence that the Union Grinding Wheel was electrified in the 1940s, after which the drum pits would no longer have been used.

A great variety of production is represented by the material recovered during excavation, which is consistent with the suggestion that the Wheel was occupied by relatively small-scale independent concerns that let space from the Union Grinding Wheel Company. Of the two workshops examined in detail, one revealed evidence for a great variety of knife blade production, along with

The eastern end of the Union Grinding Wheel under excavation   © ARCUS

production of scissor blades, files and some evidence for saw grinding; the other revealed evidence for tool production, along with evidence for smithing or forging, and polishing of finished tools. The number and variety of items discarded noticeably increased between the earlier and later phases of the Wheel's life, reflecting the introduction of mass production. Perhaps the reduction in time and effort invested in machine blanks rather than hand-forged items made it more likely that little effort would be made to recover those accidentally dropped.

Centred at Grid Reference SK 353 881

**From reports by Mark Douglas and
Steve Baker, ARCUS**

KELHAM RIVERSIDE 2 (KELHAM ROLLING MILLS), ALMA STREET, SHEFFIELD

Following earlier assessment and building appraisal (see '*Archaeology in South Yorkshire Number 12*') a series of archaeological investigations took place here for the Raven Group. Detailed building recording in April 2006 recorded the former time house/weigh office/boiler house and associated octagonal brick chimney at the west end of the site. Originally built in the mid 19th century, these were incorporated into the expanding Kelham Rolling Mills by 1890. After the Mills' closure in the early 20th century, the buildings were modified and expanded for use by the Kelham Island (firebrick) Works and

A possible chimney and flue at Kelham Riverside 2, Alma Street © ARCUS

were identified. One find of interest recovered was a short length of flat-bottomed metal rail that may be a very early example of its type from the mid-19th century.

Detailed excavation of three areas followed in October and November 2006. The central area revealed extensive remains associated with the Kelham Rolling Mills, which is thought to have been built in the 1830s and had ceased trading by 1921. Remains included the bases of a series of rolling stands, the base of a Lancashire boiler, the base of an octagonal chimney, engine bases and a possible wheel pit, and several drainage culverts. One find of interest recovered was a sledgehammer found in association with one of the rolling bases. This appears to be of a type specifically developed for forges and rolling mills, to mark or sever the slightly deformed end of each rolled bar of steel.

latterly formed part of Turton Tyzack's works. At the east end of the site, Prospect House, which was built c.1890-1903 on a brick arch over Millsands Goit, formed part of a late re-organisation of the Rolling Mills and is thought most likely to have been built as a combined office and store. Latterly this building formed part of Samuel Staniforth's Smithfields Works. These buildings are to be retained within the new scheme.

Four evaluation trenches were excavated in September 2006 and industrial remains were identified in each. As well as early 19th century structures associated with the Kelham Rolling Mills, remains associated with the later Kelham Island (firebrick) Works

At the eastern end of the site a smithy and associated boiler house shown on the 1853 OS map were investigated. These may pre-date the incorporation of this land into the Rolling Mills, but they continued in use until the early 20th century when the structures were demolished and several concrete machine bases inserted. An unusual find recovered from the demolition/levelling layers was a fragment of Prattware clay pipe bowl. This would have been produced c1790-1830 and takes the form of a sea serpent's head. Originally this would have been attached to an elaborately glazed, coiled pipe – a high status item.

At the western end of the site part of a flue system possibly associated with the

Kelham Rolling Mills was identified, along with structures associated with the early 20th century Kelham Island Works. These later remains almost certainly relate to a kiln or furnace used for the production of firebricks.

Centred at Grid Reference SK 353 881

From reports by Richard O'Neill, Stephen Duckworth and Tegwen Roberts, ARCUS

SHEFFIELD INNER RELIEF ROAD

Following earlier assessment and evaluation (see *'Archaeology in South Yorkshire Number 11'* and *'Number 12'*), a detailed programme of building recording and excavation was undertaken for Sheffield CC, in advance of construction works starting. A general watching brief was also maintained once construction commenced.

Building recording took place at: the retaining wall at Bridgehouses goods yard, the crozzle wall on Brunswick Street, 83 Spring Street (former townhouse), 198a Gibraltar Street (former warehouse), Corporation Inn on Corporation Street, and Nag's Head PH on Shalesmoor. Building recording and excavation, following demolition, took place at: Soho Grinding Wheel on Bridge Street, Shalesmoor warehouse (formerly housing), the Greyhound PH on Gibraltar Street, 195-213 Gibraltar Street (formerly housing and possible steelworks), Corporation Saw Mills on Spring Street, Spring Street warehouse (formerly housing), the Central Ambulance Station (formerly an iron foundry), 65-67 Corporation Street

(formerly a warehouse and brass foundry), the site of Love and Manson Works on Moorfield (steelworks), Wicker Ironworks on Spital Hill, Nursery Wheel on Stanley Street (edge tool works), Talbot Works on Brunswick Road (edge tool works), and Snow Machine Tool Makers on Andrew Street (edge tool works). Excavation also took place at the sites of: Bower Spring (steel) Works on Bower Spring, the saw mill on Plum Lane, Russell Roller Mills on Russell Street, Millsands Steelworks on Corporation Street, and the Gaiety Music Hall.

It is clear that the results of this extensive suite of investigations will provide much information about the development of this area of Sheffield. Research aims set out as part of the mitigation strategy were: pre-industrial environments (what can the results tell us about this area before it became part of the urban centre of Sheffield); industrialisation and technology (what can the results tell us about the origin and growth of Sheffield industries, particularly the steel-making, edge tool, cutlery and tableware industries); urban geography (what was the character and function of this area of the town); working, dwelling and identity (what was the relationship between domestic and industrial spaces here).

Two of the excavated sites produced some evidence for the pre-industrial landscape. Three sites produced significant evidence for steel production and processing, including six cementation furnaces and two crucible furnaces. One of these crucible furnaces was originally part of the Bower Spring Works and would have formed part of the industrial complex containing the

Recording the crucible furnace at Bower Spring as part of the Inner Relief Road scheme   © ARCUS

Bower Spring cementation furnaces, now scheduled as an ancient monument. Two sites produced evidence for steam-powered grinding (this area developed as industry moved away from the traditional water-powered sites). Evidence for redevelopment following earlier municipal improvement schemes was seen, following the construction of Corporation Street and the widening of Gibraltar Street in the late 19th century. As expected, several sites produced evidence for a close mix of industrial and domestic properties. As the post-excavation process continues, the extent to which the information recovered will allow the original research aims to be met will become clear.

Centred at Grid Reference SK 355 880

From reports by Oliver Jessop and Sean Bell, ARCUS

LAND AT BRIDGE STREET, SHEFFIELD

A desk-based assessment was prepared in January 2006 for Studio One Architects, to inform a planning application for redevelopment. The proposal area was meadowland or fields until the late 18th century. By the 1820s a steel and tool works had been constructed on the site, which included a 20-hole crucible furnace. The works went through periods of expansion and change of use throughout the 19th century, becoming a confectionary works by 1890. This pattern of expansion and change of use continued in the 20th century, with the site becoming an engineering works by the 1950s. The extant buildings date from the mid 20th century and are not archaeologically significant, but below-ground remains of earlier structures may survive.

Grid Reference SK 354 879

From a report by Rowan May, ARCUS

ST GEORGE'S CLOSE, NETHERTHORPE, SHEFFIELD

Following an earlier desk-based assessment (see '*Archaeology in South Yorkshire Number 12*') four evaluation trenches were excavated in November 2005, for the Opal Property Group. Remains uncovered included cellars associated with mid 19th century back-to-back housing, and wall foundations and floors from the late 19th century Atlantic Works, which produced cutlery. However, generally archaeological preservation was poor.

Centred at Grid Reference SK 345 876

From a report by Sean Bell and Steve Baker, ARCUS

35 AND 54 WELL MEADOW STREET, SHEFFIELD

Possible redevelopment led to a buildings appraisal on behalf of Earle Hainsworth Architects Ltd. Both buildings are listed and fall within the boundary of a proposed Conservation Area. Number 35 was known as Well Meadow Works and number 54 was known as Well Meadow Steel Works. A large part of Well Meadow Steel Works had been built by the time of the 1850 Ordnance Survey; the Well Meadow Works are shown on the 1890 Ordnance Survey map, although it seems likely that the majority of the works was built in the 1860s to early 1870s. Trade directories indicate that both works were occupied by a number of small metal trades businesses, a common Sheffield practice.

Both works are considered to be important examples of integrated works and incorporate crucible furnaces and associated workshops. Well Meadow Steel Works was also found to contain a small forge; Well Meadow Works also contained grinding hulls with grinding wheels steel in place. The southern range of Well Meadow Steel Works was found to consist almost entirely of a terrace of early 19th century houses, which had been incorporated into the expanding works. Both works retain important evidence of the whole process of steel production and manufacture, from casting through to the preparation and dispatch of finished items.

Grid Reference SK 346 877

From a report by Oliver Jessop, ARCUS

LAND AT WELL MEADOW DRIVE, SHEFFIELD

A desk-based assessment was prepared in January 2006 for Studio One Architecture and Design, to inform a planning application to redevelop the site. The proposal area was developed by the late 18th century. A plan of 1792 shows two blocks of housing, one of which was named Jericho, later becoming Jericho Street before being renamed Well Meadow Drive in the 1960s. The remainder of the area was relatively undeveloped until the mid 19th century, but by 1890 a Methodist chapel, small workshops and housing had been built. Redevelopment in the 20th century saw clearance of all earlier buildings and the survival of below-ground archaeology will be dependent upon the extent of sub-surface disturbance during these works.

Grid Reference SK 346 877

From a report by Rowan May, ARCUS

UPPER ALLEN STREET / WELL MEADOW DRIVE, SHEFFIELD

A desk-based assessment was prepared in July 2006 for Coda Studios Ltd to inform a planning application for redevelopment. The site was undeveloped until the late 18th/early 19th century after which a series of domestic courts were built, including one known as Crossland's Square. By 1923, much of the area had been cleared; the final court was cleared by

1950. The present buildings on the site, known as the Norfolk Works, were probably built before the Second World War, with an inter war and later addition. The area of the last courtyard cleared has remained undeveloped and probably has the most potential for below-ground survival.

Grid Reference SK 346 877

**From a report by Dan Slatcher,
John Samuels Archaeological Consultants**

STEPHENSON BLAKE TYPE FOUNDRY, SHEFFIELD

Extensive archaeological works were carried out at this site between April 2005 and December 2006, for Watkin Jones Construction (see *'Archaeology in South Yorkshire Number 12'* for earlier assessment and building appraisal). Excavation of an area between the former Marsden Lane and Edward Street took place between April and August 2005. This revealed the remains of three courts associated with early to mid 19th century back-to-back housing. Slight differences in room size between the three courts suggest that they were built as separate enterprises, perhaps at separate times. One court was particularly well preserved because of the sloping nature of the site. Here, ground floor rooms with internal features, yard structures and drainage/sewerage structures all survived. The back-to-back houses were probably three storeys high originally. Doorways in the rear wall of the ground floor rooms would have led to steps down to the coal store and to the

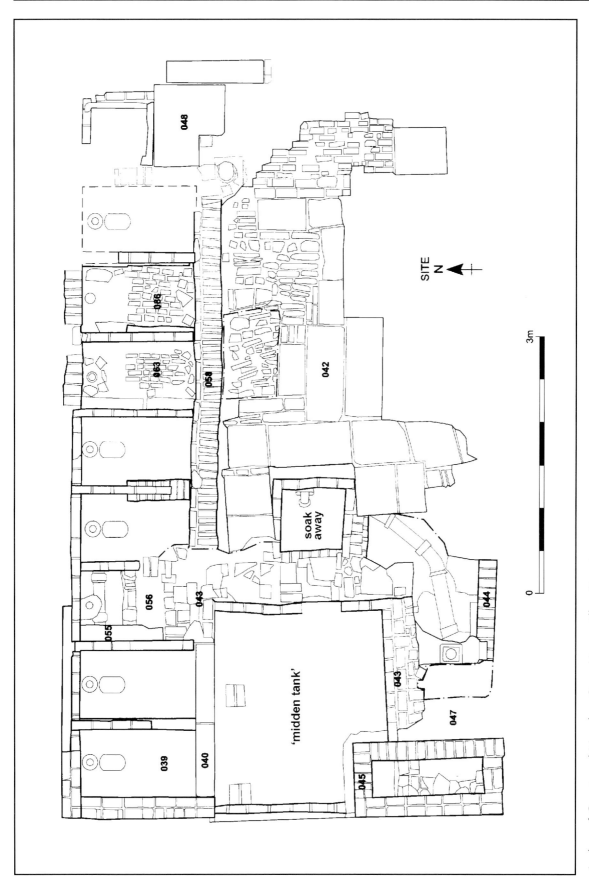

A plan of Courtyard Number One, Upper Allen Street © ARCUS

Photograph of the Stephenson Blake buildings © ARCUS

stairway to rooms above. The ground floor rooms contained chimneybreasts with an oven and side boiler. Late in the 19th century stone sinks were added, with drainage to the central yard. Stone flag floors appear to have been introduced into the houses sometime after 1862. The uniform nature of these alterations suggests the court buildings remained in a single ownership throughout their existence. The courts were demolished by 1941, allowing the firm of Stephenson Blake to expand their works into this area.

Finds included a concentration of butchered rabbit bones from beneath the floor of one of the houses, presumably representing casual discard on an earlier earthen floor. Another concentration of finds was recovered from the fill of a soakaway shaft in the yard. This contained significant amounts of pottery including late 19th century toys and a commemorative mug; these had presumably accumulated as waste material during the associated privies' use. The soakaway's fill was rich in fish bones, indicating fish was an important component of people's diets.

In July and August 2006 detailed recording took place of the standing buildings and historic fittings of the type foundry. This remained in use for a century and a half and was the last such works operating in Britain. The standing buildings represent six major phases of construction from the early 18th century to the mid 20th century, as the company expanded their works onto neighbouring plots and re-ordered existing buildings. The earliest phase of construction was identified at the centre of the Upper Allen Street frontage. This building has recessed window bays between brick piers. This is an unusual form in Sheffield where works buildings tended to use plain vernacular styles. The style was perpetuated in modified form in later buildings, giving a coherent appearance to the works frontage. Although production machinery had been removed by the time of the survey, a variety of fittings survived including line shafting and wall boxes. Typeface storage racking was also present.

Between September and December 2006 excavation took place of a further area of land off Edward Street that was incorporated by the type foundry during the 20th century. This revealed the remains of another court of early 19th century back-to-back housing, and two courts associated with the Kenyon Cutlery Works, which was established in 1868 and demolished in the 1890s. The cutlery works had been truncated below ground floor level during demolition but still preserved line shaft structures and remains of the associated power drive leading to a series of grinding troughs. The site of the engine that provided power to the works was also identified, along with the remains of a chimney. Evidence for the expansion of the cutlery works into the adjoining residential court was noted. An anvil with a large sandstone base, which

was probably used for working cutlery blade sized items, was found adjacent to the threshold of a vaulted cellar of an earlier house.

Centred at Grid Reference SK 347 876

From reports by Stephen Duckworth, James Thomson, Steve Baker and Duncan Alexander, ARCUS

LAND AT SOLLY STREET, SHEFFIELD

A desk-based assessment was prepared in November 2005 for Merlin Estates ahead of proposed redevelopment for residential use. The proposal area was undeveloped land until the last quarter of the 18th century when it began to be developed, primarily for industrial use. An exception to this was the land at 196-212 Solly Street, which was laid out as a garden and remained largely free of structures until the 20th century. The retaining wall supporting the north side of the plot featured a viewing platform constructed of re-used stone that was recorded as part of the programme of investigations at the Cornhill Works (see below and *'Archaeology in South Yorkshire Number 12'*). Demolition of the majority of the 19th century structures occurred in the late 20th century and earlier upstanding remains are limited to the building at numbers 164-168 Solly Street. There is some potential for the survival of earlier sub-surface remains.

Grid Reference SK 347 875

From a report by Mark Stenton, ARCUS

CORNHILL WORKS, EDWARD STREET, SHEFFIELD

Building recording and excavation was reported in *'Archaeology in South Yorkshire Number 12'*. Since that publication, detailed reports on both pieces of work have been produced for Merlin Estates. The surviving 5-storey building, which is listed, appears to date from the late 19th century and is one of the few surviving examples of integrated grinding and cutlery workshops in Sheffield. It operated as a single complex until the end of the 19th century, when the upper and lower floors were separated into two works, accessed separately from Solly Street and Edward Street respectively.

The first floor is supported by brick jack arches on cast iron columns and rolled steel joists. This is a technique that was widespread in large cotton mills, to act as a means of fireproofing factory floors. In Sheffield this construction technique seems to have been particularly associated with grinding hulls. Recessed arches at ground level indicate the provision of ground level power transmission, another feature of grinding hulls. The first floor is likely to have housed machinery involved with cutlery and edge-tool production that required no grinding or hot working. The upper three floors were all well provided with windows and small hearths. Activities relating to assembly, finishing and packing of cutlery and edge tools is likely to have taken place here.

The excavation on adjoining land identified several phases of activity. The

Exterior shot of the Cornhill Works   © ARCUS

earliest was a buried soil horizon from which a mid 17th century token and sherds of Cistercian ware pottery (c1450-c1600) were recovered. This represents the remains of the former fields or open land present here until the end of the 18th century. The foundations of a rectangular building first shown on a plan of 1818 as under the ownership of William Stones, razor manufacturer, were identified. The foundations of further buildings added throughout the 19th century were also identified. The majority of these were amalgamated under the name of Cambridge Works in 1889 and then Cornhill Works in 1898.

These had all been demolished by the mid 20th century and their remains truncated by the construction of a loading bay and associated access ramp. Documentary evidence shows that the site was occupied by a variety of small-scale cutlery-related manufacturers throughout the 19th century, but it was not possible, from the archaeological evidence, to determine the exact processes being undertaken or the exact items being produced within individual buildings.

Centred at Grid Reference SK 347 876

From reports by Oliver Jessop, Tegwen Roberts and Richard O'Neill, ARCUS

LAND AT EDWARD STREET, SHEFFIELD

A desk-based assessment was prepared in September 2005 for AQH Micklegate Developments Ltd, to inform a planning application for redevelopment. The proposal area was part of the medieval Town Field and had been enclosed into small fields by 1637. Development of the area took place in the late 18th century, in the form of back-to-back housing around courtyards, small metal trade workshops, shops and a public house. Larger industrial premises comprised the Paxton Works horticultural tool manufactory, and a scissors manufactory. Modern works buildings currently occupy the site and survival of earlier sub-surface archaeology will be dependent upon the extent of disturbance by their construction.

Grid Reference SK 348 877

From a report by Rowan May, ARCUS

FORMER RAB SITE, EDWARD STREET, SHEFFIELD

A desk-based assessment was prepared in July 2006 for Race Cottam Associates to inform a planning application for residential redevelopment. The site was part of the open Town Field during the medieval and early post-medieval period and was set out for building by 1789. Development of industrial, retail and domestic premises took place during the late 18th/early 19th century, including the St. George's Works and the Lincoln Castle Public House. The site was cleared of buildings during the 1930s and survival of sub-surface archaeology will depend on the degree of intrusive works since then.

Grid Reference SK 349 874

From a report by Mark Stenton, ARCUS

29-65 GARDEN STREET, SHEFFIELD

A scheme of archaeological works was carried out in response to a planning application by Merlin Estates to refurbish and demolish buildings on Garden Street. A desk-based assessment identified the proposal area as lying within the medieval Town Field, an area of land farmed in common by the townspeople. By 1637 most of this had been enclosed into smaller closes and crofts. A one-room Sunday School was built on the site in 1789 and this was rebuilt in classical style in 1873, by which time the surrounding area comprised back-to-back housing and small industrial premises. The school, known as St Luke's National School, is the only surviving 19th century building on the site and has been in light industrial use since demolition of the surrounding houses in the 1930s.

Proposals to partially demolish the building led to a building appraisal in February 2007. National schools were set up by the National Society for Promoting Religious Education, which was established by the Church of England to provide elementary education to the children of the poor, prior to the establishment of a state education system. This school is one of only two National Schools known to survive in Sheffield and was found to contain a significant number of original features, which allowed its original layout to be determined. The first floor housed one large and one small classroom and the ground floor two rooms with a folding screen between them. The two floors could be accessed separately, suggesting the ground floor rooms operated as classrooms during the day and meeting rooms out of school hours.

Excavation of three evaluation trenches in February 2007, on land adjoining the school building, identified structural remains from a cellar and walling thought to relate to the 19th century Peace Brothers steel works. Associated artefacts included clay tobacco pipes, crucible production waste, and 18th/19th century domestic pottery sherds. Notable amongst the latter was a relatively high proportion of bone china, unusual for such a site in Sheffield.

Centred at Grid Reference SK 348 875

From reports by Rowan May, Stephen Duckworth and Isabelle Kendall, ARCUS

LAND AT HOLLIS CROFT, SHEFFIELD

A proposal to build apartments with basement car parking led to preparation of a desk-based assessment in March 2006 for Esharoth Ltd. The proposal area was part of the Town Field until the mid 18th century when urban development began. Cutlery manufacture took place here from the early 19th century, with a large cutlery works shown on the Ordnance Survey map of 1890. Much of the rest of the site appears to have been occupied by smaller scale cutlery workshops. The site was cleared of all buildings in the 20th century and comprised areas of car parking at the time of the assessment. Below-ground archaeological remains can be expected to survive.

Grid Reference SK 349 876

From a report by Mark Stenton, ARCUS

LAND BETWEEN SCOTLAND STREET AND SOLLY STREET, SHEFFIELD

An application for residential development led to the preparation of a desk-based assessment in March 2007, on behalf of St. Vincent's Partnership. The proposal area was part of Sheffield's Town Field and remained open land until it was developed in the late 18th or early 19th century. By the mid 19th century the site comprised a mix of housing and commercial premises built around courtyards, alongside Nowill's Cutlery Works. Clearance in the 20th century removed all these buildings but exposed brickwork suggests that walls may survive below an embankment and that there is potential for remains associated with the cutlery works to survive.

Grid Reference SK 349 877

From a report by Mark Stenton, ARCUS

LAND OFF TENTER STREET, SHEFFIELD

Further phases of investigation were carried out on this redevelopment site between November 2005 and October 2006, for Axis Architecture (see *'Archaeology in South Yorkshire Number 12'* for the first phase of work). Proposed demolition of the Osborne Works led to a photographic survey in November 2005. The building was constructed between the inter war years and 1963 and is considered of little archaeological interest. Evaluation of the same area following demolition found that this building had severely truncated earlier below-ground remains. However, parts of several 19th century cellars were recorded, along with a single truncated pit that probably related to late 18th/early 19th century activity.

Five further evaluation trenches focused on land at the upper end of the development site, bordered by White Croft, Solly Street and Baker's Lane. These trenches revealed the well-preserved remains of 19th century buildings and courtyards. In places these were found to seal 18th century features. Subsequent excavation recorded pits, postholes, probable drainage ditches

Cementation furnace with crucible furnace in background, Tenter Street   © SYAS

and a highly compacted black deposit containing many inclusions of clay pipe and pottery from this earlier phase of occupation. This earlier activity mainly related to small-scale industrial working on the site, possibly involving forging, smelting and cutlery working. In the late 18th or early 19th century development included the construction of a single-hole crucible furnace. Evidence for smelting, forging and grinding was also recovered. An almost complete crucible with partially melted contents, including small blades and scissor parts, was found. The small size of the crucible is consistent with an early 19th century date and its contents imply that recycling of small amounts of steel was taking place here at the time. Later in the 19th century the area was fully developed with a series of courtyards and housing, although small-scale industrial activity probably continued.

A final phase of evaluation and excavation took place on the site of the former Central Steel Works, off Solly Street, between September and October 2006. These works developed from those built by William Parkin in the late 18th century or very early 19th century; they were used for both converting and refining steel. The works had been demolished by the mid-20th century and the site was subsequently redeveloped. The evaluation trenches were located in areas where documentary evidence suggested both cementation and crucible furnaces had been located. The results led to further excavation. The remains of one cementation furnace (out of an original four) were identified, although it had been damaged by later construction of a crucible furnace. An eight-hole crucible furnace is shown on a sketch plan of the works from 1834, but excavation revealed a crucible furnace with up to fourteen melting holes. It was not clear if the earlier furnace had been extended, or simply replaced, perhaps after the works changed hands in the 1840s.

Centred at Grid Reference SK 351 876

From reports by Alex Rose-Deacon,
Oliver Jessop, Dr Ben Chan and
Helen Holderness, ARCUS

JOHN WATTS WORKS, LAMBERT STREET, SHEFFIELD

Building appraisal of this metals trade works was reported in '*Archaeology in South Yorkshire Number 12*'. Between July and November 2005 detailed building recording was carried out in advance of residential conversion, for Westside Development. The first property acquired by John Watts here, in 1872, was the central one of five that the works eventually extended to. All buildings to the rear of this first street frontage range had been demolished and a single storey north-lit workshop range constructed by 1890. This workshop was provided with a lineshaft drive from the outset and it is assumed, although no direct evidence for it was noted, that a small engine and boiler, to provide steam power, must have been located somewhere within the workshop range itself. Multi-storeyed workshops are more usually found on urban sites, but it is assumed that Watts took advantage of a more spacious plot to develop on one level, thus ensuring high light levels throughout the workshop.

Watts acquired properties to the west and east in 1879 and 1892, respectively. The first expansion saw reorganisation of the street frontage range for additional office and workshop space. The second expansion involved the acquisition of the former Norbury scissor workshop and provided a property that required little alteration for cutlery production, but the opportunity was taken to expand the north-lit workshop range across the width of the new property. Later in the 19th century John Watts constructed a two-storey north-lit machine hall on the site of former workshops, on the western plot.

The fourth phase of expansion was the purchase of a further plot to the east in 1910, which allowed the largest single phase of expansion. This entire plot was cleared and replaced by a basement warehouse and ground floor workshop, with an entirely glazed roof, with offices on the street frontage. It is thought that electric power was used from the outset in this range and that the lineshafting in the west machine hall was converted to electric motor drive at the same time. The final expansion was the purchase of a further plot to the west in 1916, which allowed increased office provision and the construction of additional workshops.

Excavation of areas of proposed new build at the rear of the site revealed remains of late 18th- and early 19th-century courtyard housing. The later mid-19th-century modification of these structures for the creation of small-scale industrial workshops was clear, through either conversion or reconstruction. A possible single-hole crucible furnace found in a workshop within a domestic courtyard indicates the level of integration between domestic and industrial life during the 19th century.

Grid reference SK 352 877

**From reports by Stephen Duckworth,
Tegwen Roberts and Chris Breeden, ARCUS**

117-119 West Bar, frontage of the listed building with 1794 date stone in the centre
© ARCUS

frontages were developed by 1736 and further development took place in the 1790s, illustrated by the datestone of 1794 on the surviving historic building. All other 18th/19th century buildings in the proposal area were demolished in the 20th century but there is potential for sub-surface remains of these and earlier structures to survive.

Grid Reference SK 352 877

From a report by Rowan May, ARCUS

LAND AT WEST BAR AND LAMBERT STREET, SHEFFIELD

A desk-base assessment was prepared in March 2006 for West Bar Developments Ltd, to inform a planning application for commercial and residential buildings. West Bar formed the northwest limit of the medieval town of Sheffield and some buildings were recorded here, on what was then known as West Bar Green, in the 17th century. The street

137 WEST BAR, SHEFFIELD

A desk-based assessment was prepared in July 2006 for Mooreland Properties Ltd, to inform a planning application for redevelopment. The proposal area includes the location of Samuel Shore's cementation furnace, which is first recorded in 1716 and may have been the first built in Sheffield. The furnace had been demolished by 1828 and the area was then redeveloped with shops and housing. The standing building on the site dates from the 1950s. If sub-surface archaeology relating to Samuel Shore's furnace has survived this later redevelopment it will be important.

Grid Reference SK 352 878

**From a report by Rowan May,
ARCUS**

WESTON TOWER, WEST BAR GREEN, SHEFFIELD

A desk-based assessment was prepared in February 2006 for Hallana Ltd, to inform a planning application to redevelop the site. The area formed the northwest limit of the medieval town and some buildings were recorded in the area in the 17th century. The street frontages of West Bar, West Bar Green and Silver Street had been developed by 1771, though much of the northern end of the site was redeveloped in the 1790s when most buildings were demolished and replaced.

In the 19th century, warehouses, a wheelwright's and a mineral water factory with covered reservoir occupied the site. The site was cleared in the 20th century and survival of sub-surface archaeology will be dependent on the extent of disturbance during construction of the present buildings.

Grid Reference SK 352 872

**From a report by Rowan May,
ARCUS**

LAND AT BROAD LANE, SHEFFIELD

A scheme of archaeological works was carried out between November 2006 and January 2007 for Watkin Jones Construction ahead of site redevelopment. An initial desk-based assessment identified that Broad Lane had been a significant medieval route, possibly acting as a drove way into town. The proposal area itself was developed in the late 18th/early 19th century and by 1853 comprised back-to-back buildings with a mixture of domestic and commercial use. By the mid 20th century most of the site had been cleared of early structures and a modern tool works and Rockingham House were constructed.

A watching brief during the lifting of concrete slabs, following demolition, revealed a sandstone-flagged yard and lime mortared wall foundations. Subsequent excavation exposed the remains of domestic courts built in the late 18th century and occupied throughout the 19th century. A well was found to contain late 19th century backfill, indicating the date when piped water was probably introduced to these courts. The remains of a midden tank were similarly found to have been backfilled in the late 19th century, indicating the date when sanitary improvements were made; analysis of leather shoes from these deposits date this episode more precisely to the 1860s and 1870s.

Buried soils below the courts were found to contain artefacts dating from the 13th to the 18th century and probably

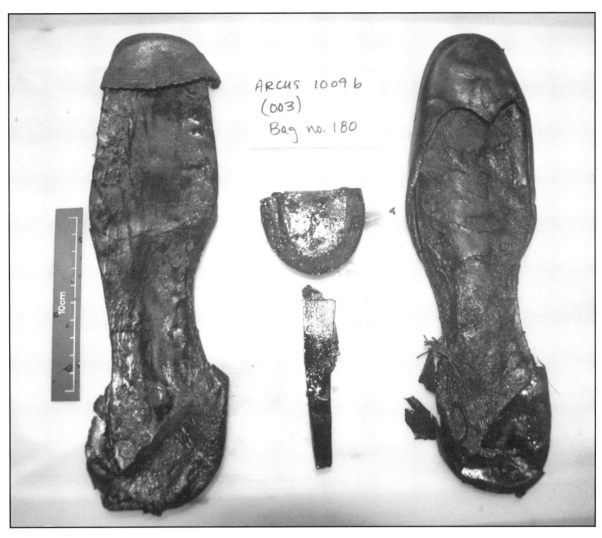

ARCUS 1009 b
(003)
Bag no. 180

19th century leather shoes from Broad Lane, Sheffield   © ARCUS

represent former plough soils. The high percentage of mid-medieval pottery recovered may support the theory that Broad Lane was a medieval drove way. These buried soils were found to seal a number of pits and post-holes that contained no finds. One sample was submitted for radiocarbon dating and this returned a date of 1600BC to 1300BC.

Grid Reference SK 349 874

**From reports by Mark Stenton and
Duncan Alexander, ARCUS**

LAND BETWEEN ROCKINGHAM STREET AND NEWCASTLE STREET, SHEFFIELD

A desk-based assessment and building appraisal was carried out on behalf of Shepherd Developments in August and September 2005 in advance of proposed redevelopment. The proposal area was enclosed fields until the late 18th century when development into mixed residential and commercial premises began. By 1953 much of the site had been re-developed and the only standing building of note is the purpose built tool factory built in 1939, which retains a frontage redolent of that period. The lack of basements in the more recent buildings offers good potential for survival of sub-surface archaeology from earlier domestic and small industrial structures.

Centred at Grid Reference SK 358 874

**From a report by Daniel Lee,
Archaeological Services WYAS**

LAND AT TOWNHEAD STREET, SHEFFIELD

A desk-based assessment was prepared in November 2005 for Princeton Investments, to inform a planning application for residential redevelopment. The area was partly developed as tenements from at least the 17th century and may have been occupied earlier as the site lies on the western limit of the medieval town of Sheffield. By the mid 19th century these tenements had been demolished and replaced by cutlery workshops. These buildings were themselves demolished in the late 20th century. There is potential for below-ground archaeology to survive. Wells are recorded as being discovered during 19th century building works here, which offers tantalising potential for survival of deposits containing medieval artefacts and environmental remains as have been recently discovered elsewhere (see Carmel House, Fargate, on page 141).

Grid Reference SK 351 874

From a report by Rowan May, ARCUS

ANGLO WORKS, 23-33 TRIPPET LANE, SHEFFIELD

A series of archaeological investigations was carried out between February 2005 and May 2006 during redevelopment of the site, for Elmopark Ltd. An initial desk-based assessment identified the site as possibly being developed by the 17th century. By the late 18th century it was occupied by a structure known as Jarvis Brady's new house, and the Brown Cow public house, which stayed in use as a public house until 1909. Redevelopment during the later 18th and 19th centuries saw the construction of what is now the Grade II listed Anglo Cutlery Works on the footprint of Jarvis Brady's house. At the time of the assessment standing buildings included the former Brown Cow, the Anglo Works (latterly occupied by William Trickett & Company, silver and tableware manufacturers) and a 1940s electricity sub-station.

Building recording was carried out before part demolition and conversion. This confirmed that the former Brown Cow building was the oldest part of the complex, containing 18th century elements. Analysis of the Anglo Works showed that several elements of the original house (shown on a plan of 1790) had survived later alteration and additions. Structural instability necessitated removal of the roof of the Anglo Works and planning/recording of the roof trusses was carried out. The trusses were found to be of suspended king post design, originally having no ironwork used in their construction and relying on carpentry joints for structural integrity.

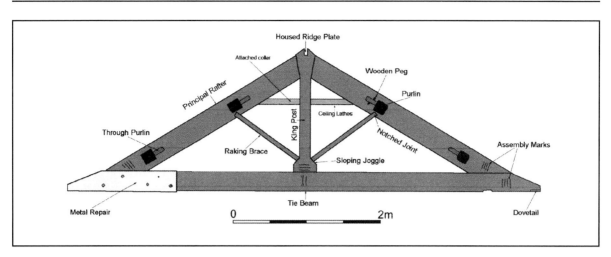

Illustration of a truss from the Anglo Works showing the main features © ARCUS

Trial trenching on land to the rear of the Brown Cow, on what had been the site of their stables, revealed a series of earlier pits and gulleys cut into made ground. Further excavation allowed more of the area to be investigated. The pits produced pottery and clay pipes dating from 1720-1850 AD and it seems reasonable to assume they represent rubbish pits in use from the early 18th century, when this was an area of open ground. Several of the pits contained industrial waste, suggesting small-scale non-ferrous metalworking was taking place nearby. The later pits, which contained basic utilitarian pottery, probably represent disposal of rubbish from the Brown Cow and suggest a degree of poverty in the local area. The made ground, into which these features had been cut, appeared to be backfill of a quarry pit. The late 17th century and early 18th century clay pipes and pottery recovered from these deposits hint at occupation in the vicinity at that date.

Grid Reference SK 351 873

**From reports by Christine Ball,
Stephen Duckworth, Oliver Jessop,
Mark Douglas and Chris Swales, ARCUS**

LAND AT HODGSON STREET, SHEFFIELD

A desk-based assessment was prepared in July 2006, for Citta Developments 2 Ltd, to inform a planning application for redevelopment. The proposal area was developed in the second half of the 19th century, mainly with back-to-back housing, but with a cutlery works situated in the southeast corner. The housing was demolished in the 1960s and much of the site is now occupied by 20th century development.

A three-storey building standing on the corner of Headford Street and Milton Lane may represent part of the original cutlery works and warrants further investigation. There is also potential for survival of sub-surface archaeology relating to the mid 19th century development.

Grid Reference SK 348 866

**From a report by Rowan May,
ARCUS**

LAND AT MILTON LANE, SHEFFIELD

A desk-based assessment was prepared in December 2005 for Axis Architecture, to inform a planning application for residential development. The site was cultivated land until the early 19th century, but had been developed for back-to-back and terraced housing, shops and industrial works by 1879. These structures were demolished during the 1960s and the survival of earlier sub-surface archaeology will be dependent on the extent of groundworks at this time.

Grid Reference SK 348 866

From a report by Mark Stenton, ARCUS

THE MOOR, SHEFFIELD

Following an earlier desk-based assessment (see '*Archaeology in South Yorkshire Number 12*') evaluation trenches were excavated within an open yard off Cumberland Way, in October and December 2006. Remains of a crudely constructed wall and a possible pit were found and considered likely to relate to 19th century terraced housing. Excavation of a further trial trench, in December 2006, took place in advance of the demolition of 156 Eyre Street. This found structures thought to relate to the former Albion Foundry, which is shown on the OS first edition map of 1850-1. A small assemblage of non-ferrous metal artefacts, probably nickel silver, relate to the manufacture of table knife handles. Archived designs suggests

that these date to the early 20th century.

Centred at Grid Reference SK 351 866

From reports by Alistair Webb, Andrew Walsh, and Marina Rose, Archaeological Services WYAS

LAND OFF CARVER STREET, SHEFFIELD

A further desk-based assessment of the NUM building was prepared in November 2005 for Wilson Bowden Developments (see '*Archaeology in South Yorkshire Number 12*' for earlier assessment). The NUM building is built on the yard of the former Sheffield Waterworks Co. This area was pastureland until the 1780s when it was laid out for offices and an underground reservoir for the Waterworks Company, being used later by the Tramways Company and Sheffield Transport Traffic Department. The buildings were retained until the late 1960s but the site is now occupied by the late 1980s NUM building, which has a basement car park and can be considered to have a low archaeological potential.

Grid Reference SK 351 871

From a report by Rowan May, ARCUS

NEW RETAIL QUARTER, SHEFFIELD

Desk-based and archive assessments were prepared for RPS PTE in May 2005

A fireplace with cast iron grate in the east range of Leah's Yard, Cambridge Street
© ARCUS

and July 2006, to inform an outline planning application for redevelopment of the area around Burgess Street and Cambridge Street. The area lies on the edge of the city's historic core and first saw development in the 18th and 19th centuries. The proposal area contains three listed buildings: the mid 19th century piercing and stamping works of Leah's Yard; the mid 19th century former Bethel Sunday School (now the Cutlers Public House, see photograph overleaf); and the late 19th century Salvation Army Citadel. Up to thirty other buildings may be considered of some significance and warrant more detailed appraisal, including the former Trafalgar Works and Kangaroo Works.

No intrusive archaeological investigations have been conducted in this area, so information on below-ground survival is limited, but there is certainly potential for survival of industrial remains as well as for evidence for post-medieval occupation. The archive assessment identified several locations within the proposal area that may have significant buried archaeological potential. Notable amongst these are possible sub-surface remains associated with Staniforth's cutlery factory in the 20th century, remains of a late 19th century furnace house/stamping house and workshops associated with Sorby's Tool Works, and structures associated with various 19th century 'little mesters' workshops.

November 2005 saw a survey of historic fixtures and fittings within the buildings at Leah's Yard, for UK Estates. The works are shown as the Coalpit Lane Horn Works on the 1850s OS map and had been extended and renamed the Cambridge Street Horn Works by the time of the 1890s OS map. The complex is now named after Henry Leah & Sons, silver stampers, who worked here in the 1960s. Features recorded included remains of lineshafting, workbenches and a domestic fireplace. Further recording of these listed buildings took place in December 2005. Annotated floor plans and cross-sections through the buildings and central yard were produced, alongside the completion of a photographic record.

Centred at Grid Reference SK 351 870

From reports by Tegwen Roberts, Mark Stenton, Anna Badcock, Stephen Duckworth, Alex Rose-Deacon and Oliver Jessop, ARCUS

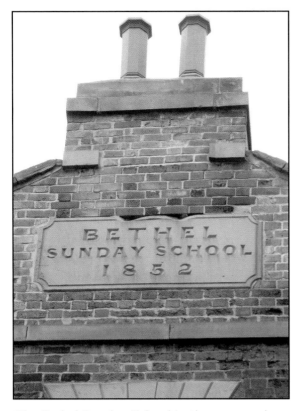

*The Bethel Sunday School in the proposed
retail quarter*   © ARCUS

SHEFFIELD CATHEDRAL, SHEFFIELD

A Conservation Plan was drawn up in April 2005 for the Cathedral Chapter, to determine the heritage significance of the cathedral building in relation to any future management plans. Elements considered of exceptional significance were: fragments of Norman decoration, the remains of the 15th century church in the present east end and the remains of 16th century monuments to the Earls of Shrewsbury.

Excavation in the northwest car park took place between November and December 2004 and was followed up by further excavation between August and September 2006; a watching brief

was maintained on subsequent groundworks for the new community resources centre (see *'Archaeology in South Yorkshire Number 11'* for earlier assessment). A total of 100 graves, containing the remains of 186 articulated individuals, were identified. The churchyard was closed to burials following the 1855 Burial Act. Dating coffin furniture, clay tobacco pipes, pottery and glass recovered from the grave fills gives a date range of between the 18th and mid 19th century for the majority of the graves recorded. Earlier material was recovered, but always as residual material in later deposits. Analysis of skeletal remains and coffin furniture suggests the population represented was predominantly working class with a higher mortality rate amongst young adult females than males.

Just under half of the skeletons recovered showed no observable pathologies. Where pathologies were identified, a high percentage related to spinal joint diseases. Identified pathologies also included at least one example of trepanation and one lobotomy. During the period of use of this cemetery dissection was legalised by the passing of Warburton's Anatomy Act, in 1832. This mostly affected the poor, as the Act allowed surgeons to access the bodies of those who died in the workhouse, prison or hospital and whose bodies were unclaimed.

Grid Reference SK 354 875

From a report by Rochelle Ramey, Field Archaeologist Specialists Ltd (Conservation Plan) and Richard O'Neill, Katherine Baker and Diana Swales, ARCUS (excavation and watching brief)

A photograph of the medieval well being excavated at Carmel House © ARCUS

CARMEL HOUSE, FARGATE AND 2-8A NORFOLK ROW, SHEFFIELD

Following earlier building appraisal and evaluation work (see '*Archaeology in South Yorkshire Number 12*'), further work was carried out between January and September 2005, for the Hermes Property Unit Trust. Building recording and a watching brief during demolition enabled reconstruction of major elements of the original layout of Carmel House and established that number 2 Norfolk Row retained much of its original layout from the 1830s/40s, but that number 4-6 had been extensively remodelled in the 20th century.

Archaeological monitoring of the site strip, following demolition of the standing buildings, revealed one feature of significance in an area of the site not affected by cellaring. This proved to be an unlined well sunk over 2 metres into the sandstone bedrock (it is estimated that the well would originally have been about 0.8m deeper, but it had been truncated). An important assemblage of medieval pottery was recovered from the deposits within the well. Sherds from a Hallgate C3 jug from the base of the well indicate that it was in use by the 11/12th century. Rapid silting in the 15th/16th century was followed by deliberate infilling with soil later in the 15th/16th century; Coal Measures Purple ware was present in all these deposits. Waterlogging of the deposits within the well meant that fragments of leather were also recovered. Two of the leather pieces were clump pieces used to repair shoes, whilst the third may have been from the neck of a leather-covered powder flask. The environmental evidence provided by plant macrofossils, charred plant remains, pollen and insects is consistent with the well being located in a back plot on the very edge of the medieval town, with open country beyond.

Grid Reference SK 354 872

From reports by Stephen Duckworth, Oliver Jessop and Steve Baker, ARCUS

ROYAL MAIL BUILDING, FITZALAN SQUARE, SHEFFIELD

A proposal to convert the former Post Office buildings led to a desk-based assessment and building appraisal in June 2005, on behalf of Assael Architecture. The buildings are Grade II listed. The first phase of the Post Office was purpose built in 1893. At that time it stood next to the Queen's Plate and Cutlery Works. After 1909, when the works were demolished, the Post Office building was expanded to the north and west. A further extension took place in the 1960s, to the south. The buildings are still largely intact and are an important part of Sheffield's heritage. Although it is likely that the various phases of building activity will have removed much buried archaeology, there are still areas where buried remains could survive.

Grid Reference SK 357 873

From a report by Blair Poole, L-P Archaeology

UPPER CHAPEL, NORFOLK STREET, SHEFFIELD

A scheme of archaeological works was carried out for Pro-Active Project Management between February and September 2006, as part of the redevelopment of the adjoining Carmel House. The works comprised recording of human burials in the former Unitarian burial ground that would be affected by the construction of an electricity sub-station and a watching brief on associated groundworks.

The burial ground was active between c.1700 and 1855. Four burials were recovered and the presence of multi-occupancy family graves and possible gold shroud pins may indicate that these related to a relatively high status community. A buried medieval soil was also discovered and this contained a significant assemblage of 13th – 15th century pottery, representing one of the largest assemblages of medieval pottery recovered in Sheffield. The pottery included waster sherds and fragments of kiln furniture implying that pottery production took place nearby.

Grid Reference SK 354 872

From a report by Katherine Baker and Steve Baker, ARCUS

ST PAUL'S PLACE, SHEFFIELD

A desk-based assessment was prepared in May 2005 for CTP St James Ltd, to inform proposed redevelopment of the site. The

Two grave cuts at the Upper Chapel, Norfolk Street   © ARCUS

site was still rural in 1736, but is shown laid out for development on Fairbank's 1771 map and as fully developed by 1797. The first structures built on the site were residential but these were replaced by industrial development towards the end of the 19th century. Small businesses occupied parts of the site but three large buildings dominated it: the Eyre Street Brewery, the Royal Works, and Walker and Hall's Electro Works. During the late 20th century the area was subject to major development associated with the construction of the Town Hall extension and the construction of the Registry Office.

Building recording of the Yorkshire Grey Public House took place in March 2006 prior to its demolition. The building dated from 1937/1938 and occupied the site of an earlier public house. A watching brief during geotechnical test pitting in May 2006 suggested that the site has little potential for below-ground archaeology.

Centred at Grid Reference SK 354 871

From reports by Laura Broughton and Isabel Mason, Scott Wilson Kirkpatrick & Co Ltd

BUTCHERS WHEEL, 72 ARUNDEL STREET, SHEFFIELD

Following an appraisal of previous research (see *'Archaeology in South Yorkshire Number 12'*) detailed recording of this important cutlery

143

Courtyard view of the Butcher Works before renovations © Sheffield City Council

factory was carried out between September 2005 and January 2006, for J F Finnegan. This survey established that several buildings from the early 19th century survive within the complex, one of which contains the sealed cellars and blocked stairwells of a former back-to-back dwelling. By the latter part of the 19th century the Butcher Works had acquired more land on Arundel Street and covered its present footprint.

Expansion included the construction of purpose built four-storey ranges of grinding troughs with workshops on the upper floors. These were built using a brick jack-arch structure. All of the earlier buildings displayed evidence of having been enlarged from two-storeys,

by the addition of upper floors. In this way, the footprint of the works was retained while allowing capacity to increase.

Grid Reference SK 354 868

**From a report by Stephen Duckworth,
ARCUS**

58-60 ARUNDEL STREET AND 118-138 CHARLES STREET, SHEFFIELD

Following an earlier desk-based assessment (see '*Archaeology in South Yorkshire Number 12*') building recording of the former Canada Works, numbers 118 – 138 Charles Street, was carried out in November 2005. This range was the last surviving component of a suite of 19th century workshops, most of which were demolished in the 20th century.

Excavation in January and February 2006 revealed workshops within the former works and the cellars of domestic buildings. Between 1823 and c.1890 the Canada Works was occupied by saw and knife manufacturers, it was then taken over by a file manufacturer. The layout of the site is typical of many in Sheffield with domestic terraced housing backing onto a courtyard and works buildings.

Grid Reference SK 355 868

**From reports by Stephen Duckworth,
Alex Rose-Deacon and Duncan Alexander,
ARCUS**

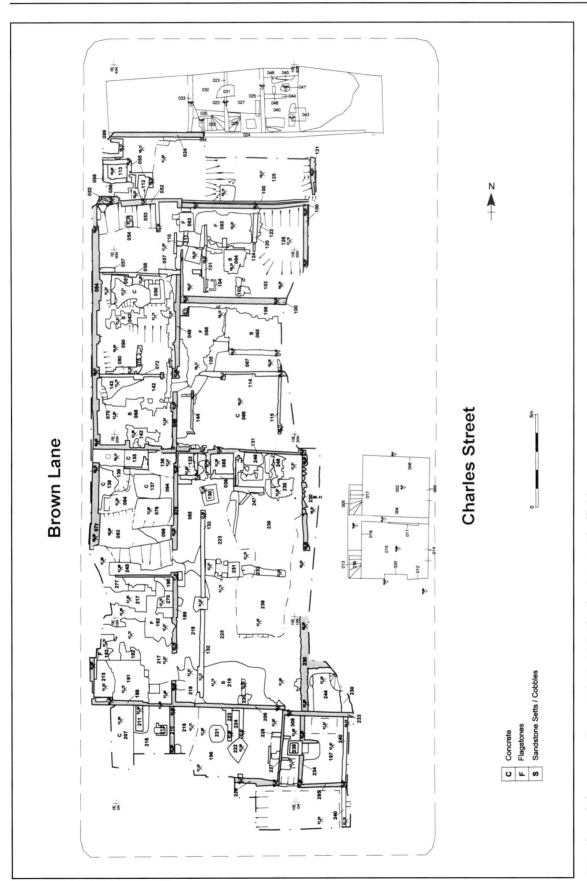

Site plan of the excavations at 118-138 Charles Street, Sheffield   © ARCUS

145

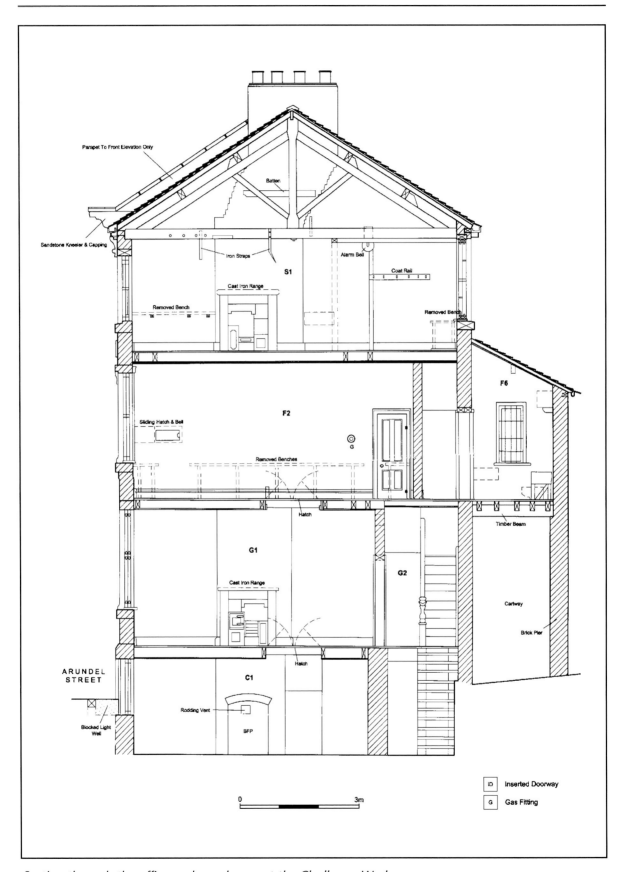

Section through the office and warehouse at the Challenge Works   © ARCUS

CHALLENGE WORKS, 94 ARUNDEL STREET AND 47 EYRE LANE, SHEFFIELD

Further recording of these late 19th century metal trades buildings took place in February 2006 (see '*Archaeology in South Yorkshire Number 12*' for an earlier appraisal). The buildings were used as offices, workshops and warehousing. Details recorded included the remaining items of machinery in the workshops, which included two 19th century drop hammers and several rotary stamps. A watching brief during the site strip for a new rear range revealed a possible single-hole crucible furnace. This was covered and left *in situ*.

Grid Reference SK 354 867

From a report by Stephen Duckworth, ARCUS

FORMER PEARL WORKS, 17-21 EYRE LANE, SHEFFIELD

A desk-based assessment was prepared in December 2006 for Bolsterstone plc to inform a planning application to redevelop this site. The majority of this area, which had formed part of Sheffield deer park, remained as undeveloped pasture into the post-medieval period. Housing was built in the late 18th or early 19th century but by 1890 this had been absorbed into the Arundel Works cutlery factory. By 1923 these buildings had been replaced by the current Pearl Works cutlery factory. These standing buildings were found to be in poor condition and of little archaeological significance.

Grid Reference SK 353 867

From a report by Mark Stenton, ARCUS

44 EYRE LANE AND 161-163 ARUNDEL GATE, SHEFFIELD

A desk-based assessment and building appraisal was carried out in March and April 2005 for Sheffield City Council in advance of proposed demolition and development. The site was open land until the early 19th century, when back-to-back housing and shops were built. Over time these buildings were replaced by larger industrial buildings. The extant buildings are predominantly of mid-20th century date, but one building was found to contain late 19th century wrought-iron columns. This may be a remnant of a larger courtyard building, shown on historic maps, that was probably built by W & S Butcher as an addition to their main complex, on the other side of Eyre Lane. However, it is possible that these earlier columns have been re-used in a later building. A watching brief was maintained during demolition in November and December 2005 and additional details recorded. Limited evidence for survival of cellars from the back-to-back housing was also noted.

Grid Reference SK 354 869

From reports by Mark Fletcher, Matrix Archaeology

ARUNDEL GATE AND FURNIVAL STREET, SHEFFIELD

A series of archaeological works was carried out between January and June 2006 for Turner and Townsend Project Management Ltd, in response to proposals for redevelopment. A desk-based assessment identified that the area was first developed in the 19th century. Works buildings were present by 1828 and back-to-back housing by 1854. By the 1870s the works incorporated a brass and silver foundry, cutlers works, chandelier manufactory and packing case manufactory. The housing was demolished in the late 1930s, the other 19th century buildings in the 1970s and the site was subsequently built over.

Evaluation trenches found two domestic cellars and the subsurface remains of a small workshop. The trench along the Arundel Street frontage revealed a small crucible furnace with three melting holes. Their linings had traces of copper and iron slag adhering to the sides and bases. When it went out of use, the furnace had been backfilled with material that included bundles of copper wire. The furnace may have related to the brass and silver founder, or the wire gauge manufacturer, who are recorded as working at this site from the 1870s.

Grid Reference SK 355 868

**From reports by Rowan May
and Helen Holderness,
ARCUS**

FURNIVAL SQUARE, SHEFFIELD

A desk-based assessment was prepared in June 2006 for McAleer & Rushe Ltd, as part of a proposal to redevelop the site. The site was pasture land until the late 18th century and by the mid 19th century was occupied by the Trinity Cutlery Works and Wallace Steel Works. These were demolished in 1968 to make way for the Furnival Square roundabout. The site was later occupied by a store and associated car parking. Some potential for sub-surface archaeology was identified and further investigation is likely.

Grid Reference SK 353 867

**From a report by James Brightman
and Jessika Shakarian,
Archaeological Research Services Ltd**

LAND AT FURNIVAL STREET AND SIDNEY STREET, SHEFFIELD

Proposals for redevelopment led to a scheme of archaeological works between June 2005 and July 2006 for Jefferson Sheared Architects. A desk-based assessment identified the proposal area as being first developed in the early/mid 19th century. A Sunday School associated with the Howard Street Chapel occupied the Furnival Street frontage from 1850. In the late 19th century, the southwest of the site was developed for workshops used by cutlery manufacturers. The whole site was subject to redevelopment in the mid/late 20th century. Evaluation revealed the cellar of the Sunday School and sub-surface remains associated with the 19th century workshops.

Grid Reference SK 355 868

From reports by Rowan May and
Helen Holderness, ARCUS

LAND OFF EYRE STREET, SHEFFIELD

A proposal to relocate the fire station as part of the New Retail Quarter development (see page 138 of this volume) led to a scheme of archaeological works being carried out between January 2006 and January 2007 on behalf of Hammerson UK Properties plc. An initial desk-based assessment showed that the site was part of a field until the early 19th century when it was laid out as part of the Alsop Fields development, comprising back-to-back housing, small retail premises, and small workshops. These were demolished in the 1930s and the site was vacant until 1946 when a factory and offices were built. These were in turn demolished late in the 20th century and the site was then used for car parking.

A watching brief during geotechnical test-pitting revealed the foundations of stone and brick built walls and probable floors, thought likely to be associated with cellars from the 19th century structures. Subsequent excavation of three evaluation trenches confirmed that courtyards and associated buildings, corresponding to the known

locations of 19th century buildings, survived on parts of the site.

Grid Reference SK 352 865

From reports by Rowan May, Michael
Klemperer and Steve Baker, ARCUS

SHEAF VALLEY DEVELOPMENT, SHEFFIELD

Initial phases of work in advance of the redevelopment of the area around the train and bus stations were reported in '*Archaeology in South Yorkshire Number 12*'. Further archaeological works comprising a watching brief during geotechnical trenching and excavation of trial trenches were carried out on land adjoining the bus station between February 2005 and November 2006. The geotechnical trenching exposed the in-filled Bamford goit that had served forges and mills to the north of the site in the late 18th/early 19th century. The subsequent evaluation trenches revealed remains of mid 19th century back-to-back houses, represented by stone and brick foundations. Extensive remains of the mid to late 19th century cutlery works were found, comprising two wings of a building, a cellar, cobbled floor and a machine base. The early 19th century Sheaf Island Grinding Wheel had been much altered in the 20th century and no remains of internal activities were revealed. Limited remains of the former Sheaf Saw Mill were found, probably dating from the late 19th century. Remains from the mid to late 19th century Central Hammer Works comprised external and internal walls and a drop hammer base. In one area the 19th century developments had been built over layers of made ground that sealed an 18th century wall, a cobbled surface and a possible pond. Further investigation is clearly warranted.

A watching brief during groundworks in the car park area fronting the train station found more evidence for features recorded in the earlier excavation. A section of the brick-built culvert was removed revealing further features relating to the New Pond Tilt. These included the sidewall of the wheel pit and several earlier brick culverts. These features were left *in situ* following recording. Part of the former access road to the station was also noted.

Centred at Grid Reference SK 358 872

From reports by Louise Martin and Daniel Lee, Archaeological Services WYAS

SHEAF STREET, SHEFFIELD

A desk-based assessment was prepared in November 2006 for CTP St. James Ltd, ahead of proposed redevelopment. The earliest evidence for activity in the area is post-medieval, when water from the River Sheaf was diverted into a series of goits and reservoirs to power tilt hammers and mills; the site lies adjacent to the site of the Old Pond Tilt. By the late 18th century, this area was a mix of residential, commercial and industrial buildings. These uses continued through the 19th century, but the 20th century saw demolition of all earlier buildings. The site is now occupied by Sheffield Hallam University's Nelson Mandela student union building and the

landscaped area of Sheaf Square. Test boreholes were sunk in January 2007 and found evidence of significant recent disturbance and deep areas of made ground.

Grid Reference SK 357 869

From a report by Laura Broughton, Scott Wilson Ltd

LAND OFF SYLVESTER STREET, SHEFFIELD

A desk-based assessment prepared in September 2005 was followed by evaluation and limited excavation between February and July 2006 for Roy Peters Estates, in advance of residential redevelopment. This was the site of a water-powered cutler's grinding wheel, the Sylvester Wheel, recorded from 1650. In the early 18th century the works were small, and only 4 grinding troughs are documented, but by 1794 they had been extended to contain 20 troughs. A change of ownership early in the 19th century saw further enlargement of the works and culverting of the goit, with demolition of the original wheel building after 1864, by when cutlery production was steam-powered. A small iron foundry was built at this time, and workshops were added during the late 19th/early 20th century. Most of the 19th century works buildings had been demolished by 1989.

An initial evaluation trench was extended to allow detailed recording of features that would be affected by the new development. This work revealed evidence for the dam, bypass goit, and flywheel pit from the Sylvester Wheel.

Archaeologists working on the site of the Sylvester Wheel, the grinding workshop can be seen in the foreground with the flywheel pit and the southern external wall of the Sylvester Wheel behind © ARCUS

The earliest structures recorded were dated to the mid or late 18th century. Significant structural remodelling associated with the conversion to steam power between 1830 and 1850 were identified. Despite this re-ordering of the power source and transmission system the internal organisation of the Sylvester Wheel appears to have remained fairly constant. Internal structures recorded included a grinding workshop (4 grinding troughs were identified) and a boiler or forge associated with bone handle manufacture. Artefacts recovered from the site included bone material relating to the manufacture of cutlery handles, knife blades and grindstones. These suggest that blades for table knives formed the primary output of the Sylvester Wheel. A quantity of clay pipe fragments and pottery was also recovered. Amongst the latter were some white glazed balls that are likely to have been used in the popular 19th century game of 'Knurr and Spell'.

Grid Reference SK 352 864

**From reports by Rowan May and
Steve Baker, ARCUS**

RENOWN WORKS, SYLVESTER STREET, SHEFFIELD

A desk-based assessment was prepared in July 2006 for AQH Micklegate Developments Ltd, to inform a planning application for redevelopment. The site remained open until the early 19th century when a grid of new streets was laid out for the Duke of Norfolk, part of the Alsop Fields development. By 1832 the proposal area was fully occupied by back-to-back houses and courtyards, small workshops, shops and a tavern. Initial clearance of the site had occurred by the 1880s, continued in the 1920s, and was completed c1939. The site remained an empty plot until the mid 1950s when modern light industrial premises were built, including the Renown machine knife works. There is potential for sub-surface remains where modern building foundations have not been intrusive.

Grid Reference SK 353 865

From a report by Stephen Duckworth, ARCUS

LAND OFF SYLVESTER GARDENS, SHEFFIELD

A desk-based assessment and building appraisal was carried out in March 2006 for John Seifert Architects Ltd, to inform a planning application for redevelopment. In the early 19th century, the site contained Ward's Wheel, a grinding wheel. By the late 19th century, this had been replaced by the Porter Island Works, also a grinding wheel. The industrial use of the site continued to expand, replacing earlier residential courts. The majority of the site is now occupied by 20th century buildings. However, one earlier building survives – the western part of the Porter Island Works. This building is a complete and discrete former workshop with little internal alteration; it has probably escaped previous attention because it is hidden from the street behind more modern structures.

Grid Reference SK 353 864

From a report by Richard Sheppard, Trent and Peak Archaeological Unit

MATILDA TAVERN, 100-102 MATILDA STREET, SHEFFIELD

A desk-based assessment and building appraisal were carried out in August 2006 for Wireframe Studios Ltd, ahead of proposed redevelopment. The tavern was built between 1839 and 1841 as a coaching stop, with a stable yard to the rear accessed via a cart passage. The adjoining property, number 102 Matilda Street, originally comprised two back-to-back houses. Although the buildings have seen later extension and alteration, they have the potential to contain features relating to their original uses.

Grid Reference SK 354 865

From a report by Rowan May and Oliver Jessop, ARCUS

FORMER MARY STREET STEEL WORKS, SHEFFIELD

A desk-based assessment and building appraisal was carried out for Franklin Ellis Architects, in February 2006, as part of proposals to refurbish and redevelop the site. The standing buildings were part of Mary Street Steel Works, which was a crucible steel works built in the 1870s that continued in use as a steel works until the 1970s. Surviving structures from the steel works include the former melting shop (with evidence for 20 melting holes) and an original office and warehouse range, although both have been altered and adapted to some degree.

Grid Reference SK 353 864

From a report by Richard Sheppard, Trent and Peak Archaeological Unit

LAND AT MARY STREET, SHEFFIELD

A desk-based assessment was prepared in November 2005 for Escafeld Design to inform a planning application for redevelopment. A goit carrying water from the Porter Brook to the dam of Cinderhill Wheel, which was first recorded in 1588, is known to have crossed the site. The goit was an open channel until at least 1850 and may have been infilled when Cinderhill Wheel was demolished in 1866. The mid/late 19th century saw development of much of the site including the construction of the Cyprus Works file manufactory and the Hammer Works tool factory. Further development in the 20th century saw part of the site occupied by the Guion Works, late the Union Works machine knife manufactory.

Despite re-modelling, standing buildings at the time of the assessment retained some 19th century features. Survival of below-ground remains relating to the goit and 19th century

works will depend on the degree of intrusion of later construction activities.

Grid Reference SK 354 866

From a report by Mark Stenton and Mark Douglas, ARCUS

LAND OFF SHOREHAM STREET, SHEFFIELD

Six evaluation trenches were excavated in June 2005 for S Harrison Construction Ltd, ahead of construction of apartments. Structural features were found in all trenches, predominantly relating to 19th century domestic and retail buildings. A small pottery assemblage comprised both domestic and industrial wares, the latter including sherds from Brown Glazed Coarsewares. This vessel type has been previously recorded only from excavations at the nearby Leadmill in Sheffield and, as a result, is thought to have had a role in the manufacture of red and white lead. The vessels were recovered from a dump of material and do not relate to industrial activity on this site.

Grid Reference SK 355 865

From a report by Owen Raybould, ARCUS

GIBSON PEWTER WORKS, ST MARY'S ROAD, SHEFFIELD

Following earlier archaeological assessment (see '*Archaeology in South Yorkshire Number 12*') a watching brief was commissioned in December 2006, to allow recording during alterations to these 19th century metals trades buildings and on the excavation of service trenches. These works confirmed evidence for internal re-arrangement during the 20th century, but were unable to identify the former cart passage, which had been identified by map regression.

Grid Reference SK 348 876

From a report by Stephen Duckworth, ARCUS

ST MARY'S GATE, SHEFFIELD

Following on from investigation of Phase 1 of this site (see *'Archaeology in South Yorkshire Number 12'*) evaluation of Phase 2 was undertaken in November 2006, for Tiger Developments Ltd. The trial trenches revealed extensive groundworks associated with an aborted 20th century development that had not been picked up by the earlier assessment.

Limited foundations of an earlier building are thought likely to be remains of the Bridgefield Works, but their relatively insubstantial nature meant that it was not possible to determine their function. A single sherd of creamware from an adjoining pit dates this earlier phase to mid 18th - mid 19th century.

Grid Reference SK 348 864

From a report by Marina Rose, Archaeological Services WYAS

LAND OFF BLONK STREET, SHEFFIELD

Following an earlier desk-based assessment (see *'Archaeology in South Yorkshire Number 12'*) a series of investigations took place across this site. Three evaluation trenches were excavated in June 2005 on land adjoining the Wicker. All of these exposed walls from buildings shown on the 1896 Goad Fire Insurance Plan, but two of the trenches also contained earlier structures, possibly shown on Fairbank's 1782 plan of the Wicker. Foundations from the Clyde Steel Works, which was in operation from the late 19th century to the 1980s, were also identified. Excavation of two areas followed, in March to April 2006, for Bowmer & Kirkland Ltd. The first re-examined the area of possible 18th century structures adjoining the Wicker, but these were found to have been heavily disturbed by later activity – including the culverting of the Blonk or Wicker goit in the 19th century. The second area examined found extensive remains of the Clyde Steel Works, incorporating parts of the earlier Castle Mills. Features identified included the base for a machine - possibly an engine - the base of a boiler (probably a Lancashire boiler), chimney and flues, and a large 20th century concrete cellar.

In July 2006, following an updated desk-based assessment, two further evaluation trenches were excavated on land adjacent to the River Don. This area also formed part of the Clyde Steel Works and the trenches were sited to test the locations of cementation furnaces and a forge house, and

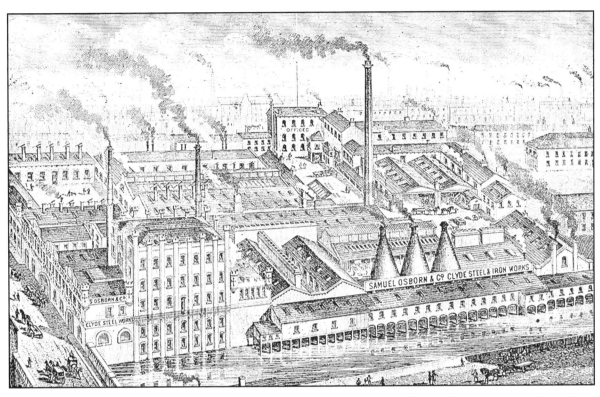

Publicity engraving of the Clyde Steel Works, c1870, viewed from the south bank of the River Don

furnace, shown on the 1896 Goad plan. Both trenches revealed remains of interest associated with steel production and processing. More detailed excavation, therefore, followed in September to October 2006. The work was carried out for Artisan Construction. Two crucible furnaces recorded on the 1896 plan were noted but three vaulted coal cellars were all that remained of the associated cementation furnaces. The well-preserved remains of a later thirteen-hole crucible furnace, built over the earlier cementation furnaces, were also revealed. A series of hearths, flues and chimneys were thought likely to relate to experimental developments in steel production in the mid to late 19th century, relating to a gas converter and later Siemens Regenerative furnace. Significant archaeometallurgical finds recovered included a possible bar of

Swedish iron and an early railway wagon wheel dating from c1810-1840.

Centred at Grid Reference SK 358 878

From reports by Owen Raybould, G Davies, M McCoy, Mark Stenton, Rowan May and Neil Dransfield, ARCUS

SMITHFIELD CAR PARK, SHEFFIELD

A desk-based assessment was prepared and evaluation trenches excavated on behalf of Holiday Inn Royal Victoria. The proposal area was undeveloped until the 18th century when a cutler's grinding wheel was built on the northwest part of the site in 1731. This was known as the Simon Wheel, after its first tenant, Peter

Plan of trench 1 at Smithfield Car Park. Wall 1035 represents the early part of the Simon Wheel
© ARCUS

Simon, or as Castle Orchard's Wheel. By 1787 a new wheel with a larger reservoir had been constructed further to the north, and the original wheel converted to tenement housing. This survived until the mid 19th century when the site was cleared. It was then used as the Smithfield Cattle Market. By the mid 20th century the site was being used as a steel stockyard and since then as a car park. Evaluation trenches exposed the remains of Simon Wheel in the form of sandstone foundations at some depth, associated with remains of a water management system and a contemporary road. These had been sealed by clay and rubble that had provided a stable surface for the 19th century cattle market.

Centred at Grid Reference SK 359 878

From reports by Rowan May and Richard Jackson, ARCUS

LAND AT SHEAF QUAY, SHEFFIELD

A proposal for redevelopment led to the preparation of a desk-based assessment in January 2006, on behalf of Ant Marketing. The proposal area was part of the Little Park, a subdivision of Sheffield's medieval Great Park, created by the Lords of the Manor for deer hunting. Following 18th century 'disparkment' the area became fields until it was developed in the early 19th century. The 1890 Ordnance Survey map shows the buildings here as 'Canal Stores'. An 1893 directory lists the site as the stores of the Manchester, Sheffield and Lincolnshire Railway Company, who had purchased the canal basin in 1848. The site was broken up into different uses in the early 20th century, including an upholstery works and a confectionary company. Redevelopment of the site in the late 20th century removed all earlier buildings and removed the 19th century road layout. Extensive landscaping at this time is likely to have severely impacted on any below-ground archaeology.

Grid Reference SK 361 878

From a report by Mark Stenton, ARCUS

LAND OFF SAVILE STREET, SHEFFIELD

A desk-based assessment was prepared for Pinnacle Consulting Engineers Ltd in February 2007, to inform a planning application for redevelopment. The earliest known building within the proposal area was Hall Carr House, which is identifiable on maps from 1736. By 1894 it had been replaced by two small cottages that were in turn replaced by a goods warehouse for Wicker Station in the early 20th century. Part of the Wicker Station itself covered some of the site from 1838 until its demolition in 1978. Car showrooms presently cover the site. Below-ground survival of earlier remains will be dependent on the extent of intrusive groundwork associated with demolition and subsequent construction.

Centred at Grid Reference SK 361 882

From a report by Helen MacQuarrie, AOC Archaeology Group

SAVILLE HOUSE, SAVILE STREET, SHEFFIELD

Following an earlier desk-based assessment (see '*Archaeology in South Yorkshire Number 12*') four evaluation trenches were excavated in February and March 2007, on behalf of Nathan Incorporated. These revealed extensive and well-preserved industrial remains, including a mid 19th century cementation furnace with surviving barrel vaulted coal chamber, as well as machine housings and brick flues. The results indicate that further investigation will be required.

Centred at Grid Reference SK 361 881

From a report by Ben Reeves, York Archaeological Trust

The early travelling crane from Park Iron Works, to a design of 1892   © ARCUS

PARK IRON WORKS, ATTERCLIFFE, SHEFFIELD

A desk-based assessment and building appraisal was carried out in May 2006, with follow-up recording in January 2007, for Prospect Estates Ltd, to inform a planning application for redevelopment as offices and industrial units. The site represents the western half of the former Park Iron Works and contains large workshops built between c1885 and 1915 for the engineering firm Davy Brothers. By 1890, Davy's are recorded as engineers, boiler and steam hammer makers, and as sheet and rod steel rollers; by the end of the 19th century they had added hydraulic presses to their range of products. Overhead cranes, nine of which still survive, dating between 1892 and 1953, facilitated movement of heavy items in the workshops. The firm moved to new premises in Darnall in the 1950s and the site has more recently been occupied by the Tempered Spring Co. Ltd, who made only limited alterations to the buildings.

The first development in this area was Smith's or Georgia Wheel, a grinding wheel built c.1753 with a narrow adjoining dam. In 1782 William Booth & Co. leased the wheel and constructed one of the earliest blast furnaces in Sheffield (along with a much larger dam, now under Foley Street). An 1810 survey by Fairbank shows a smaller secondary wheel on land to the north west of the

1883 Kelly's Directory; Davy Brothers' advert illustrating steam hammer

main wheel, which would have been used to power ancillary machinery. Survival of this secondary wheel and associated buildings will depend on the degree of intrusion by later construction (the earlier wheel site lies outside the present development plot).

Centred at Grid Reference SK 367 881

From reports by Stephen Duckworth, ARCUS

DARNALL WORKS, SHEFFIELD

Following an earlier desk-based assessment (see *'Archaeology in South Yorkshire Number 11'*) an evaluation trench was excavated in October 2005, focusing on the probable location of the 18th century glass cone identified. Redevelopment proposals included construction of a new access route here. The evaluation showed that a complex series of demolition and rebuild activities had occurred since the late 18th century. Two structures did display evidence of damage from high temperatures and were thought to be remains associated with the glass furnace.

Grid Reference SK 384 885

From a report by Sean Bell, ARCUS

LAND OFF DARNALL ROAD AND ELEANOR STREET, ATTERCLIFFE, SHEFFIELD

A desk-based assessment was prepared in April 2006 on behalf of Haslam Homes Yorkshire, ahead of proposed residential redevelopment. The Attercliffe New Pottery, which manufactured earthenware pottery, occupied part of the site from around 1823 until the late 19th century. By

Ongoing evaluation at Darnall Works © SYAS

1903 the pottery buildings had been demolished and a brick works had been built in the central part of the site, with associated clay pits to the north. The brick works were converted to a cement works in the 1960s. Terraced housing had been built on the southwest edge of the site by 1895 but this was cleared in the late 20th century.

Centred at Grid Reference SK 386 886

From a report by Rowan May,
ARCUS

GRIMESTHORPE ROAD, BURNGREAVE, SHEFFIELD

Works to retain a bank running alongside Grimesthorpe Road were the subject of a watching brief in March 2007 for Sheffield City Council. The road follows the course of the 'Roman Ridge', an enigmatic ditch and bank feature that runs between Sheffield and Mexborough. The earthwork was documented in 1854 as running along the north side of Grimesthorpe Road and Leslie Butcher recorded a section through it during road widening works in the 1940s. However, no evidence of the earthwork was observed during the watching brief. It was noted that the bank was made up of a sandstone scarp, implying that in this area the 'Roman Ridge' incorporated this natural feature.

Grid Reference SK 363 884

From a report by Jessika Shakarian,
Archaeological Research Services Ltd

JENKIN ROAD, WINCOBANK, SHEFFIELD

Additional building works led to excavation of a further evaluation trench in June 2006 (see '*Archaeology in South Yorkshire 1995 – 1996*' and '*Number 11*' for earlier work). The site lies on the postulated route of the Roman Ridge, but no archaeological deposits were found.

Grid Reference SK 383 912

From a report by Sean Bell, ARCUS

STAYBRITE WORKS, WEEDON STREET, SHEFFIELD

Proposals to construct a car showroom led to a desk-based assessment in July 2005 on behalf of Barlow and Associates. The proposal area was in agricultural use until the late 19th century and a farmhouse is shown in the southwest corner of the plot on a map of 1795. A brick & tile works was present by the early 20th century but this, and the earlier farmhouse, was demolished prior to the construction of the Tinsley Works of Thomas Firth & Co. Ltd, between 1906 and 1917. These works originally consisted of crucible furnaces and rolling mills and by the 1930s were being used exclusively for production of stainless steel under the name of the Staybrite Works.

Partial demolition took place in the 1980s but some historic buildings remain and there is also potential for survival of sub-surface remains, which will require further investigation.

Grid Reference SK 392 904

From a report by Rowan May, ARCUS

LAND AT SHEFFIELD ROAD, TINSLEY, SHEFFIELD

A desk-based assessment was prepared in May 2006 for Ordic Investments, to inform a planning application for construction of commercial buildings. The earliest structures on the site appear to have been a row of cottages adjacent to the Sheffield and Tinsley canal, identified on the OS map of 1892 as Wharf Row. These were demolished sometime before 1934. The remainder of the site was developed early in the 20th century and by 1923 comprised the Standard Steel Works, the British Abrasive Wheel Works, the Simplex Motor Works and a complex of terraced housing. Industrial use of the site expanded during the 20th century, but by 1991 the site had been cleared. The site is considered to have a low potential for below-ground archaeology.

Centred at Grid Reference SK 400 913

From a report by Duncan Hawkins, CgMs Consulting

LAND OFF CITY ROAD, SHEFFIELD

A desk-based assessment was prepared in September 2006 on behalf of Coda Studios, to inform a planning application for redevelopment. The site lies within the former Sheffield Park, in an area known to have been worked for coal from at least the 18th century. However, archive evidence suggests that the nearest area of coal mining lay further to the west, at Heeley Side. This site was part of a field until the late 19th century when a belt of woodland was planted. It remained woodland until sometime after 1935, when workshops for a monumental stonemason were constructed (the site lies opposite City Road cemetery).

Grid Reference SK 372 859

From a report by Margaret Bennett-Samuels, John Samuels Archaeological Consultants

MANOR OAKS, MANOR LANE, SHEFFIELD

A proposal to restore Manor Oaks farmhouse, as part of the wider restoration of Manor Lodge and its surrounding open space, led to building recording and a watching brief during conversion and demolition works between January and December 2005, on behalf of Green Estates Ltd. The recording exercise identified four main phases of construction within the farmhouse, between the 17th and the 19th centuries (see phase plan on page 187 of the colour section). The earliest element is the stone-built section of the farmhouse, the structure of which implies it was originally a large agricultural building, possibly dating to the late 17th century. At some point in the 18th century this building was

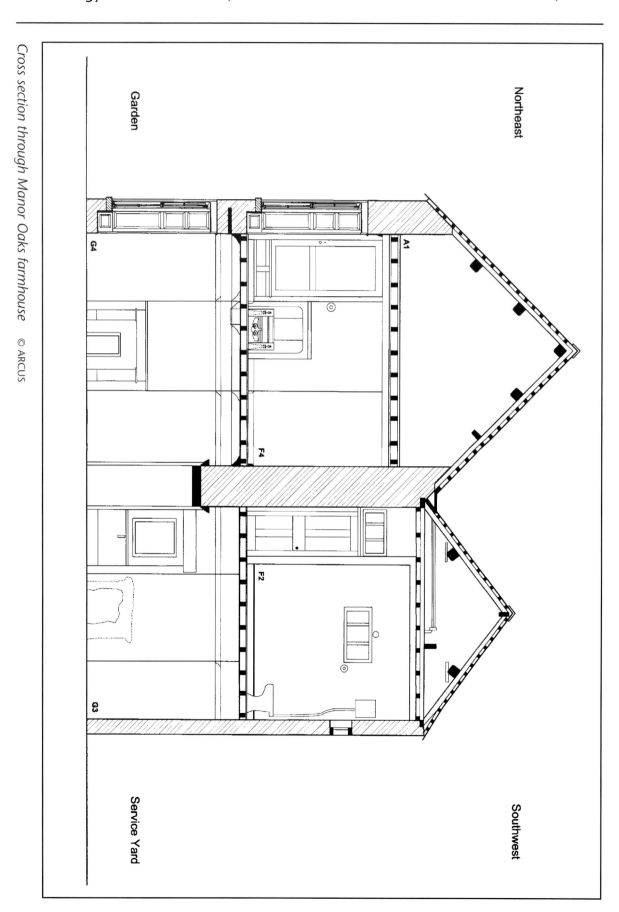

Cross section through Manor Oaks farmhouse   © ARCUS

A view of Manor Oaks farmhouse © ARCUS

converted into a dwelling, with an extension to the northwest, refacing of the northeast elevation and the insertion of larger windows. At the same point, construction of additional outbuildings, a ha-ha and garden enclosures created a large self-contained complex designed to impress. Later developments in the mid 19th century considerably expanded the main house and probably relate to the property's purchase by William Bradley, owner of the Soho Brewery, Sheffield.

Grid Reference SK 376 868

From reports by Oliver Jessop and Mark Douglas, ARCUS

ASH HOUSE FARM, MYRTLE ROAD, SHEFFIELD

Further archaeological works were carried out here between July and November 2005, in advance of proposed housing development (see '*Archaeology in South Yorkshire Number 12*' for earlier assessment and building recording). A geophysical survey (magnetometer) produced evidence only for ferrous debris in the soil. Excavation of trial trenches similarly found evidence only of modern activity. The subsequent excavation, therefore, focused on the farmhouse site itself. This identified features from three phases of activity.

The earliest phase consisted of a cellar from a late 17th century farmhouse and remains of the barns that had been archaeologically recorded prior to demolition. The second phase of activity related to the rebuild of the farmhouse in the 18th century, which building had been recorded prior to demolition; a few low sections of farmhouse wall were identified, along with yard walls, sandstone paving, a culvert and two gullies. The final phase related to activity in the 19th century and later, and consisted of features in the garden and yard, comprising a cold store, waterhole and spread of domestic waste (although the waterhole and cold store may have had earlier origins - no known water supply to the original farmhouse being known). Artefacts recovered included pottery consisting of two different components: a group of 18th century utilitarian tablewares, and a group of 19th century tablewares and utilitarian wares. Other finds include a variety of ferrous objects such as parts of buckets or tubs, parts of spades or shovels, and several pieces of table cutlery.

Grid Reference SK 361 849

From a report by Daniel Lee, Archaeological Services WYAS

Stone-built cold store, with later 19th century water tank at Ash House Farm   © AS - WYAS

NEWFIELD RAVINE AND NEWFIELD SCHOOL, SHEFFIELD

Proposals to rebuild Newfield School led to a walkover survey within the adjoining ravine in December 2005, on behalf of Sheffield CC; the ravine could be affected by an amended access route. Several potential archaeological features were identified, including a possible Q-pit, for making white coal (dried timber used in the lead industry). Geotechnical test-pitting on the school site itself showed that extensive terracing has taken place and that little of the original ground level survives, reducing the potential archaeological impact of the scheme.

Centred at Grid Reference SK 360 834

From a report by Dr Ben Chan, ARCUS

MEADOWHEAD SCHOOL, SHEFFIELD

A desk-based assessment was prepared for SDA Partnership in June 2006, to inform a planning application for redevelopment. The site was part of the common land of Greenhill Moor in 1724 but was in agricultural use by 1842. The first development here was in 1916, when German Prisoners of War were used to build a repair depot associated with the Royal Flying Corp Landing Ground at nearby Coal Aston. The site was sold in 1922 and later use included engineering works and a bakery until construction of the present school in the 1960s and 1970s. The standing buildings were considered of little archaeological significance, but some potential for below-ground remains relating to earlier uses was identified. A watching brief during test-pitting and subsequent groundworks, for Aedas Architects Ltd, found no evidence for archaeologically significant features or finds.

Centred at Grid Reference SK 354 812

From reports by Mark Stenton, Oliver Jessop and Chris Swales, ARCUS

LAND AT VINE GROVE FARM, MOSBOROUGH, SHEFFIELD

An application for redevelopment led to the preparation of a desk-based assessment in October 2005, for Barclays Bank Trust Company Ltd. The site was undeveloped until the early 20th century when a pair of kilns were built, associated with the Mosborough Brick and Tile Works, which started business between 1875 and 1887. No standing features relating to the works are evident on this part of the site.

Grid Reference SK 427 812

From a report by Rowan May, ARCUS

Photograph of the kilns with bricked in arches, Vine Grove Farm, Mosborough. © ARCUS

WOODHOUSE JUNCTION, BEIGHTON, SHEFFIELD

A desk-based assessment was prepared for Network Rail, as part of an application to regenerate existing railway sidings as a fleet maintenance facility. Sites within, or close to, the proposal area include Ryknild Street Roman road, evidence for medieval ridge and furrow cultivation, and the possible location of the medieval Beighton Castle. However, as the proposed works would affect an existing railway track bed, the archaeological impact was considered low.

Centred at Grid Reference SK 439 846

From a report by Jacobs Babtie

ST DOMINIC'S CRAG, SPROTBROUGH, DONCASTER

A proposal to build four houses within the grounds of the former Sprotbrough Hall led to a series of archaeological works between August 2005 and May 2006, on behalf of ADS. The desk-based assessment highlighted the discovery of 10th/11th century pottery in a ditch immediately north of the site and the proximity of the site to the church of St Mary, which may have had an Anglo-Saxon precursor. The icehouse associated with Sprotbrough Hall stood within the proposal area; its remains are incorporated into the present house on the site. The remains were surveyed in March 2006, prior to the demolition of the house; it is intended that the icehouse will be preserved within the new scheme.

Geophysical surveys (magnetometer and resistivity) carried out in December 2005 found a circular high resistance feature that was considered worthy of further investigation. A subsequent evaluation trench found no archaeological features or finds of interest.

Grid Reference SE 540 018

**From reports by Jill Stephenson
and Colin Merrony,
Hallam Environmental Consultants Ltd**

101 PARK DRIVE, SPROTBROUGH, DONCASTER

Proposals for construction of a residential dwelling to the rear of this property led to the excavation of a single evaluation trench in May/June 2006 for Greg Braithwaite Associates. The property lies between the parish church and the former stable block of Sprotbrough Hall. A single feature was discovered. This had been cut into the limestone bedrock, clay lined, and filled with dump deposits containing sherds

of 18th or early 19th century formal tableware. It is suggested that the feature represents part of a pond associated with Sprotbrough Hall. Its absence from early Ordnance Survey maps implies that it was backfilled before the mid 19th century.

Grid Reference SE 540 020

**From a report by Colin Merrony,
Hallam Environmental Consultants Ltd**

PARK DRIVE, SPROTBROUGH, DONCASTER

Proposals for residential development by Barratt Homes Ltd led to a desk-based assessment and field evaluation in January and April 2006. The proposal area is a remnant of the former Sprotbrough Park, associated with Sprotbrough Hall. However, no archaeological features or finds were recovered during excavation of seven evaluation trenches. The evidence suggests that this area was woodland throughout most of its recent history.

Grid Reference SE 547 021

From reports by Ian Mellor, Field Archaeology Specialists Ltd (desk-based) and William Munford, Pre-Construct Archaeology (evaluation)

WENTWORTH CASTLE AND STAINBOROUGH PARK, STAINBOROUGH, BARNSLEY

Stainborough Castle is an 18th century garden folly within the Wentworth Castle estate. A topographical survey

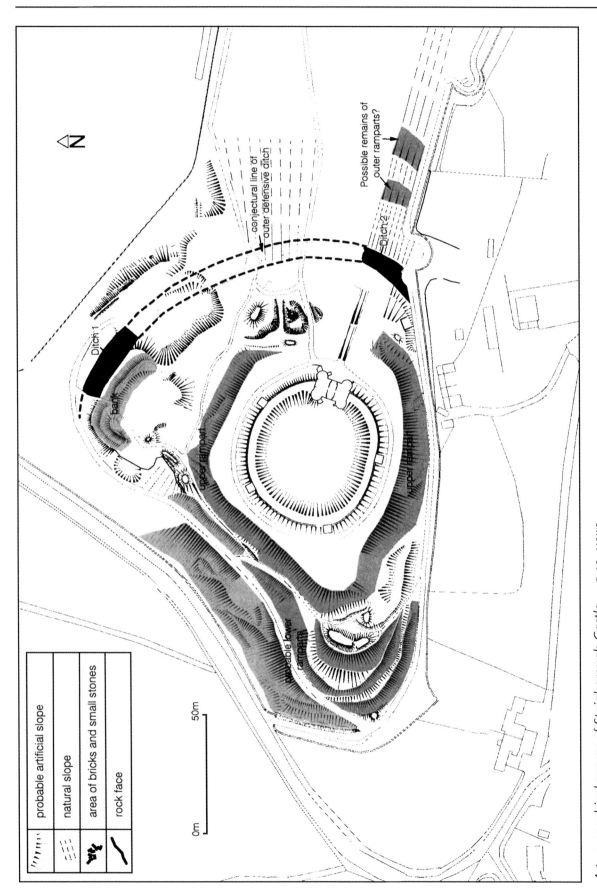

N

probable artificial slope

natural slope

area of bricks and small stones

rock face

0m

50m

conjectural line of outer defensive ditch

Possible remains of outer ramparts?

Ditch 2

Ditch 1

bank

upper rampart

upper rampart

probable lower ramparts

A topographical survey of Stainborough Castle   © AS - WYAS

was carried out around the folly between February and May 2006, to aid future management of the site (for earlier investigations carried out during the restoration programme at Wentworth Castle and Stainborough Park see *'Archaeology in South Yorkshire Number 12'*). The results suggest that the extensive earthwork terraces on which Stainborough Castle stands pre-date its construction; they may be remnants of an Iron Age hillfort or of medieval fortification.

Geophysical survey (magnetometer) was carried out on three plots within the park, where works are proposed, in April 2006. A cropmark visible on aerial photographs at the southern end of the South Avenue was identified as a curving anomaly, but there was no evidence that it continued into the adjoining arable field. The anomaly may represent an infilled and levelled ornamental feature, or an enclosure ditch. Along the line of a proposed access road, a number of anomalies were identified that could indicate buried archaeological features – possibly forming part of an enclosure.

Centred at Grid Reference SE 319 035

From reports by Alistair Webb and Mitchell Pollington, Archaeological Services WYAS

HATFIELD MAIN COLLIERY, STAINFORTH, DONCASTER

Following a desk-based assessment of the former colliery site (see *'Archaeology in South Yorkshire Number 11'*), a borehole survey was carried out in July 2006 for Powerfuel plc. This identified a

sedimentary sequence of probable Late Devensian sands and gravels overlain by Holocene alluvium deposits. These deposits were not considered to have palaeo-environmental potential.

In August and September 2006 seventeen trial trenches were excavated, to test whether the extensive alluvial deposits identified sealed earlier archaeological features. The majority of the trenches revealed only natural features, such as palaeo-channels, which were filled with inorganic silts. The only archaeological feature identified was a ditch and associated bank that represents a field boundary shown on the Stainforth Enclosure map of 1826.

Centred at Grid Reference SE 649 115

From reports by Dr Malcolm Lillie and Claire Twiddle, WAERC (borehole survey) and Jonathan Tabor, Northern Archaeological Associates (evaluation)

STOCKSBRIDGE NURSERY AND INFANT SCHOOL, STOCKSBRIDGE, SHEFFIELD

A watching brief on geotechnical works was carried out in February 2007, for Sheffield City Council. The investigative works on the school playing fields were needed to test for the presence of former mine workings, prior to the development of a proposed children's centre. The site lies opposite the former Bolsterstone glass and pot works and associated features, e.g. waster dumps, could have been located here (see map on page 188 of colour section). However, no archaeologically significant features or finds were exposed, although a series of former mine workings were identified at a depth of between 1.5 and 2m.

Grid Reference SK 266 981

From a report by Jessika Shakarian and Brian Marshall, Archaeological Research Services Ltd

CRODA BITUMEN WORKS, SWINTON, ROTHERHAM

Proposals by the Woodford Group to develop the former Croda Bitumen Works led to the preparation of a desk-based assessment in April 2006. The development of the site began in 1886 with the establishment of the Don Chemical Works, a tar distillery. This works expanded until it covered much of the site by the mid 20th century. The works accepted tar, creosote and latterly crude petroleum for distillation to produce pitch, creosote and associated oils. The site closed in 1997 and all above-ground structures have since been demolished. Some potential for the survival of buried features from the early works was identified.

Centred at Grid Reference SK 465 985

From a report by Mary Lakin, Northern Archaeological Associates

LAND OFF MAWSON GREEN LANE, SYKEHOUSE, DONCASTER

A geophysical survey (magnetometer) was carried out in September 2006 on

View of the cart shed/dovecote at Glebe Farm, Tankersley © CS Archaeology

behalf of Carter Jonas LLP, ahead of the proposed creation of fishponds. The site is close to the location of a late prehistoric/early Roman enclosed settlement and the medieval moated site of Warren Hill. However, no anomalies of probable archaeological origin were identified.

Centred at Grid Reference SE 646 172

From a report by T S Harrison and M Pollington, Archaeological Services WYAS

GLEBE FARM, TANKERSLEY, BARNSLEY

A desk-based assessment and building appraisal was prepared for Mr D Yeardley in September 2006, ahead of renovation and redevelopment of the farmstead. Glebe Farm lies within a series of moats that are thought to have once contained the medieval manor house of Tankersley. This indicates that significant archaeological below-ground deposits could be preserved on the site. All the present buildings are post-medieval in character and most were probably constructed in the late 18th century. One of the upstanding buildings, the cart shed/dovecote, built in 1735, is a Scheduled Ancient Monument. At the time of its construction, the building would have been a highly visible feature in the landscape, as the surrounding area was mostly recently enclosed land (rather than woodland). Other 18th century elements present are a barn and cow-house, or mistal.

Grid Reference SK 348 997

**From a report by Chris Scurfield,
CS Archaeology**

LAND OFF NORTH EASTERN ROAD, THORNE, DONCASTER

Proposals for the construction of new houses led to archaeological investigation in August 2006 for Patley Homes Ltd. Far Post (corn) Mill is recorded at this location on the 1851 Ordnance Survey map. However, the site was found to have been disturbed by previous development and excavation revealed no features or finds of archaeological interest.

Grid Reference SE 682 138

**From a report by Marina Rose,
Archaeological Services WYAS**

LAND OFF COULMAN ROAD, THORNE, DONCASTER

A desk-based assessment was prepared in January 2007 for Haslam Homes, to inform a planning application for residential redevelopment. The proposal area was part of Thorne's North Common until enclosure in 1825 and then remained in agricultural use until the mid 20th century. A factory is shown here on mid-late 20th century OS maps, but this has since been demolished. This 20th century development is likely to have disturbed any earlier archaeological deposits.

Centred at Grid Reference SE 695 141

From a report by Mark Stenton, ARCUS

BRADHOLME FARM, THORNE, DONCASTER

A desk-based assessment was prepared in July 2005, for Turley Associates. The proposal site consists of a series of large fields surrounding the farmstead, which may have medieval origins; the name 'Bradholme' is first recorded in a document of 1324. The area is generally low lying and the farm is sited on a slight rise. A series of boreholes was sunk across the site in March 2007 to test the palaeo-environmental potential of the lower-lying areas and to look for other areas of higher ground that might have attracted ancient settlement. The survey revealed a complex pattern of deposits. The south-central part of the site comprised shallow channel features, the southwest and north of the site showed evidence of a deep channel of water, all these surrounding the central area of raised ground, which comprises sands and gravels, some possibly representing marginal deposits from the late Devensian Lake Humber.

Centred at Grid Reference SE 693 116

From reports by Archaeological Services WYAS (assessment); Tim Robinson (borehole survey), On-Site Archaeology

ELM HOUSE, STONEGATE, THORNE, DONCASTER

Following an earlier desk-based assessment (see *'Archaeology in South Yorkshire Number 12'*) two evaluation trenches were excavated in the grounds of Elm House in June 2005. The work was carried out for Building Design Ltd. Two features cut into the subsoil were found to contain fragments of 19th century hand-made bricks. A small quantity of late medieval/early post-medieval pottery was recovered, but this is likely to be residual or intrusive.

Grid Reference SE 690 130

From a report by Ben Chan, ARCUS

FORMER EXPRESS DAIRY DEPOT, QUEEN STREET, THORNE, DONCASTER

An application for residential development led to the preparation of a desk-based assessment and subsequent watching brief during excavation of foundation trenches, on behalf of Building Design Services. The work was carried out between May and September 2005. The site lies on the edge of the historic core of the town and may not have been developed until the late 18th or early 19th century. The current depot was constructed in the 1980s. The watching brief during development identified an 18th or 19th century wall cutting through buried soils that contained 15th-17th century pottery, confirming that this site was developed late in Thorne's history.

Centred at Grid Reference SE 695 133

From reports by Mark Stenton and Duncan Alexander, ARCUS

LAND AT FIELDSIDE, THORNE, DONCASTER

A desk-based assessment for this former school site, which lies on the edge of the town's historic core, was prepared in March 2005. The first development on the site seems to have been the construction of a Board School in 1876. This gothic building still survives but in a derelict condition. Later school buildings have been demolished.

Four evaluation trenches were excavated for Bluestone plc in April 2005, to inform a planning application for a proposed health centre and residential development. The only archaeological features identified were two ditches that represent field boundaries shown on the 1824 Enclosure map. A small quantity of medieval pottery was

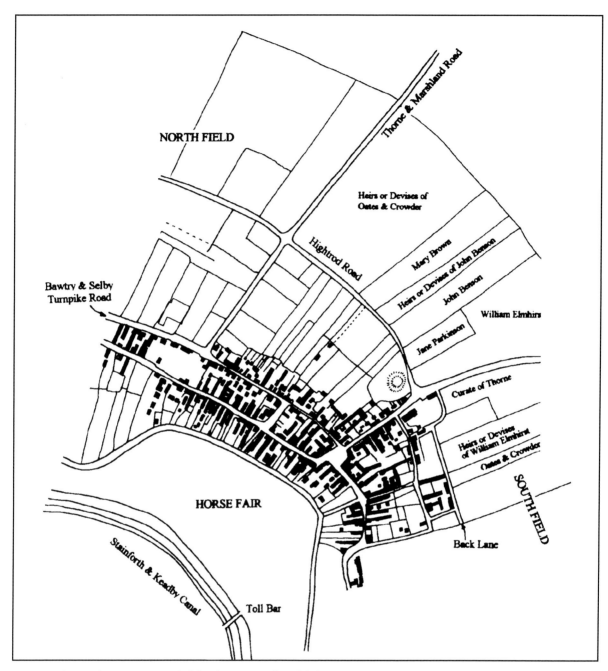

Excerpt from the 1825 Hatfield, Thorne and Fishlake Enclosure Map showing Thorne   © ARCUS

recovered but this is thought to have been redeposited.

Centred at Grid Reference SE 685 136

From reports by Christine Ball, Tim Cooper and Glyn Davies, ARCUS

GRAMMAR SCHOOL, THORNE, DONCASTER

A further phase of evaluation was carried out in May 2005 (see '*Archaeology in South Yorkshire Number 12*' for earlier work). Three trenches were excavated, focused on earthworks that were thought possibly associated with Peel Hill motte, which stands on land to the west of the school site. Only modern dump deposits were revealed, suggesting that the earthworks represent former quarrying, recorded in this area on the 1906 OS map.

Grid Reference SE 692 135

From a report by Aaron Goode, Pre-Construct Archaeology

1-2 MARKET PLACE AND 8 SILVER STREET, THORNE, DONCASTER

An assessment of these standing buildings was carried out in April 2005 for Commercial Development Projects Ltd, ahead of planned demolition and redevelopment of the site. No.1-2 Market Place may be 17th century in origin; no. 8 Silver Street was a purpose built Police Station built in the mid-late 19th century. The majority of the interiors of the properties have been altered and original features removed; the rear wing of the older property has also been part demolished.

Grid Reference SE 688 132

From a report by Mark Chambers and Martin Griffiths, M&M Archaeological Services

LAND OFF CASSONS ROAD, THORNE, DONCASTER

In January and February 2006 eight evaluation trenches were excavated for

Remains of Thorpe Salvin Hall with the later cottages to the right © AS - WYAS

Tolent plc ahead of site development. The proposal site lies on a sand ridge that raises it above the surrounding low-lying area and could have made it attractive to ancient settlement. However, the only archaeological feature identified was a ditch representing a former field boundary.

Centred at Grid Reference SE 682 141

From a report by Duncan Alexander, ARCUS

OLD HALL COTTAGES, THORPE SALVIN, ROTHERHAM

Building recording of the cottages and a subsequent watching brief during their demolition was carried out for Mr P Moody between February and August 2006, as a condition of planning consent to build a house and garage. The cottages stood adjacent to the site of the 16th century Thorpe Salvin Hall and were probably constructed in the 18th century, but had undergone significant changes since then. The earliest part of the buildings was a section of the southeast wall shared with the hall boundary wall. Here, a chamfered doorway could indicate that the wall was originally part of a building contemporary with the hall.

Grid Reference SK 521 812

From a report by A C Swann, Archaeological Services WYAS

LAND NORTH OF THURNSCOE, BARNSLEY

A proposal to build houses on two fields north of Thurnscoe led to the preparation of a desk-based assessment in April and May 2006, for the Chevin Housing Association Ltd. Archaeological features identified within the proposal area were limited to medieval or post-medieval ridge and furrow, visible on aerial photographs, and the site of a modern building. The assessment noted that earlier archaeological evidence could be being obscured by this later activity.

Centred at Grid Reference SE 459 061

From a report by Chris Scurfield, CS Archaeology

HOYLE MILL, THURLSTONE, BARNSLEY

A desk-based assessment was prepared in March 2006, for Mr J Hutchings, to determine the impact of proposed redevelopment of this mill site. The first known activity on the site was the

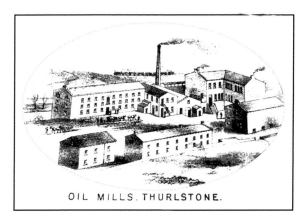

OIL MILLS. THURLSTONE.

A bill head for Hoyle Mill, dating from about 1900

construction of an oil mill here in the 1740s and the site was known until recently as Oil Mill. This mill would have been used to crush flaxseed for the manufacture of paint and dyes. The original water-powered mill building was either rebuilt or enlarged in 1761 and had been converted for wool production by 1845; it was probably used for fulling and scribbling. At the same time a new mechanised hand-spinning mill was erected alongside the river. At some time in the 1920s, the original mill was demolished and the former dam infilled. By this time, the complex was being used for rug manufacture, but its association with the textile industry ended after the Second World War. Subsequent use has removed or altered many of the historic elements, reducing the importance of the surviving 18th and 19th century structures. However, the buildings warrant a photographic survey prior to any demolition.

Grid Reference SE 237 036

From a report by Shaun Richardson and Ed Dennison, Ed Dennison Archaeological Services Ltd

Photograph of one of the glasshouses at Hesley Hall, Tickhill   © AS - WYAS

HESLEY HALL, TICKHILL, DONCASTER

Proposed redevelopment of the nursery west of the hall, formerly a walled garden, led to an evaluation and building recording in 2006, for the Hesley Group (see *'Archaeology in South Yorkshire Number 11'* and *'Number 12'* for earlier work at the hall). Two evaluation trenches were excavated but no archaeological features of interest were recorded. The Edwardian glasshouses, possibly under threat of demolition, were recorded and found to have sophisticated opening mechanisms for temperature control.

Grid Reference SK 616 956

From reports by Marina Rose, Andrew Walsh and Andy Swann, Archaeological Services WYAS

LAND OFF BARNSLEY ROAD, WATH-UPON-DEARNE, ROTHERHAM

Proposed redevelopment led to a scheme of archaeological investigation between April 2005 and July 2006, for McInerney Homes Yorkshire. The

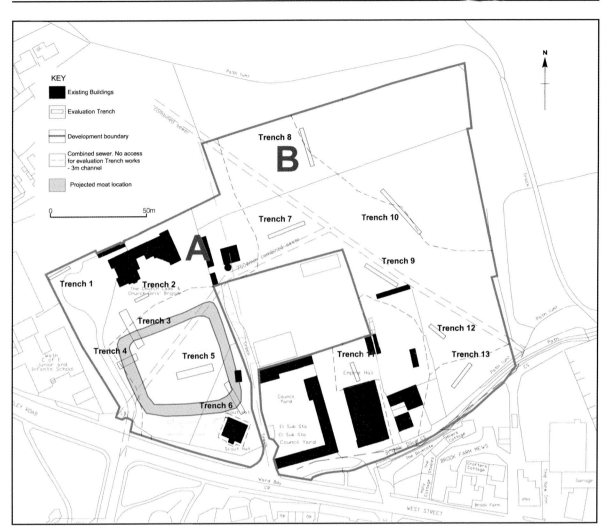

Figure showing the location of evaluation trenches and projected location of the moat at Wath-upon-Dearne   © AS - WYAS

remains of a medieval moat, thought to be the location of the former manor house, lies within the western part of the development site. Documentary records show that the manor was given to the Rector of Wath in 1325 and that a vicarage was built in 1410. This building may have been located within the moated enclosure, or have been sited near the present vicarage, to the north.

Magnetometer and resistivity surveys were carried out across the site. Several linear areas of high resistance were located within the moated enclosure, suggesting the presence of sub-surface structural remains. These results were then tested by trial trench evaluation. The trenches confirmed the presence of a large square-shaped moat, which had been re-cut at least once. A substantial stone retaining wall was found to line the island side of the moat; this feature may be a later formalisation of an earlier earth banked moat. Stone foundations on the island represent two phases of construction. Finds were very limited, but sherds of 13th to 16th century pottery indicate activity on the island throughout the medieval period. A watching brief during geotechnical test pitting further confirmed the extent and layout of the moated enclosure.

Centred at Grid Reference SE 432 011

From reports by Andy Mayes and Nick Finch, Scott Wilson Ltd (assessment and watching brief); T P Schofield, A Webb, Daniel Lee and Luigi Signorelli, Archaeological Services WYAS (geophysics and trial trench evaluation)

WHARNCLIFFE CHASE, WORTLEY, BARNSLEY

Two areas of woodland at the southern end of Wharncliffe Chase were surveyed in March 2007 on behalf of the Rural Development Service (DEFRA), as part of an Agri-Environmental Scheme Higher Level Agreement, which included proposals for planting and woodland regeneration. Wharncliffe Chase was a medieval hunting park established c1252 and now comprises mixed areas of heathland, moorland and woodland. The remains of a buck shed and deer pen associated with hunting deer were identified during the survey. The buck shed is shown on the 1855 OS map; the deer pen is thought to be earlier. A pond and goit thought to relate to water supply for the buck shed or a lost hunting lodge were also identified. To the north of the proposal area is Wharncliffe Rocks, a Scheduled Monument where late prehistoric/Roman quern manufacture took place. Probable areas of quern manufacture were noted within the proposal area; circular hollows on

earthfast boulders near Wharncliffe Farm are likely to be from production of beehive querns.

Centred at Grid Reference SK 307 956

From a report by ASE Ltd

177

COLOUR SECTION

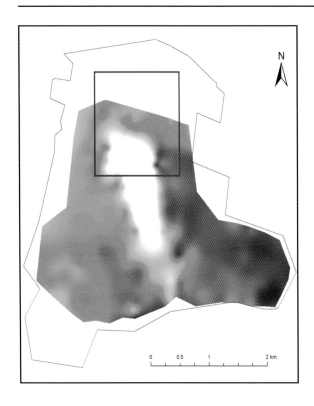

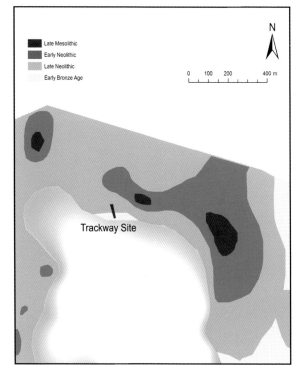

Terrain modelling of Hatfield Moors showing the Neolithic trackway in relation to surrounding landform and peat development   © Birmingham University

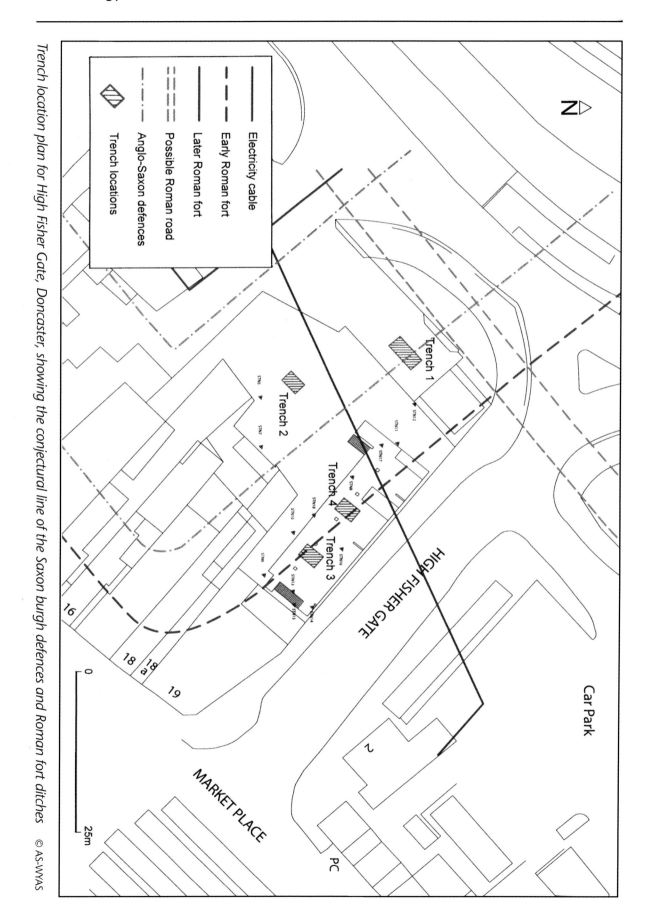

Trench location plan for High Fisher Gate, Doncaster, showing the conjectural line of the Saxon burgh defences and Roman fort ditches　© AS-WYAS

Legend:
- Electricity cable
- Early Roman fort
- Later Roman fort
- Possible Roman road
- Anglo-Saxon defences
- Trench locations

N

HIGH FISHER GATE

MARKET PLACE

Car Park

PC

Trench 1

Trench 2

Trench 4

Trench 3

16　18　18a　19

0　25m

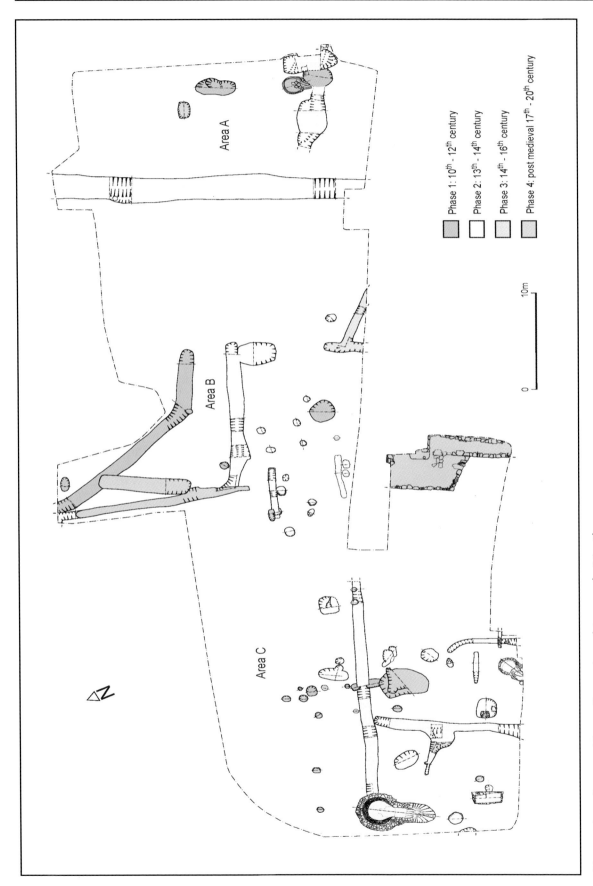

Area A

Area B

Area C

N

10m

0

Phase 1: 10th - 12th century

Phase 2: 13th - 14th century

Phase 3: 14th - 16th century

Phase 4: post medieval 17th - 20th century

Phase plan, Rectory House Farm, Laughton-en-le-Morthen   © AS-WYAS

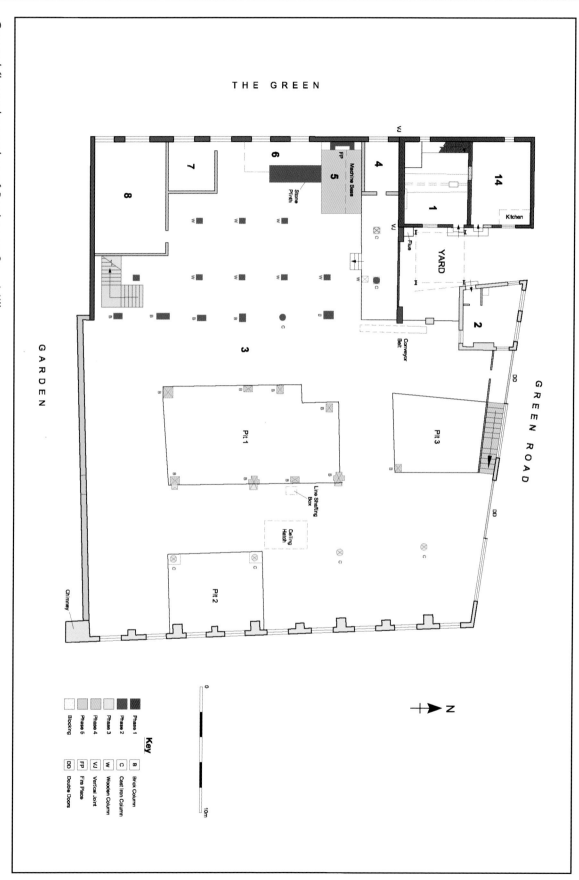

Ground floor phase plan of Penistone Saw Mill © ARCUS

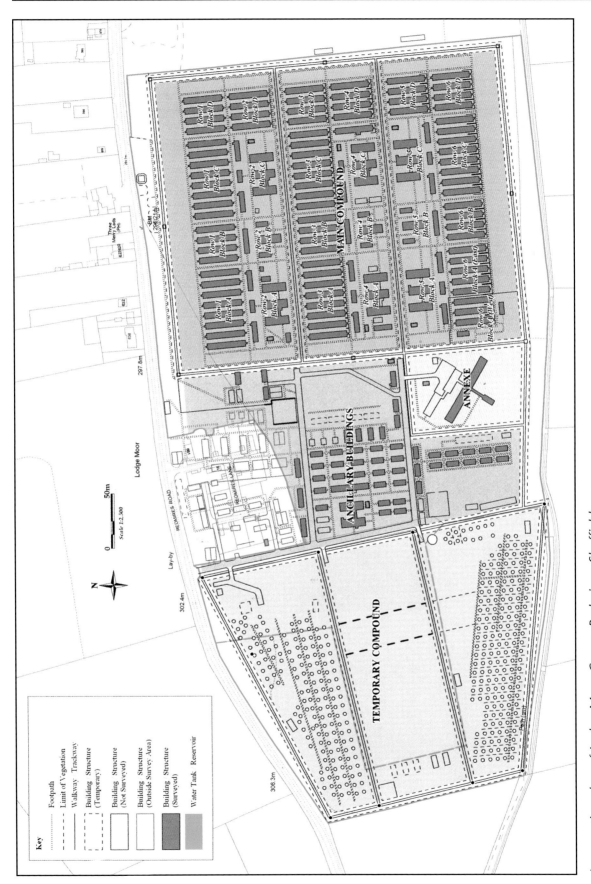

Interpretive plan of Lodge Moor Camp, Redmires, Sheffield © ASE Ltd.

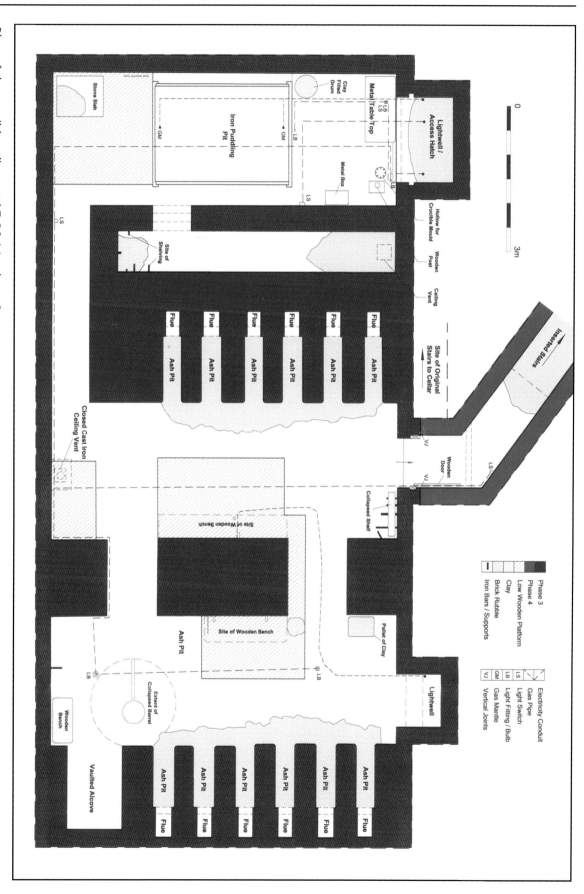

Plan of the crucible cellars at 17-39 Mowbray Street   © ARCUS

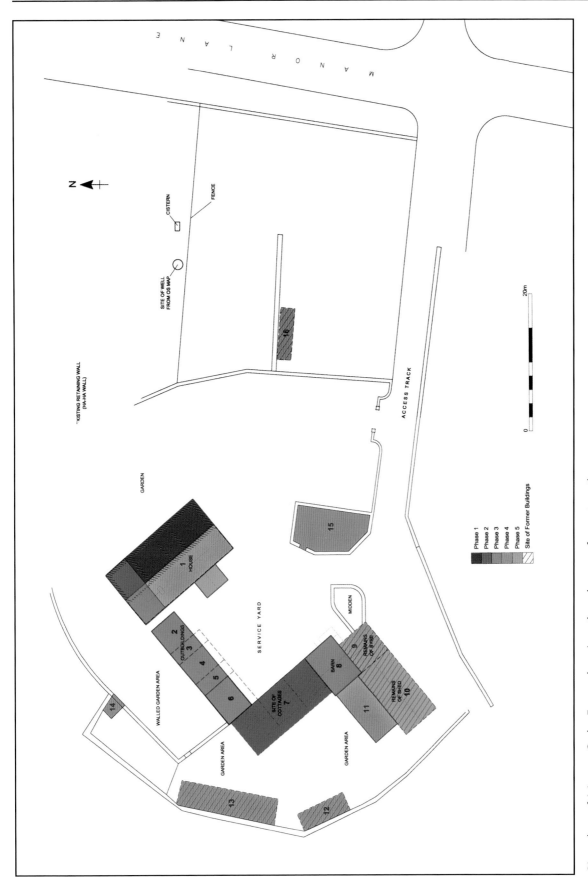

Site plan of Manor Oaks Farm showing the phases of construction © ARCUS

187

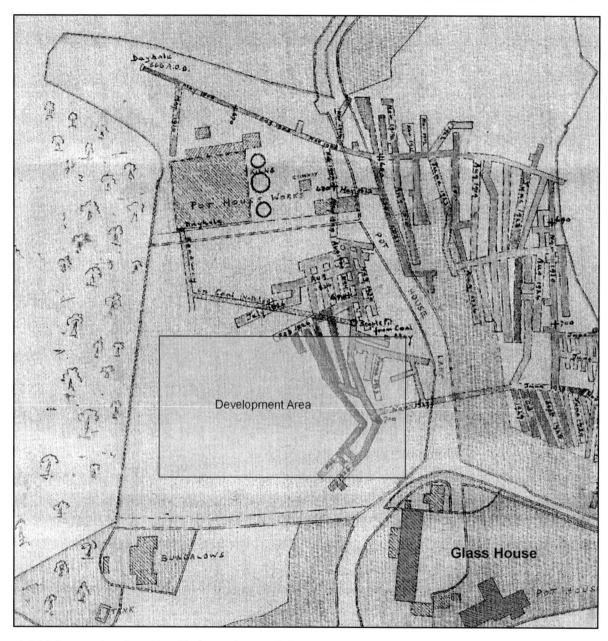

A 1926 map showing Clay Shale workings of the Halifax Middle Coal Bed, in the area of Stocksbridge Nursery and Infant School © ARS Ltd

CONTENTS

Fair's Fair
by Leon Garfield

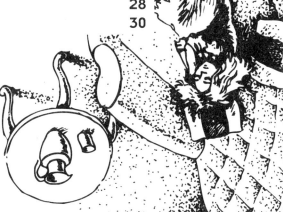

CREDITS

Published by Scholastic Ltd,
Villiers House,
Clarendon Avenue,
Leamington Spa,
Warwickshire CV32 5PR
Text © Sue Dean and Alan Howe
© 1997 Scholastic Ltd
1 2 3 4 5 6 7 8 9 0 7 8 9 0 1 2 3 4 5 6

Authors Sue Dean and Alan Howe
Editor Kate Pearce
Series designer Lynne Joesbury
Designer Rachel Warner
Illustrations Brian Hoskin
Cover illustration Stewart Lees

Designed using Aldus Pagemaker
Printed in Great Britain by Hartnolls Ltd.

British Library Cataloguing-in-Publication Data
A catalogue record for this book is available
from the British Library.

ISBN 0-590-53732-6

ACKNOWLEDGEMENTS

Berlie Doherty for the use of text from *Street
Child* by Berlie Doherty © 1993, Berlie Doherty
(1993, Hamish Hamilton).
**Heinemann Educational Publishers, a division
of Reed Educational and Professional
Publishing Ltd** for the use of an extract from
Victorian Children by Jane Shuter © Jane
Shuter (Hamlyn).
John Johnson (Authors' Agents) Ltd for
photograph of Leon Garfield and the
permission for educational use of *Fair's Fair* by
Leon Garfield © 1981, Leon Garfield (1981,
Macdonald and Co. (Publishers) Ltd).
Wayland Publishers Ltd for permission to use
the cover of *Fair's Fair* by Leon Garfield © 1991,
Illustration, Brian Hoskin 1991 (1991, Simon and
Schuster).

INTRODUCTION

Fair's Fair
by Leon Garfield

WHAT'S THE PLOT OF THE STORY?

It is the week before Christmas. Jackson, homeless and starving, is sitting in a doorway in a street in Victorian London. Just as he's warming his hands around a hot pie, and deciding whether to eat it straightaway or save it, along comes a big black dog. Jackson's life starts to change from that moment.

WHAT'S SO GOOD ABOUT THIS BOOK?

This is a mystery story, set in a time when many children had difficult lives, fending for themselves on the streets of cities. As you read, you will begin to wonder about all sorts of questions. Where does the black dog come from? Where is he leading Jackson? Is Jackson's luck about to change? Or is he being led towards danger? The writer, Leon Garfield, keeps us guessing. He also describes people and places really well. You will enjoy finding out what happens.

ABOUT LEON GARFIELD

Leon Garfield was born in 1921 and died in 1996. His most famous children's book is *Smith*, also set in the past, in London during the 18th century. He more recently wrote the scripts for the BBC series of Shakespeare plays presented as animations.

Find the story

● Look at this book cover. The title and author of the book have been removed.

● Study the picture carefully and make a list of what you can see. What clues do these give you about the book?

I can see	Clues about the book

● Who do you think the boy might be? Look at his clothes and where he is. Write your ideas here.

● Now read what is written on the back cover of the book:

It's a week before Christmas, and Jackson is frozen and starving. But the big black dog looks just as thin and hungry as he does. So Jackson gives the dog half of his pie. Little does the street urchin know what this one generous act will lead to...

What do you think the title of the book is?

Title talk

The title of a book usually gives you some clues about the story. The title of this book, *Fair's Fair*, is an everyday saying. What do you think it means?

● Fill in your ideas on the spider plan. Look at the front cover illustration with the boy, the pie and the dog to get you thinking.

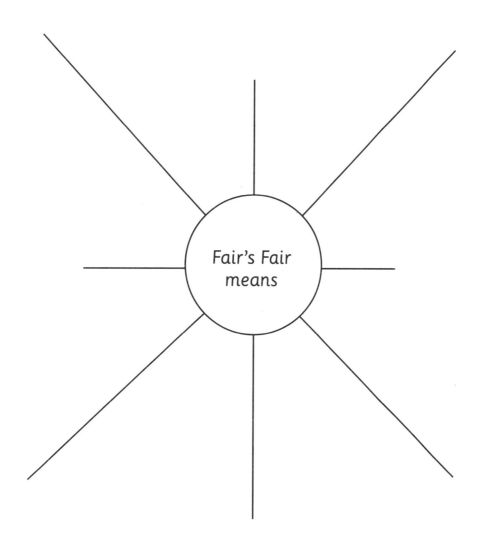

Fair's Fair
means

Work out the story

● Look at the following illustrations. They all come from *Fair's Fair*.

Jackson sitting in the cold street about to eat a hot pie.

● What do you think is happening in the story? Write a caption for each picture.

● These illustrations don't tell the whole story, though! What questions do you have about the story? Write them in the box below.

On the streets

Read the start of the story up to '... he vanished one day and was never seen or heard of again.' Think about why Jackson has ended up on the streets.

Who are Jackson's parents?
Perhaps...

● His mother is a servant in a big house.
● His father is a sailor who hardly ever visits England.
● His mother is a rich lady in the town.
● His father is a soldier.

What unhappy event happened to Jackson?
Perhaps...
● His mother died in childbirth.
● His mother couldn't keep both her baby and her job.
● His parents had lots of children and no work.

● Why do *you* think Jackson lives on the streets? Write your ideas here.
Perhaps...

_____

_____

_____

_____

_____

_____

_____

A word picture of the dog

Read up to the words '... when the black dog came.'
● Now read the passage below. Some of the verbs (doing words) and adjectives (describing words) have been missed out to make you think carefully about the dog Jackson meets.

Huge: as _____ as a donkey, nearly, with eyes like street

lamps and jaws like an oven door. Down the street it _____,

with a glare to the right and a glare to the left, and a _____

twitch of its _____ _____ nose. Somebody _____ a

window and _____ a bucket of _____ water down; and

the black dog _____ with rage. Up it came to the doorstep

where Jackson sat and steamed. It _____ and _____

while the snow flakes _____ on its nose.

● Fill in the gaps with words that make sense. Now read the passage as Leon Garfield wrote it. Did he choose different words to you?

● Complete these two lists and then compare your verbs and adjectives with Garfield's.

Verbs		Adjectives	
mine	**Garfield's**	**mine**	**Garfield's**
	padded		big
	opened		savage
	threw		great
	snarled		black
	glared		dirty
	growled		
	fried		

● Which version do you like best? Why? Write your ideas on the back of this sheet.

Street urchin

● Read this passage about another Victorian child. Some of the words are missing. See if you can make sense of it without the missing words.

Jim Jarvis hopped about on the edge of the road, his feet blue with cold. Passing carriages _____ muddy snow up into his face and his eyes, and the swaying horses slithered and skidded as they were _____ on by their drivers. At last Jim saw his chance and made a dash for it through the traffic. The little shops in the _____ street all _____ yellow with their hanging lamps, and Jim _____ from one light to the next until he came to the shop he was looking for. It was the meat pudding shop. _____ boys and _____ dogs hovered round the doorway, watching for _____. Jim pushed past them, his coin as hot as a piece of coal in his fist. He could hear his stomach _____ as the rich smell of hot gravy met him.

(from *Street Child* by Berlie Doherty)

● Fill in the gaps in the passage, using the words below. Make sure it makes sense when you have added the words.

hungry   flung   whipped   gurgling
skinny   dodged   glowed   scraps   dark

● What picture do you have in your head of the place that Jim lives in and the kind of life he leads? Write or draw your ideas below. Continue on the back of this sheet if you need more space.

Would you or wouldn't you?

Read up to the part where Jackson says to the dog, 'Now shove off!'

● If you had been Jackson, what would you have done? Write it here.

● Why do you think Jackson behaves as he does to the dog? Write it here.

● Think of some questions to ask Jackson at this point in the story. You can write your questions in the boxes.

● Now think about how Jackson might answer your questions. Work with a partner. One of you should pretend to be Jackson and one of you the interviewer. Take it in turns to ask and answer questions in your roles. Then swap over.

'You got a key!'

Read up to '... and his knuckles still raw from his last scrubbing.' What do you think this mystery key will open? ... a gate, a box, a door...?

● Write a different idea in each key. Using that idea, jot down under each one how the story might continue and how it might end. Keep in mind the clues that Leon Garfield has already given in the story:
● the title, *Fair's Fair*;
● how Jackson disappears and never returns, 'And nobody *did* miss him when he vanished one day and was never seen or heard of again.'

So, what might happen is _____

_____

_____

So, what might happen is _____

_____

_____

So, what might happen is _____

_____

_____

'Doors'

Read up to the words '... and gates with nothing at all inside.'
● Re-read the description of the doors Jackson tries to open. Practise reading it aloud a few times.

> The doors he tried! Short fat doors with panels all over like a poacher's pockets; tall thin doors with iron studs down the middle, like a bishop's buttons; doors with little windows, doors with fanlights, doors with pillars, doors with porches, doors with horrible knockers and doors with brass letter-boxes that had eyes inside them when you looked through.

● Use a dictionary to look up these words if you are not sure of their meanings:

panel   poacher   fanlight   pillar   porch

● Choose one of the doors Jackson tried to open and draw a picture of it inside this door-frame.

● Label your picture using words from the book.

Telling the story so far

Read up to '... with an iron letter-box as thin as a miser's mouth.'

● Use some of these key words to tell someone the story so far. You have only 30 seconds!

Jackson   homeless   weather
        pie   dog   key
    sharing   search   streets

Remember! Your listener has an important job too. Your listener should decide:
● whether all the important parts of the story have been included;
● what has been left out.

The story so far...

Has anything been left out?

● Now swap roles and listen to your partner telling the story. Who remembered more about the story? Who was quicker?

Writing a 'found' poem

A 'found' poem is when you use words or phrases from something you have read to make up your own poem. This 'found' poem uses words and phrases from the first description of the dog.

Black Dog

Huge black dog
Eyes like street lamps
Jaws like an oven door
Pads down the snow-filled street.
It glares around
Snarls with rage
A hunger deep in its belly.
It stoops, sniffs the air, turns and
Sees Jackson with his pie.
Steadily it pads towards him
As snow flakes fry on its nose.

> huge
> black dog
> padded
> glared
> snow flakes fried on its nose
> snarled with rage
> eyes like street lamps
> jaws like an oven door

Read up to '... small, thin, dirty, tattered, angry little girl!' Using the description of the house, list any interesting words and phrases.

● Now use your list to write a 'found' poem called
The Deserted House

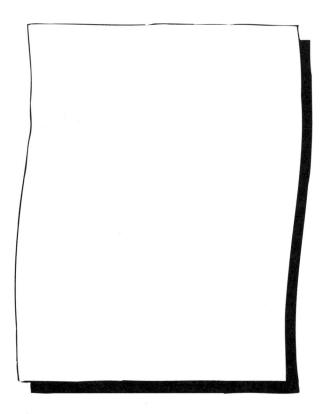

Missing!

Read up to where Jackson says 'I'll do the grate and the kitchen floor.'

Imagine somebody notices that Jackson and Lillipolly have gone missing and asks the police to find them. The police might issue a 'Missing' poster like this:

● Make a list of everything the police would need to know about Jackson and Lillipolly.

	Jackson	Lillipolly
last seen at		
appearance		
what to do if seen		

● Now design your 'Missing' poster for Jackson and Lillipolly, using the information you have listed. How will you make it eye-catching? Think about the size and shape of the lettering and how you will display your information on the page.

● Draft your poster design in the space below. Check the details carefully. Have you included them all? Can you improve it?

'I wonder'

Read up to '... Jackson and Lillipolly were fast asleep.'

● Fill in the boxes with your answers to these questions.

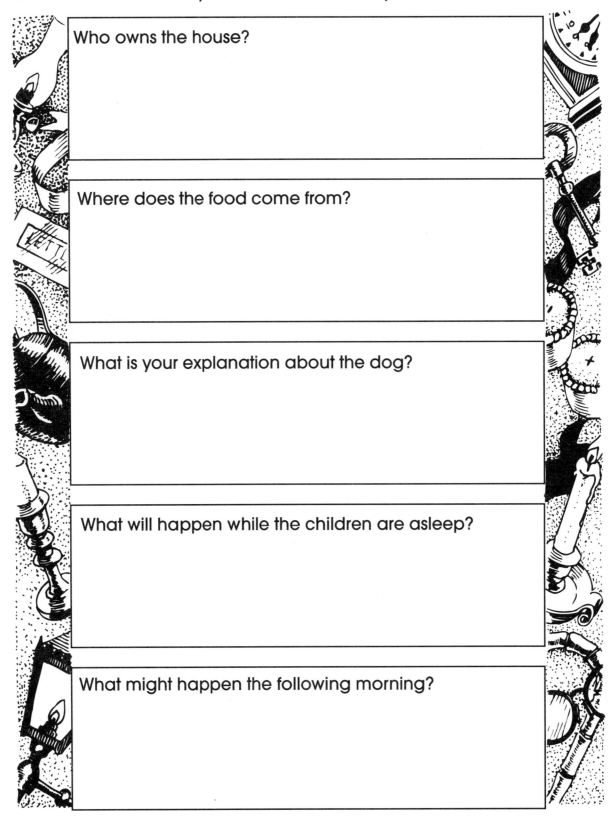

Who owns the house?

Where does the food come from?

What is your explanation about the dog?

What will happen while the children are asleep?

What might happen the following morning?

The two men

Read up to 'The two men looked at each other; then the first one clapped his hands.'

● Work as a word detective. Use a dictionary and discuss with a partner the meaning of each of these words.

kind   brave   patient   honest   generous

● In the spaces below write what Jackson and Lillipolly have done since they entered the house that shows that they are:

kind	
brave	
patient	
honest	
generous	

Here's the last bit you read:
'The two men looked at each other; then the first one clapped his hands.'

● What do you think happens next? Are the two men evil robbers? Or is there a different explanation? Write your ideas below.

● Now work with a partner and practise telling the next bit of the story, based on your ideas. Make it as interesting and exciting as you can.

The ending

Read to the end of the book.

In 'You got a key!' you made three guesses about how the story might continue and end. Now you know what really happens, how close were your guesses?

I thought...	What really happened was...

● Now that you have read all the story, why do you think the book is called *Fair's Fair*? Add your ideas to this spider plan.

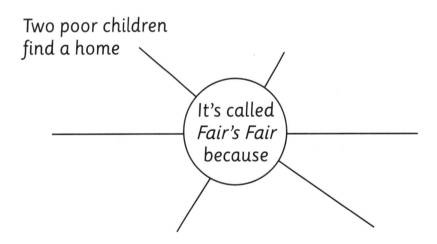

Two poor children find a home

It's called *Fair's Fair* because

● Do you think the title suits the story? Write your reasons here:

Can you identify?

● Test how much you have remembered of the story! Match these quotations with the characters and places in *Fair's Fair*. Check back in the book if you're not sure.

Who

'stank like a drain'?

was 'as big as a donkey'?

was 'small, thin, dirty, tattered'?

were 'ragged, fearful, old and wild-looking'?

Who said

'I cleaned all the silver and polished the table'?

'And *I'm* froze and hungry!'?

'You're spifflicating me!'?

Where is this?

'... ghostly houses twinkled among ghostly trees, and ghostly coaches with tall white hats rolled silently by.'

'As long as a street, nearly, and tall and wide to match!'

● Look at these descriptions. What do you notice about them?

'Dreadful weather, as hard and bitter as a quarrel.'

'... an iron letter-box as thin as a miser's mouth.'

'... his face screwed up like a piece of dirty paper...'

They are similes. A **simile** is a way of describing one thing by comparing it to something else, using the words 'like' or 'as'.

● Fill in these explanations, using the descriptions above to help:

A quarrel is

A miser's mouth is

A piece of dirty paper is

● Now make up some similes youself, using these beginnings. RULE: it must 'fit' by sounding right. Try to think of descriptions that nobody else will think of!

As white as   A headache like

Eyes like   As hot as

Rich and poor

Jackson is a 'street urchin', which means that he has no home and lives on the streets. *Fair's Fair* is set in Victorian London, between the years 1850 and 1900. To help you understand what life was like, read these extracts about the life of Victorian street children.

Children working in mines, factories and on farms had a hard life. But there were some children, especially in London, who had an even harder life. These were children living on the very edge of starvation. They were forced to beg or steal to live. Or they had to fish for wood, coal and other things out of the disease-ridden mud of the River Thames, to sell for a few pennies. Many of them died before reaching adulthood.

There were many children like this because they were orphans; they had run away from cruel parents; they had run away from cruel masters.

The very poorest families could not pay rent for a house and were homeless. They could either sleep on the streets and beg for a living, or they could go to the workhouse.

● Now fill in this grid. Look back at the information to make sure that you don't miss anything important.

What street children did for:		Reasons why there were street children:	
food		1.	
money		2.	
shelter		3.	

Here is some more information about rich and poor children.

Rich people lived on large country estates and also had big houses in fashionable towns like London or Bath. They had servants to do everything for them, even bring up the children. Rich children had

lots of toys and clothes and were well fed, but they were brought up very strictly. Boys were sent away to private schools from the age of seven. Girls stayed at home to be a rich man's wife.

Poor children had to work. They lived in the slum areas of the cities, which were crammed with badly built houses. Often there were several families living in one room.

Children of wealthy parents did not have to find work. They were well looked after. They stayed at home, playing or reading books.

● Complete the chart to show what you know about the different ways rich and poor children lived.

Poor children	Rich children
lived on the streets	lived in big houses

● Now use what you have found out to write a short report about Victorian children. Use the starter sentences given in the frame opposite to help you plan your writing.

Report on Victorian Children

I want to tell you about...

In Victorian times, some children...

However, other children...

Some children were very poor because...

So now you can see...

An exchange of letters (1)

Mr Beecham Chambers wants to help two homeless and deserving children. He asks his lawyer, Mr Chuter & Ede, to help him set a test to find two such children.

● Imagine that you are Mr Beecham Chambers. Write a letter to your lawyer, asking for his help. Use this letter outline to help you draft your ideas.

> 1 The Mansions,
> Hampstead,
> London
>
> Dear...
> I have been thinking for some time about...
>
>
> I would like you to help...
>
>
>
> I have an idea that I could use Growler to...
>
>
>
> I would be most grateful for your opinions...
>
>
>
> Yours sincerely

● When you have drafted your ideas for the letter, present it so that it looks old. Remember when the story takes place. Think about the paper you should use and the style of handwriting.

An exchange of letters (2)

● In the story, Mr Beecham Chambers asks his lawyer, Mr Chuter & Ede, to help him find two homeless and deserving children. Imagine you are Mr Chuter & Ede. You have received a very interesting letter from your client, Mr Beecham Chambers, but you are not sure that his plan will work! Reply to his letter, using this letter outline to help you with your ideas:

1 The Law Courts,
Temple Inn,
London

Dear...

I read your letter, received today, with the greatest of interest.

Your idea of using Growler to...

is...

But I am uncertain about....

because...

I would be most obliged if we could meet to discuss...

Yours sincerely

● When you have drafted your ideas for the letter, present it so that it looks old. Remember when the story takes place. Think about the paper you should use and the style of handwriting.

Picturing the story

● First, jot down on scrap paper all the important things you can remember about the story. Think about:

the characters	what they say	what they do
what happens	where it happens	problems they have
solutions they find	the beginning	the ending

● Now choose the six most important things on your list. Using the picture board below, draw your six important things in the order they occur in the story. Give each picture a brief caption, using no more than ten words for each.

● Use your picture board to tell the story to someone.

Passing the test

Mr. Beecham Chambers set Jackson and Lillipolly a 'test' to see if they were **kind, brave, patient, honest** and **generous.** They were rewarded when they passed his test.

There are lots of stories with 'tests'. Read this one:

There was once a rich man who was dying. He had three sons, and couldn't decide which one should inherit his wealth. So he set them a test. He called them to him and told them that he would leave all his wealth to the son who could fill his empty storeroom by the end of that day.

So the three sons set off. The eldest went to a farmer and bought a cartload of straw. 'That'll surely fill the room,' he said to himself. The second son rushed off to the town and bought twenty sacks of feathers from the market. 'These will surely fill the room,' he said to himself. But the third son just sat at home thinking. Finally he had an idea. He went out and bought two small things.

That evening all three sons arrived back. 'What have you brought?' asked the father of his eldest son. The son unloaded the cart full of straw. But it only filled a third of the storeroom. The second son smiled. He could do better then that. Once the straw had been cleared away, he shook out the twenty sacks full of feathers. They swirled around and seemed to fill the room at first, but soon settled and only filled it halfway up the walls. 'Can you do better than that?' the old man asked his youngest son. The third son stepped forward with the two small things he had bought. In a moment the room was filled, and his father gladly bestowed his wealth upon him.

Can you work out what the third son brought to fill the room so quickly

and easily? _____

What quality do you think the father was testing?_____

What qualities did the third son show?_____

Have you read any other examples of 'test' stories? Write their titles on

the back of this sheet.

Story ingredients for *Fair's Fair*

The 'ingredients' of a story are its characters, plot, setting and themes. Look at this example of the 'story ingredients' in *Little Red Riding Hood*.

Setting	Plot
Little Red Riding Hood's cottage. The forest. Grandma's cottage.	Little Red Riding Hood sets out for Grandma's. Talks to wolf in forest. Grandma gets locked in cupboard. Wolf dresses as Grandma. Little Red Riding Hood visits Wolf/Grandma. Wolf attacks Little Red Riding Hood. Woodcutter saves the day!
Characters Little Red Riding Hood. Wolf. Grandma. Mum and Dad. The woodcutter.	
Themes Don't talk to strangers.	

● Now sort through the story ingredients for *Fair's Fair* using this chart.

Setting	Plot
Characters	
Themes	

● Check carefully to make sure that you have included everything.

READ & RESPOND
26

What I think of *Fair's Fair*

When I first started to read *Fair's Fair* I thought that

_____

_____

_____

_____

The best moment in *Fair's Fair* for me was

_____

_____

_____

_____

Fair's Fair really got me thinking about

_____

_____

The most interesting character was _____

because _____

_____

The sort of person who would enjoy this book is

_____

because _____

_____

The most important thing about the book for me is

_____

_____

Fair's Fair by Leon Garfield was first published in 1981. It is an unusual book in that it is written for a younger readership than was Garfield's usual target audience. Set in Victorian London, its simple storyline ('What will happen to Jackson?') carries a complex set of meanings which explore the themes of generosity and 'right action'. It has Garfield's characteristic writing style, with vivid descriptive passages and lively colloquial dialogue.

MANAGING THE READING OF *FAIR'S FAIR*
The first 'Ways in' activity has been designed to be carried out before children have seen the title of the book. Children then read the book in 11 short sections. Each short section is supported by at least one 'Making sense' activity. This structure enables children to look very closely at the way the story is constructed, and to use their developing knowledge of the story to make confident predictions and to anticipate events.
The 11 sections are:
• '... he vanished one day and was never seen or heard of again.'
• '... when the black dog came.'
• 'Now shove off!'
• '... and his knuckles still raw from his last scrubbing.'
• '... and gates with nothing at all inside.'
• '... with an iron letter-box as thin as a miser's mouth.'
• '... small, thin, dirty, tattered, angry little girl!'
• 'I'll do the grate and the kitchen floor.'
• '... Jackson and Lillipolly were fast asleep.'
• 'The two men looked at each other; then the first one clapped his hands.'
• up to the end.

The 'Developing ideas' activities prompt children to re-read and reflect on the story. They ask children to re-read specific sections and to explore key themes and narrative technique in the book as a whole.

CLASSROOM MANAGEMENT AND SUPPORT
Fair's Fair is best read with the whole class, in a series of carefully planned shared reading sessions. This approach both supports the least able and challenges the most able readers in your class. Intersperse reading the book as a class with discussion of the section you have read. Then introduce the appropriate activity. Many of the activities are suitable for group, pair or individual work.
The following activities will work better if children collaborate, either as pairs or in small groups of four to five children:

'Work out the story' (page 6);
'Doors' (page 12);
'Telling the story so far' (page 13).

Activities for which children need a copy of *Fair's Fair* so that they can reread key sections are marked with a 📖. It is advisable to invest in at least six copies of *Fair's Fair* so that groups and pairs can work independently. If a whole class is working on the book, plan so that some children can work on activities which do not require close text work, while others use copies of the book to work from. Make sure that you give children ample opportunity to share and discuss their work in groups and as a class if appropriate.

DIFFERENTIATION
This activity book is not designed to be worked through slavishly. It provides a range of activities for you to adapt and match to the needs and abilities of your class. Most activities are designed to be accessible to children in Years 4 and 5 and differentiation comes with their differing levels of response. One of the more challenging activities is 'Rich and poor' on pages 20–21. Less able children may need teacher support to work on this activity. Most of the activities provide the basis of response work which can be extended as you wish. The Teachers' notes give ideas for extension tasks which challenge more able readers and writers.

TIME-SCALE
A child's uninterrupted reading of *Fair's Fair* takes only about 40 minutes. The aim of *Read & Respond* is to slow down the reading of books to improve the quality of children's response. A reflective reading gives children the opportunity to delve deeper into the narrative and to practise reader-response skills – reading beyond the lines. If you make *Fair's Fair* the focus of your English work, plan to work with the book for about three hours a week over a two-week period. This time-scale gives children an intensive and satisfying experience of studying the story, without diluting their enjoyment of the book by overloading them. Once children are used to this way of working with a significant literary text, they will be able to tackle longer, more challenging books as they move through the school.

MATCHING THIS BOOK TO YOUR CLASS
Fair's Fair is a simple story, simply told. It is an excellent book for reading aloud. The story takes place in the days leading up to Christmas. A series of linked episodes tell how Jackson is led to a strange house and meets Lillipolly, who is a homeless street orphan like

himself. Food and drink miraculously appear in the house, and Jackson and Lillipolly decide to keep it clean and tidy until the owners return. They are rewarded for their virtue when two gentlemen appear in the final pages.

The narrative structure has clear links with the fairy story tradition of tale-telling, and as a read-aloud story it is thus very accessible to a wide audience.

The language of the story makes it more challenging. *Fair's Fair* is ideal for children who are just beginning to read independently, because Garfield's vivid descriptions and lively dialogue raise the interest level. Its exploration of the themes of generosity and 'thinking of others' are also of wide appeal.

These activities aim to introduce young readers to ideas and themes that lie beneath the surface of the text, and to develop key reading skills such as reading for meaning, making inferences, deductions and predictions, and evaluating and comparing stories. It is often easier for children to develop these skills in the context of a simple, accessible text. *Fair's Fair* offers ample opportunity for this to happen as its simple story carries complex language and masterly authorial effects.

TEACHING POTENTIAL OF *FAIR'S FAIR*

See the Skills Grid on the inside back cover for reading response skill areas covered by the activities.

Fair's Fair also offers the following learning opportunities:

Writing
• note-making;
• descriptive writing;
• writing poetry – composing a 'found' poem;
• report writing.

Literary understanding and response
• depiction of character;
• establishment of setting;
• understanding of narrative sequence – the genre of the traditional story;
• exploration of theme and ideas.

Responding to language
• use of descriptive language – selection of verbs and adjectives;
• use of similes.

Cross-curricular links
• History study unit 'The Victorians' – in particular the lives of Victorian street children, and rich and poor in Victorian cities;
• Art - extend illustration work begun in 'Doors' (page 12).

GLOSSARY

It is helpful (though not essential) if children know the following key terms. Always teach them in the context of an activity. Encourage children to use these terms in their own discussion or written work:
Author/writer; Character; Setting; Plot; Verb; Adjective; Simile; Report; Theme; Dialogue.

PRIOR TEACHING

Some activities may be more successful if the teacher provides a model for children to follow first. The following activities benefit from this approach:
The first part of 'Work out the story' (page 6). Provide one or two examples of captions to show how they are used to summarise events.
'Rich and poor' (page 20). Model how to read for information: to skim for the gist, scan for key words, select key information and make brief notes. Show children how to use the writing frame as a draft for a report.
'Doors' (page 12). Make sure children know how to use a dictionary.
'Writing a 'found' poem' (page 14). Model how a series of descriptive phrases can be built up into a 'found' poem. Use the 'Black Dog' example given, or work with a different passage if you prefer.
'Missing!' (page 15). Show some examples of posters and discuss design features with the children.
'An exchange of letters' (pages 22 and 23). Ensure that the children have looked at some examples of formal letters. Demonstrate how to use the writing frame.

RESOURCES

It will be helpful for children to have access to a thesaurus, a dictionary and a selection of information books on the Victorians to provide background information on the setting and historical period of *Fair's Fair*, and for specific support for the 'Rich and poor' activity.

The following wider reading books will also be useful, for more able readers, or for reading selected passages aloud.
Other books by Leon Garfield:
Black Jack (Penguin)
Smith (Penguin)
The God Beneath the Sea (Gollancz)
Devil-in-the-Fog (Penguin)
Shakespeare Stories (Gollancz)
Other books:
Street Child by Berlie Doherty (Lions)
The story of another Victorian street child. His rescue from a life of poverty and crime charts the start of the Doctor Barnardo homes.
Oliver Twist by Charles Dickens (Penguin)

TEACHERS' NOTES

WAYS IN
FIND THE STORY
Aim: to look closely at the cover for clues to possible plot lines, story themes and setting.
Teaching points: introduce this activity before mentioning the book or its title to the children. To encourage discussion children should work in pairs and share their interpretations of what they see.

TITLE TALK
Aims: to examine the cover closely; to speculate about the story based on observations about the cover.
Teaching points: children interpret the visual clues given on the cover. They consider the conundrum of the title *Fair's Fair* and what it means in relation to the illustration. Collect individuals' ideas from the group or class to show how different readers bring different sets of knowledge and experience to a book before they begin to read it.
Extension: explore other everyday sayings, for example 'as mad as a hatter'; 'bright eyed and bushy tailed', looking at their unusual language and speculating on their 'real' meanings.

WORK OUT THE STORY
Aims: to heighten interest in the story in preparation for reading it by predicting events using selected illustrations; to focus on narrative sequence and explore possible narrative developments.
Teaching points: progression is built in as children develop their initial ideas to explain and predict. Model how to retell a story by using with another well-known story. Collect questions and possible directions for the story generated from the final part of the activity, and use them as the basis for group or class discussion.
Extension: able writers can draft the opening to the story, using the first two or three illustrations as prompts.

MAKING SENSE
ON THE STREETS
Aims: to speculate about Jackson's past; to consider the lives of orphans and the poor in Victorian times.
Teaching points: each reader brings a great deal of previous knowledge and experience to a text. This adds to the reader's appreciation and commitment to the book. Speculating about a character's history helps to deepen understanding of the place and time of the story. Small groups can discuss and compare different ideas of individuals.
Extension: some small-scale research into the lives of the Victorian poor adds a cross-curricular dimension. Later on, children can write a case history for Lillipolly.

A WORD PICTURE OF THE DOG
Aims: to encourage close reading of a short piece of text; to show how verbs and adjectives aid descriptive writing.
Teaching points: discuss effective use of words in a description. Model the decision-making involved and how to re-read for understanding. Emphasise that the idea is to find the most effective words, rather than the 'right' answer. The second part demonstrates an aspect of redrafting, which many children find challenging in their own writing.
Extension: use the cloze technique for shared reading of a short text or poem to reach understanding about the way other writers achieve effects using unusual verbs and adjectives. Children choose their own animal or creature and brainstorm a list of verbs and adjectives about what it does and what it looks like. They then write their own descriptive paragraph using lists as a starting point.

STREET URCHIN
Aim: to encourage close reading of descriptive language, identifying adjectives and verbs.
Teaching points: the passage is taken from Berlie Doherty's *Street Child*. It offers another account of what life was like on Victorian streets for poor children. Allow children to read the passage two or three times before they fill in the gaps. Encourage individuals to change their selections as they work through the passage. Pairs can then discuss their choices.
Extension: using a thesaurus, children could find alternative words for the spaces. Discuss the effects different word choices have and how they change the meaning of the passage. Talk about the sounds of words and the effect of different combinations.

WOULD YOU OR WOULDN'T YOU?
Aim: to explore Jackson's character and his motivation.
Teaching points: 'hot seating' helps children 'get inside' a fictional character. Pairs or small groups could present their interview live or on tape, but it need not be presented if they are unused to role-play. Teacher in role is another possibility – taking the role of Jackson or the dog, inviting questions from the group or class before setting up pair work once children understand the activity.
Extension: children can develop interviews into a radio broadcast or a newspaper story using a software package such as *Front Page News*.

Fair's Fair

'YOU GOT A KEY!'

Aim: to predict the storyline.

Teaching points: children focus on the title and the given clues to anticipate three different versions of what might happen next. Finding the key is the 'fiction trigger' for the plot of the story. Groups or class could discuss this – what other fiction triggers do they know?

Extension: collect ideas for a display collage of possible story developments in the outlines. Check back when children come to consider the ending ('The ending' see page 18).

'DOORS'

Aim: to develop close reading skills and dictionary use.

Teaching points: encourage children to read the passage aloud, experimenting with changes of tone, pace and emphasis. Develop the sketch of the door into a more ambitious individual, pair or group artwork, or a group or class display of different individual doors.

TELLING THE STORY SO FAR

Aim: to assume the roles of storyteller and story listener as a way of recapping story events so far.

Teaching points: this is not a presentation activity but a speaking and listening activity to develop storytelling within a given framework in the teller, and purposeful listening skills in the listener. The time limit adds focus, but allow extra time for additional retellings if children wish to perfect their first attempt.

Extension: groups or class discuss what helps a reader remember a story. The 'bone patterning' technique could be introduced. This is a method of remembering a story by identifying nine key words to use as a retelling framework. Model the technique by using a familiar story.

WRITING A 'FOUND' POEM

Aim: to read a short piece of text closely and select effective vocabulary.

Teaching points: if children are unfamiliar with this technique of close reading, model the reading and drafting techniques using a shared poem before setting individuals to work.

Extension: children can present poems orally to the rest of the class or collect poems into a book for the reading area or library.

MISSING!

Aims: to review what children can remember about Jackson and Lillipolly; to re-read the story closely to select key information.

Teaching points: to test their recall, children should try to remember details of appearance, character, location, and so on. Some children may need to be reminded that the reader knows more than the police or other concerned people. Allow children to refer to the book if they need to. Introduce the design element by looking at examples of posters and discussing design and layout. Encourage them to draft the wording before they decide on the design.

'I WONDER'

Aims: to make inferences, deductions and predictions while reading.

Teaching points: pair children with a response partner to discuss each other's ideas.

Extension: children can write their own version of what happens next, using the notes they have made. It is important that they write only the next episode – no shorter than 100 words and no longer than 150. They could start it: 'Later that night, while they were still asleep...' or 'In the morning...' or 'The dog lay dozing...' Writers can redraft their continuation after discussing it with a partner and produce a final version with an illustration in the style of those in the book.

THE TWO MEN

Aims: to find textual evidence by scanning the story read so far; to predict what happens next.

Teaching points: children need to find words in a dictionary. Check that they understand how to do this.

Extension: the 'evidence' for the qualities shown by the children is summarised by Mr Beecham Chambers in the next section of the book. Children can compare their evidence with his version.

THE ENDING

Aim: to evaluate the ending and to look back over the whole story.

Teaching points: children should review the predictions they made for 'You got a key!' (page 11) and compare them with the actual ending. The aim is to help children see how all the circumstances and events in the story lead up to Garfield's ending. The second part asks them to find key evidence in the story to justify Garfield's choice of title. These are good opportunities for class or group discussion and display.

DEVELOPING IDEAS
CAN YOU IDENTIFY?

Aim: to focus on Garfield's use of language to characterise and describe; to introduce children to the use of similes.

Teaching points: *Fair's Fair* is full of poetic descriptions, vivid imagery and striking

language. Encourage children to speculate beyond the literal meaning of the words and pick up on poetic and emotional resonances.
Extension: swap and share 'original' similes in groups or as a class to discuss effectiveness. Children can find other examples of figurative language in *Fair's Fair* and other books.

RICH AND POOR
Aims: to investigate the historical background of *Fair's Fair*; to read for information, skimming and scanning for key ideas; to select and categorise information; to represent information using a writing frame.
Teaching points: model how to set about reading for key information. You will need three different coloured highlighter pens. Read the information carefully twice. Use the first colour to highlight information about how the street children lived. Use the second colour to highlight information about why there were children living on the streets of Victorian cities and the third to highlight how better-off people lived. Demonstrate how to make succinct notes. The grid on page 20 starts pupils off but some may need more support in learning how to summarise what they have learned in note form. The 'writing frame' is designed to support children as they turn their notes into a piece of connected writing. Encourage the children to write with the frame alongside them, incorporating the starter sentences into their own writing. They can alter the frame by adding or amending it as necessary. It is not a worksheet, but a support for their writing.

AN EXCHANGE OF LETTERS
Aim: to speculate on events 'outside' the text using the story as a basis for speculation.
Teaching points: the letter frames support children's writing. One half of the class could write the letter and send it to the other half who then write the reply.
Extension: collect a range of formal letters and discuss the different ways that they are structured and the kinds of phrases used. Children can formulate their own set of 'rules for writing formal letters'. They can create personal frameworks for different kinds of letters as guidelines for their own later use or for other classes.

PICTURING THE STORY
Aim: to reflect on and develop an overview of the key elements of the story.
Teaching points: after reading, children reflect on key images and ideas in the book. They can then share others' responses. Making a picture board aids understanding of narrative structure and also helps to develop response

and encourage evaluation. Group or class discussion of key moments and vivid visual images created by the story encourages reflection on and understanding of different, but equally valid, 'readings' of the same story. Model captions and caption writing if children are unfamiliar with these.

PASSING THE TEST
Aim: to draw attention to the similarities between *Fair's Fair* and other traditional stories.
Teaching points: The story is a traditional tale from the Middle East. The 'answer' to the riddle is that the youngest son bought a box of matches and a candle – once lit, it filled the room with light! What quality the father was testing is harder to establish: quick-wittedness? resourcefulness? intelligence? Ensure that children explore various possibilities and explain how their ideas are borne out by the story.

STORY INGREDIENTS FOR *FAIR'S FAIR*
Aim: to develop understanding of the structure of narrative.
Teaching points: the worked example shows that narrative structures can be looked at in many ways, not just the familiar 'beginning, middle, and end'. To reinforce this, talk the example through with the group or class. Alternatively, work through the activity without the example, then compare the class or group version with the example given. In the second part of the activity, individuals or pairs reflect on different elements of the narrative as outlined in the framework.
Extension: use the framework with other stories to familiarise children with the useful vocabulary of literary response. Collect other completed frameworks within genre categories (adventure, myths) to focus on similarities and differences in structure. Children can also use the framework as a story planner for writing their own stories.

EVALUATION
WHAT I THINK OF *FAIR'S FAIR*
Aim: to record personal evaluation of *Fair's Fair*.
Teaching points: the starter sentences give support for individual responses, beyond a superficial review. If children are unused to working with frames, model an example with a different but familiar story.
Extension: children use completed frames as the basis for oral book recommendations. Adapt the frame to fit other review activities, not only in reading but to evaluate activities in other curriculum areas.